*Public Politics in
an Authoritarian State*

Public Politics in an Authoritarian State

MAKING FOREIGN POLICY
DURING THE BREZHNEV YEARS

RICHARD D. ANDERSON, JR.

CORNELL UNIVERSITY PRESS

ITHACA AND LONDON

First published 1993 by Cornell University Press.

International Standard Book Number 0-8014-2900-5
Library of Congress Catalog Card Number 93-15240
Printed in the United States of America
*Librarians: Library of Congress cataloging information
appears on the last page of the book.*

⊗ The paper in this book meets the minimum requirements
of the American National Standard for Information Sciences—
Permanence of Paper for Printed Library Materials, ANSI Z39.48-1984.

*For Richard D., Jeanette O.,
and Judith L. Anderson*

Contents

Preface

Eduard Shevardnadze, the former Soviet foreign minister, recalls that in order to lead *perestroika*, Mikhail Gorbachev "constantly had to choose among constituencies."[1] Or does Shevardnadze say that? Where the English reads "constituencies," the Russian original uses *opory*—"supports," in the sense of bridge abutments or other structural underpinnings.[2] The metaphors are parallel but the referents are not. Constituencies provide support and so do opory, but a constituency is an electorate. As general secretary of the Communist Party, Gorbachev never ran in any general election.

Was Shevardnadze translated accurately? Many observers of the Soviet Union would answer no. There is compelling reason to deny the presence of constituencies in Soviet politics. By the rules of the Communist Party, the general secretary and the Politburo, which until 1990 held the power to decide policy on any question of Soviet politics, were formally accountable only to the few hundred voting members of the Central Committee. That body was composed almost entirely of the Politburo's appointees to the highest offices of the Communist Party and the state, the exceptions being meritorious citizens who were also Politburo nominees. Choosing its

1. Eduard A. Shevardnadze, *The Future Belongs to Freedom*, trans. Catherine A. Fitzpatrick (New York: Free Press, 1991), xix.
2. Eduard A. Shevardnadze, *Moi vybor: V zashchitu demokratii i svobody* (Moscow: Novosti, 1991), 25.

own electors, the Politburo decided its own composition. Formal accountability might be present, but the case is not comparable to an elected politician's representation of a constituency of voters whom the politician does not choose.

Despite the plausibility of the argument that Politburo members depended on no individual constituencies beyond the Central Committee, Shevardnadze's translator did capture the intention of a man who knew the politics he had lived. The objection to the translation is emblematic of a larger quandary about how to compare the Soviet Union's distinctive institutions with those of an electoral polity. Because the formal rules prohibited Soviet bureaucrats from voting on or even discussing Politburo members' personal suitability for office, observers have been unable to collect direct evidence about the attitudes of officials. Consequently they have failed to discern the dependence of Politburo members on larger bureaucratic constituencies, including Central Committee members but extending far deeper into officialdom. No matter how valuable, direct evidence of constituency attitudes is not the only possible ground for inferring the presence of constituencies. Observers could also have examined Politburo members' own behavior to see whether they engaged in activities known from the study of more accessible polities to serve the purpose of recruiting constituents.

Linkage from observations to inferences depends on theory. The study of Soviet politics has profited by past efforts to introduce social science concepts originating elsewhere, as in the study of interest groups and in institutional analysis, into empirical research on the USSR. Constituency-seeking by electoral politicians is within the purview of the theory of competitive politics, to which I turn in this book. This theory forms hypotheses about two activities by politicians: going public and bargaining.

Tenure in office in an electoral polity is won by public campaigning. A politician secures office by advocating distinctive themes in the hope that the rhetoric will attract constituency support. The candidate's themes include both material appeals to voters' self-interest and, crucially, attitudinal appeals that identify the candidate with symbols that through repeated reinforcement have come to define a collective identity for a group of voters.

Having secured office by going public, political competitors formulate policy by bargaining. As candidates, they make their distinctive themes concrete by recommending the adoption of specific policies. Differences between their recommendations define issues.

After election, the winning candidates resolve their disagreements on the issues by bargaining to a compromise policy. Because a favorable distribution of voter opinion supplies leverage in the bargaining over policy, competitors continue to go public even between elections. Success in bargaining in turn reinforces a candidate's appeal to constituents by enabling the candidate to claim credit for the enactment of policies materially or symbolically beneficial to them.

If evidence of going public and bargaining by Politburo members cannot be found, then we can be confident that political competition in the USSR, if it existed at all, took a form not comparable to electoral competition. It might have been, as some analysts have suggested, the courtier politics of currying favor with the general secretary in the hope of holding office by display of loyalty. But evidence that Politburo members did go public and did choose policy by bargaining raises a pointed question: If tenure in the Politburo was not dependent on the approval of bureaucratic constituencies, why did the members trouble to appeal to bureaucrats?

To accept the implication of the observations of going public and bargaining, observers need not find that Politburo members' behaviors exactly duplicated those familiar in electoral polities. To investigate whether constituency politics preceded the advent of perestroika, the Politburo membership examined here is that of the early Brezhnev years. Differences between the rhetoric of the Politburo in those years and the familiar rhetoric of electoral politics are already well known. In contrast to electoral candidates, who obey a live-and-let-live rule that each determines the content of his or her own speeches, the Politburo enforced prior review of public speeches by the speaker's peers. Moreover, the Politburo's speeches displayed an arcane stylistics that has occasioned extensive commentary. Markedly distant from the Russian vernacular, the Politburo's rhetoric sounded wooden to its audiences and clouded its meaning. When translating the Politburo's Russian, I have abandoned the translator's convention of rendering foreign speech into the natural English of a native speaker. Instead I have opted for an English that retains the clumsiness and obscurity of the Russian original. The pursuit of felicity or clarity by past translators has imposed analysts' meanings on the speakers' words. As a result, the reading of these texts has seemed far less problematic than it is, and many observers have fallen into an unjustifiable certainty about their interpretations.

The differences between the Politburo's rhetoric and an electoral rhetoric should not be discounted. But rather than contradict an inferred dependence on constituencies beyond the Central Committee, these differences offer a vital clue to the identity of the constituents. Enforcement of mutual restrictions on speechmaking and of an artificial rhetoric, as Jeffrey Tulis has noted, served in nineteenth-century America to reinforce the estrangement of the mass public from politics.[3] The Politburo's determination to restrict mass participation is well established, and the differences signal an effort to confine its appeals to bureaucrats.

Others have made significant contributions by examining public speeches by Politburo members and contemplating the effects of co-alition bargaining on Soviet policy, but the full implications of their observations have gone unrecognized. Evidence of going public and bargaining would justify revision of our explanations for two key developments: the Politburo's inability to abandon self-defeating policies that drove the Soviet Union through unsuccessful reform to collapse, and as an instance of those policies, its self-frustrating attempt to combine East-West cooperation on some issues with confrontation of the West in the developing world.

A theory of competitive politics explains self-defeating policies in general as a cost of maintaining the cohesion of a political collectivity. By offering material benefits and by symbolic personification of voters, a politician induces constituents to recommit their allegiance at intervals to the polity. By compromising with one another, the winning politicians continuously reconstitute the coalition of their constituencies that is the polity. Both symbolic politics and bargaining distort the adaptiveness of policy to the objective circumstances facing any government. Symbolism that appeals to constituents displaces objective problems as the target of policy proposals, while logrolls that ease politicians' search for compromise authorize a combination of policies with mutually interfering substantive consequences that prevent accomplishment of each policy's declared objective. If the Soviet Union adopted a variety of self-defeating policies during the late Brezhnev years, it was because individual Politburo members were relying on different symbols to attract bureaucratic constituents and were logrolling to resolve the resulting disagreements over policy.

Self-defeating foreign policies originate in competitors' use of foreign policy issues to sharpen the contrast among their political iden-

3. Jeffrey Tulis, *The Rhetorical Presidency* (Princeton: Princeton University Press, 1987).

tities and thus to attract constituency support. The focus of the empirical research in this book is a self-defeating foreign policy that Jack Snyder has called "offensive détente":[4] the effort after 1969 to couple superpower détente in bilateral and European issues with interventionism in Third World conflicts, an aggressive arms build-up, and exclusion of Western influence from Eastern Europe. By antagonizing U.S. voters, the offensive elements of this policy package ultimately contributed to the election of the most anti-Soviet president in history, who ended efforts to achieve détente in favor of resurgent military spending and an armed global crusade against the spread of Soviet influence. The theory of competitive politics predicts that states will often enact foreign policies that frustrate their own goals. Rivals for leadership compete by going public with distinctive, symbolic issue positions, and the international arena provides a wide array of issues on which leaders can take distinctive positions that instantiate their symbolic self-presentation at home. Rooted in the symbolic visions that leaders expect to attract a constituency at home, these symbolic stands misrepresent actual world conditions. When the leaders then resolve disagreements by logrolls that combine policies regardless of mutual interference among their substantive effects, counterproductive foreign policies ensue.

A demonstration that competitive politics shaped the Soviet decision for offensive détente would not only revise views of Soviet politics but also raise a general question for theorists of international relations. Realist and many other theories of world politics interpret the behavior of states as a strategic response to objective circumstances. While admitting that domestic politics can cause a state's policy to deviate from the strategic optimum, realists argue that because institutions vary across states, no general theory of international relations can take politics within the state as its point of departure. Though an empirical finding of competitive politics in one institutional setting where it is unexpected, the Soviet Union, is far from justifying a conclusion that competitive politics will be found in all such settings, competitive politics offers a general theory of foreign policy that could be tested for any state for which an adequate documentary record is accessible. Competitive politics theory argues that the behavior of states is responsive to international conditions, but only through the impact of world events on competitors' pros-

4. Jack Snyder, *Myths of Empire: Domestic Politics and International Ambition* (Ithaca: Cornell University Press, 1991), 246–50.

pects of winning the domestic contest for constituency support. If the behavior of states in world politics were generally a strategic response to their leaders' problem of recruiting constituencies at home, then foreign policy would obey imperatives quite distinct from objective international conditions. That possibility would in turn explain what existing theories of international relations do not: why states have chosen policies that promote not their survival in world politics but their demise—as the Soviet Union did.

The findings presented in this book raise an equally general question for observers of electoral polities. An association is well established between variation in electoral institutions and diversity in the political strategies of electoral competitors. This association has been taken as evidence that the variation in electoral institutions causes the diversity in political strategies. A finding that political leaders adopt strategies similar to those of electoral competitors even in the absence of the institution of contested elections indicates, however, that the phenomenon of political strategies is more general than the institutional variation posited as their cause. What presuppositions about our own politics have led observers to attribute the phenomena of political competition to electoral institutions rather than to some more general conditions of social existence which we may share with societies organized according to very different principles?

A theory of competitive politics, unlike some earlier theories of Soviet politics, does not lose its relevance with the disintegration of the Soviet Union and the transition to democracy in Russia. One of the hardest questions to answer about the transition is the origin of mass politicians such as Gorbachev and Boris Yeltsin. Were they just natural geniuses who retained the common touch through years of bureaucratic infighting? Or did triumph in Soviet politics somehow necessitate their acquisition of the skills that win electoral contests too? Now as Yeltsin leads Russian democracy, an understanding of competitive politics will contribute to analysis of the processes that determine whether democracy survives or authoritarianism revives. Competitive politics theory cannot foretell that outcome, because the theory's expectations are path-dependent and contingent. Its predictions are "if–then" statements, whereas forecasts depend on knowledge of the "if" in advance, which the theory cannot supply. But the recognition that the results of competitive processes vary with the paths taken by those processes is itself valuable knowledge. As late as 1984, the question preoccupying observers of Soviet politics was whether the Politburo would undertake limited reforms. Not seeing

the cohesion of the Soviet Union as rooted, like that of electoral polities, in its leaders' public appeals to politically empowered social
strata, few observers (if any) contemplated a transition to democracy. A view of the Soviet Union as a competitive polity could not
have forecast this transition but would have rendered observers far
more alert to the contingent stability of Soviet institutions and therefore to the prospects for radical change.

This book constructs Soviet politics along vertical and horizontal dimensions. George Breslauer provided the vertical when he
learned how to identify authority building in the speeches of
Khrushchev and Brezhnev. John Harsanyi supplied the horizontal
by patiently instructing a nonmathematician in the foundations of
formal bargaining theory. Ernst Haas taught me how and why to
conceive a theoretical construct built of abstract horizontals and ver-
ticals. When in my enthusiasm for theory I overreached, he also
rescued the project by demanding that I discard five hundred pages.
The book would not exist without their invaluable help.

At Berkeley, Claremont Graduate School, and UCLA, many colleagues have read some and listened more. Their willingness to contemplate a new argument has sustained me through the vicissitudes
of academic publication. Among them are Glyn Morgan, James Ma-
hon, John Gilmour, Maria Cook, Donald Green, James McAdams,
Jeffry Frieden, Barbara Geddes, Miriam Golden, George Tsebelis,
David Lake, Kathleen Bawn, Steven Postrel, Stephen Ansolabehere,
and Ronald Rogowski. David Lake told me what publisher to trust.
Nelson Polsby talked to me about pluralism. When I needed a job,
Daniel Mazmanian, Thomas Rochon, and William Thompson put
faith in the project, and understood when I needed to move on. Gail
Lapidus went far beyond her obligations to find me funding when I
did not know how to ask for it. Jack Snyder provided encouragement and advice, as did Ned Lebow and Janice Stein. If my research
is thorough, no little credit is due Shulamith Roth, who taught me
the power and intricacies of computer data bases for text retrieval.
Judith Chase supplied research assistance.

I am grateful for the financial support provided by the Social Science Research Council, the American Council of Learned Societies,
the John D. and Catherine T. MacArthur Foundation, and the Institute on Global Conflict and Cooperation of the University of California.

Judith Anderson did not type, read, edit, or comment—her con-

tribution was to share her life. Without her gift, I could not have
written this book, but the chance to finish it is the least of what I
have received.

Unless I indicate otherwise, all translations are my own. References to *Pravda*, which has supplied most of the documentation, are
indicated by dates alone. All other publications are identified by
name.

R. D. A.

Los Angeles, California

*Public Politics in
an Authoritarian State*

Chapter 1

Going Public
in Soviet Politics

On October 18, 1964, President Lyndon Johnson spoke to the
nation about Nikita Khrushchev's ouster three days earlier from the
leadership of the Soviet Union. Johnson interpreted Khrushchev's
removal as a sign of stability in world politics and continuity in U.S.
foreign policy. Noting "discontent and strain and failure . . . within
the Communist bloc," Johnson said, "These troubles are not the creation of one man. They will not end with his ouster." Khrushchev's
successors, he predicted, "will be concerned primarily with problems of Communism . . . men who are busy with internal problems
may not be tempted to reckless external acts." As for the United
States, Johnson promised that "any Soviet government which is
ready to work for peace will find us ready to talk."

On October 21 a nationwide television audience heard the Republi-
can candidate for president, Senator Barry Goldwater, give a different
interpretation. In Khrushchev's removal Goldwater saw an ominous
sign of worsening world conditions that would require new U.S. policies. "The dissension in Communist ranks, brought on by a clash of
personalities, is being repaired. . . . The foreign policy of the present
Administration . . . has . . . helped the Communist world through a
time of troubles and allowed it to emerge as a greater threat than ever
to the freedom of the West." As for the United States, Goldwater
promised "to confront Communism with a firm policy of resistance."[1]

1. *Vital Speeches of the Day*, November 1, 1964, 34–38.

One day earlier readers of Pravda had seen texts of the first speeches by Khrushchev's successors, Leonid Brezhnev and Aleksei Kosygin, in their new roles as heads of Party and government. They spoke at separate ceremonies honoring cosmonauts just returned from a space flight. Each man turned the event into a symbol of Soviet relations with the United States, and each promised a policy toward the West.

Brezhnev's symbolism combined an expression of "pleas[ure] that our country leads in space research" with mockery of Westerners for approaching a "grand and serious" technological endeavor in a "gambling spirit" as a "'space race.'" Pursuing his symbolism of technological and moral superiority, Brezhnev promised that the Soviet Union would remain "steadfast" in pursuing an "incessant struggle for peace," but questioned whether "governments of other states will display an aspiration for peace in turn and observe the sovereign right of every people, large or small, to decide its own fate autonomously."

Kosygin's symbolism set East and West on more equal terms. Expressing "sincere gratitude also to foreign scholars whose scientific achievements played no small role" in the exploration of space, Kosygin said, "Let the sixth ocean—space—become an arena of international cooperation among states." He promised, "The Soviet government will multiply its efforts for the resolution of international disputes through talks."[2]

With Goldwater and Johnson locked in a contest for the presidency, their speeches were naturally read as instances of the familiar activity known as "going public." In an electoral polity, leaders go public to stress the differences between their policy proposals and those of rivals. U.S. presidents call on the public to pressure Congress; senators and representatives urge their constituents to resist presidential appeals. Going public with justifications for a distinctive policy course enhances a leaders' prospects in the next election; it also mobilizes the pressure of public opinion against political opponents for leverage in the competitive bargaining that produces policy.[3]

Should one interpret the difference between the statements by

2. Pravda, October 20, 1964. In subsequent references to Pravda I give only the date. References to other Soviet newspapers include the title.
3. Samuel Kernell, Going Public: New Strategies of Presidential Leadership (Washington, D.C.: Congressional Quarterly Press, 1986); Jeffrey Tulis, The Rhetorical Presidency (Princeton: Princeton University Press, 1987).

Kosygin and Brezhnev as an instance of going public in Soviet politics? Some critics have dismissed apparent policy differences in Politburo members' public speeches on the grounds that to focus on passages that apparently disagree is to neglect the passages that display consensus. Kosygin did in fact agree with Brezhnev that Soviet policy should combat "colonialism and neocolonialism," and Brezhnev agreed with Kosygin that Soviet policy should pursue international cooperation. Yet insertion of consensual passages into public speeches intended to underscore differences among political opponents also characterizes going public in the United States. Johnson agreed with Goldwater that the new Soviet leaders were "dedicated, dangerous Communists," held in check only by the "strength of the United States"; Goldwater agreed with Johnson that "a lasting peace" could be sought through negotiation of "concrete concessions and safeguards." Rhetorical consensus hid Johnson's differences with Goldwater from no one.

While expressing consensus on some issues, Brezhnev and Kosygin also displayed certain differences. Any difference between them over policy is expressed far less overtly than Goldwater's denunciation of Johnson's foreign policy as an "utter failure." Even so, a difference is readily discernible, and it parallels the contrast between the two presidential candidates. Brezhnev promised continuity in Soviet policy (the USSR would remain "steadfast") while Kosygin promised change (it would "multiply its efforts"). Kosygin called for "talks," while Brezhnev portrayed Soviet efforts for peace in conflictual language as an "incessant struggle." To Brezhnev, achievement of peace depended not on the Soviet Union but on whether foreign governments would "display an aspiration for peace." Brezhnev then set up a test of whether foreign governments did aspire for peace. Without needing to mention Indochina, Brezhnev could count on every Soviet reader of *Pravda* to interpret U.S. actions there as failing the test of respect for the Vietnamese people's right to sovereign autonomy. Brezhnev's use of Vietnam as a test of U.S. intentions closely paralleled Goldwater's citation of Vietnam as an indicator that Soviet interest in Johnson's proposals for negotiations was insincere.

The central question investigated by this book is whether political competition among Brezhnev-era Politburo members shaped Soviet foreign policy in a manner comparable to the effects of electoral competition on the foreign policy of an electoral polity. I answer that question by investigating whether going public over foreign policy generated rewards for Politburo members comparable to the advantages that elected politicians obtain—tenure in office and leverage in policy bargaining. The literature on Soviet politics under Brezhnev recognizes the pervasiveness of bargaining over policy, but in much of it going public appears either useless or even perilous for Politburo members. The reason is the contrast between the institution of contested elections and the procedures that secured tenure in office for Politburo members. It is certainly plausible to suppose that Politburo members, who held office by the consent of their peers rather than by the consent of mass voters, did not stand to gain by appealing to outside constituencies and might risk penalties from their peers for eroding the Politburo's established autonomy. Accordingly, much scholarship depicts members of the Brezhnev Politburo either as *infighters* using policies as weapons in a covert power struggle confined within the Politburo or as *brokers* of bargaining among interest groups composed of policy experts housed within the great bureaucracies of the Communist Party and the government. This literature does not see the members of the Brezhnev Politburo as competitive *advocates* of different policies who seek leverage in bargaining or tenure in office by going public.

Whether members of the Brezhnev Politburo acted as infighters, brokers, or advocates in turn varies one's answer to a central puzzle in the study of Soviet politics: why the Brezhnev leadership's policies so severely exacerbated the objective problems that developed into the crisis that faced Gorbachev after 1985 and ultimately resulted in the disintegration of the Soviet Union. Decisions by Brezhnev's Politburo decelerated economic expansion, damaged social morale, hypertrophied the arms industry, embittered ethnic antagonisms, encouraged official corruption, and committed the Soviet Union to a foreign policy that ultimately produced self-encirclement. The infighting school ascribes the Brezhnev Politburo's failures in managing objective problems to its members' shared ideological commitments—their loyalties to the command economy, to denial of political rights to the mass public, to a foreign policy rooted in antagonism toward the United States.[4] The brokering school attributes maladaptiveness in the face of the objective problems to an aging

4. William E. Odom, "Choice and Change in Soviet Politics," in Erik P. Hoffman and Robbin F. Laird, eds., *The Soviet Polity in the Modern Era* (New York: Aldine, 1984), 923; Harry Gelman, *The Brezhnev Politburo and the Decline of Détente* (Ithaca: Cornell University Press, 1984).

Politburo's indecisiveness—its unwillingness to make the hard choices necessary to reconcile the disagreements that naturally arise among experts whose specialized knowledge lies in different fields.[5]

If, on the other hand, the members of the Brezhnev Politburo were advocates whose bargaining influence rested on going public, the reasons why their decisions proved maladaptive to the objective problems facing the Soviet Union may resemble the difficulties that plague competitive policy making by elected governments. These difficulties arise because when leaders go public, they connect specific policies addressed to particular social problems with their larger task of sustaining the political collectivity. The practice in international relations and comparative politics of regarding the state as a fixed entity conditioning all political behavior hides the possibility of viewing the state as a resultant of continuing interactions among leaders, officials, and publics. As one of these interactions, going public does more than secure national leaders' hold on office and build their leverage on policy bargaining. By going public they also sustain the political collectivity. By presenting a choice between alternative policies, going public engages citizens' commitment to various contestants for leadership. Citizens' commitment to rivals for office simultaneously reaffirms their allegiance to the ongoing polity constituted by the stream of policy compromises among victors in the contest.

Accordingly, policies chosen by going public serve not only as adaptive responses to objective problems facing the polity but also as symbolic ties that bind followers to leaders and as solutions to the leaders' problem of continually reconstituting the polity. These additional purposes of policy making introduce three kinds of distortions into the adaptiveness of policy to objective problems facing the political collectivity as a whole. First, symbols that help leaders communicate to inattentive constituents may displace objective problems as the focus of policy. Second, leaders whose influence in bargaining

5. Jerry F. Hough, *Soviet Leadership in Transition* (Washington, D.C.: Brookings, 1980), 14; Paul Cocks, "The Policy Process and Bureaucratic Politics," in Cocks, Robert V. Daniels, and Nancy Whittier Heer, eds., *The Dynamics of Soviet Politics* (Cambridge: Harvard University Press, 1976); Timothy Colton, *The Dilemma of Reform in the Soviet Union* (New York: Council on Foreign Relations, 1984), 10–13, and "Perspectives on Civil-Military Relations in the Soviet Union," in Colton and Thane Gustafson, eds., *Soldiers and the Soviet State: Civil-Military Relations from Brezhnev to Gorbachev* (Princeton: Princeton University Press, 1990), 37–38; Thane Gustafson, *Crisis amid Plenty: The Politics of Soviet Energy under Brezhnev and Gorbachev* (Princeton: Princeton University Press, 1989), 319–333.

depends on going public often resolve their differences by logrolls that combine mutually incompatible proposals into self-frustrating policies. Third, a government's capability to adjust to changing objective circumstances may depend on the emergence of a dominant leader, one who can revise the political vision that, by motivating constituents to provide support, assured the leader's hold on office and influence on policy in the first place.

If members of the Brezhnev Politburo went public to secure themselves in office and to gain leverage on policy bargaining, then the reasons for their defective policy choices take on a new cast. *Whether* they went public is an empirical question. The empirical investigation must be guided by a more precise definition of what going public means and what its consequences are for policy compromises and for the responsiveness of policy to changing objective circumstances. I draw that definition from the theory of competitive politics—a theory abstracted from the study of electoral polities, especially of the United States. This theory explains why politicians recommend divergent policies in public, how private bargains to reconcile their public differences shape policy choices, and why politicians change their policy recommendations over time.

To accept the proposition that political competition shapes the behavior of Politburo members, one need not find that their style of going public precisely duplicates the conduct of electoral contestants. As comparison of the Johnson-Goldwater and Brezhnev-Kosygin exchanges has already shown, if Politburo members went public with policy disagreements, they did so with far more subtlety than their counterparts sometimes employ in the United States. Although the evidence presented in this book does not resolve the question why going public might have taken a more limited form in Soviet politics, a reasonable hypothesis is that bureaucrats, to whom Soviet leaders may have addressed their political appeals, are better informed and more attentive than mass voters and consequently more likely to detect less frequent, less overt differences among contestants for leadership.

The empirical questions are whether some members of the Brezhnev Politburo did go public with contrasting policy recommendations and whether their public appeals shaped policy bargains. This book presents evidence that for certain members of the Brezhnev Politburo, going public was a routine activity. Some lost by going public, but others gained, and those who went public less lost more. Whenever Politburo members did publicly differ over policy, the ultimately enacted policy consistently was a compromise among the publicly expressed positions. Incorporation of new policy recommendations into some Politburo member's public statements was associated with change in Soviet policy on the issues addressed by those new proposals, sometimes because the member's influence on those issues increased and sometimes because rivals coalesced to resist the member's expansion of his influence by changing policy in a contrary direction.

If this evidence confirms that the theory of competitive politics in electoral polities explains the behavior of Politburo members in the Brezhnev years, it raises a further question, one much more general than the characterization of Politburo members or even than the reasons for the collapse of the Soviet Union. Denials that Politburo members could usefully go public are rooted in a claim that institutional rules structured the behavior of a Politburo member dependent on the consent of his peers as surely as they are thought to shape the conduct of an elected leader dependent on the consent of mass voters. According to this claim, because electoral institutions differ so radically from the rules for selecting the Politburo, the behavior of Soviet leaders should also differ radically from the conduct of elected leaders. A finding that the behavior of at least some Politburo members conformed to the predictions of a theory of political competition among elected officials, however, would cast doubt on the presumption that institutional rules are what ultimately structures politicians' behavior in any polity.

Going Public, Bargaining, and Institutional Distinctiveness

Denials of the utility of going public for members of the Brezhnev Politburo draw plausibility from the institutional distinctiveness of the Soviet Union. Like officials of an electoral polity, Soviet authorities in the Brezhnev era chose policies by bargaining to reconcile diverging interests. But policy bargaining in the Soviet polity is often treated as "closed politics." Politburo members could not gain from going public because the Brezhnev Politburo was self-appointing. Its members' right to appoint the officials entitled to Central Committee membership supposedly enabled the members of the Politburo to keep their seats regardless of the opinion of their policies held by any public. The assertion that institutional rules could isolate policy bargaining from leaders' search for public support is the hypothesis I examine.

Jerry F. Hough's concept of "institutional pluralism" advanced one version of the argument that policy bargaining remained un-affected by going public. Hough took an explicitly comparative ap-proach, stressing resemblances between the policy processes in the United States and the Soviet Union despite profound institutional differences. He observed that policies adopted by the Brezhnev Pol-itburo regularly coincided with desiderata expressed by interested bureaucratic groups: health policy served hospital administrators, military strategy served the officer corps, ecology received short shrift because it fell within the recognized purview of industrialists, and so on. From the observed resemblance of the Soviet policy pat-tern to outcomes of interest-group bargaining in the United States, Hough inferred that bargaining was at work in the Soviet Union, too.[6]

While similar ideas became widely shared,[7] the concept of institu-tional pluralism also encountered criticism for exaggerating the de-volution of power from the Politburo to the bureaucratic interests. The critics agreed that Soviet policies displayed evidence of bargain-ing, but they argued that the bargaining was more properly de-scribed as infighting in a Politburo that used policies as weapons in a covert struggle for power. Success in the power struggle depended on whether a member's policy proposals conformed to the consen-sus opinion of the Politburo, and especially of its most senior fig-ures.[8]

Despite their disagreements over the locus of policy bargaining, both Hough and his critics concurred that the institutional rules for selecting Politburo members emancipated their tenure in office from

6. Jerry F. Hough, "Pluralism, Corporatism and the Soviet Union," in Susan Gross Solomon, ed., *Pluralism in the Soviet Union: Essays in Honour of H. Gordon Skilling* (London: Macmillan, 1983), 49–53, and *The Soviet Union and Social Science Theory* (Cam-bridge: Harvard University Press, 1977), 23–46.
7. H. Gordon Skilling and Franklyn W. Griffiths, eds., *Interest Groups in Soviet Politics* (Princeton: Princeton University Press, 1971); Darrell P. Hammer, *USSR: The Politics of Oligarchy*, 2d ed. (Boulder, Colo.: Westview, 1986); Robert V. Daniels, "So-viet Politics since Khrushchev," in John W. Strong, ed., *The Soviet Union under Brezhnev and Kosygin* (New York: Van Nostrand, 1971); Joel J. Schwartz and William R. Keech, "Group Influence and the Policy Process in the Soviet Union," *American Politi-cal Science Review* 62 (1968): 840–51; Philip D. Stewart, "Soviet Interest Groups and the Policy Process: The Repeal of Production Education," *World Politics* 22 (1969): 29–50.
8. Gelman, *Brezhnev Politburo*, chaps. 2–3; William E. Odom, "A Dissenting View on the Group Approach to Soviet Politics," *World Politics* 28 (1976): 524–67; Hannes Adomeit, "Consensus versus Conflict: The Dimension of Foreign Policy," in Seweryn Bialer, ed., *The Domestic Context of Soviet Foreign Policy* (Boulder, Colo.: Westview, 1981), 49–83; John Lenczowski, *Soviet Perceptions of U.S. Foreign Policy: A Study of Ideology, Power, and Consensus* (Ithaca: Cornell University Press, 1982), 259–75.

dependence on the consent of subordinates. Formal power to elect and remove Politburo members belonged to the Central Committee of the Communist Party. This body consisted almost entirely of appointees to the several hundred most powerful offices in the Party and government. The appointees on the Central Committee in turn selected the delegates to each Communist Party congress, who would vote to reelect them to the Central Committee. Since the Politburo chose the appointees entitled to Central Committee membership, Politburo members chose their own electors. Known as the "circular flow of power," this institutional setup ensured that retention in the Politburo depended solely on a member's standing with Politburo peers, not on support from any subordinates. At times of intense divisiveness within the Politburo, as in 1957, 1964, and 1985, Central Committee members might arbitrate Politburo conflicts, but even then the accountability of Politburo members never extended to officials below Central Committee rank.[9]

The Politburo's supposed independence of outsiders' consent shaped the views advanced by both Hough and his critics of the Politburo's role in policy making. In Hough's view, when expansion of the economy combined with acquisition of superpower capabilities to increase the complexity of the objective problems facing the Brezhnev Politburo, the freewheeling style of policy making found under Khrushchev gave way to regular consultation with bureaucratic experts, to whose specialized knowledge the Politburo began increasingly to defer. The Brezhnev Politburo began to act as a broker, reconciling disagreements that naturally arose whenever objective problems were analyzed by functionally specialized bureaucrats relying on diverse kinds of expertise. Because tenure on the Politburo was independent of the bureaucrats' attitude, Politburo members could afford to act as objective referees of bureaucratic disputes.[10] The critics saw the Brezhnev Politburo accepting the advice of bureaucratic experts but confining ultimate decision authority within the ranks of its members in order to keep policy choices available for use as weapons in their internal struggle.

9. Robert V. Daniels, "Political Processes and Generational Change," in Archie Brown, ed., *Political Leadership in the Soviet Union* (Bloomington: Indiana University Press, 1989), and "Office Holding and Elite Status: The Central Committee of the CPSU," in Cocks et al., *Dynamics of Soviet Politics*; Jerry Hough, *How the Soviet Union Is Governed* (Cambridge: Harvard University Press, 1979), 260–64, and *Soviet Union and Social Science Theory*, 44–46.
10. Hough, "Pluralism," 52, and *Soviet Union and Social Science Theory*, 28–31.

Neither as brokers nor as infighters could members of the Brezhnev Politburo gain by going public. Brokers striving to reconcile bureaucratic disagreements would not want to polarize the disputants by going public to mobilize support for one side or another. An author of an infighting model has written that the Brezhnev Politburo devoted "much of its energies" to maintenance of a "Kremlin Wall" isolating the infighting from the influence of bureaucratic subordinates. In his view, under Brezhnev the Politburo penalized, with exclusion from membership or reduction of power, any member who tried to appeal to lesser officials for support in Politburo quarrels. Losers might try to appeal for bureaucratic support but going public invariably accelerated their defeat when the rest of the Politburo members penalized this disruption of the rules guaranteeing their own hold on power.[11]

I propose to emulate Hough's approach of explicit comparisons across differing institutions and to pursue his theme that the Brezhnev Politburo's policies represented bargains that took into account the diverse interests of bureaucratic groups. At the same time I also seek to explore the implication of disagreements between his version of institutional pluralism and the concepts of other scholars who have seen more advantage for Politburo members in going public than the circular flow of power would imply. One of these disagreements offers an amendment consistent with the thrust of institutional pluralism; the other offers an implicit challenge to its claim for the institutional distinctiveness of the Soviet polity.

First, Bruce Parrott and Thane Gustafson have independently argued that a limited form of going public is fully consistent with a variant of institutional pluralism's view of the Brezhnev Politburo as a deferential broker of debate among experts. By publicly disputing the rational merits or demerits of policy alternatives, Politburo members could shape the debate among bureaucratic experts, and the return flow of expert advice could either bolster or undermine a leader's reputation for policy expertise among Politburo peers. Investigations of particular policy issues by Parrott, Gustafson, and others have revealed that public engagement in "rational deliberation" of policy was a routine practice of members of the Brezhnev Politburo.[12]

11. Gelman, *Brezhnev Politburo*, 52–55.
12. Bruce Parrott, "Political Change and Civil-Military Relations," in Colton and

Second, George W. Breslauer and others have questioned the contention that control of appointments ever sufficed to secure power in
Soviet politics. Breslauer examined "authority building" by Khrushchev and Brezhnev on domestic issues and their public disagreements with their rivals, Georgii Malenkov and Aleksei Kosygin. By
"authority building" Breslauer meant public speechmaking by Soviet
leaders intent on winning reputations among officials for competence in devising solutions to policy problems and for artfulness in
brokering the conflicting demands of functionally specialized bureaucracies. Breslauer argued that mastery of the circular flow of
power might not suffice to motivate obedience by bureaucratic officials unless a leader also supplied officials with reasons to expect
that the leader's policy program would produce results beneficial to
them.[13]

When Breslauer concludes that control of appointments was insufficient to secure power in Soviet politics under Brezhnev without
authority gained by policy leadership, his finding implies a further
question of central concern to this book: Was control of appointments even independent of Politburo members' authority among Soviet officials? The concept of a circular flow of power may neglect
the possibility that Politburo members could exercise control of appointments only because their policy stands earned them support
from below—just as an elected executive's power to appoint cabinet

Gustafson, *Soldiers and the Soviet State*, 49–51, and *Politics and Technology in the Soviet
Union* (Cambridge: MIT Press, 1983), 5, 181–305. See also his "Soviet Foreign Policy,
Internal Politics, and Trade with the West," in Parrott, ed., *Trade, Technology, and
Soviet-American Relations* (Bloomington: Indiana University Press, 1985), 35–62; Thane
Gustafson, *Reform in Soviet Politics: Lessons of Recent Policies on Land and Water* (Cam-
bridge: Cambridge University Press, 1981), esp. 32–33. See also Dina Rome Spechler,
"The USSR and Third World Conflicts: Domestic Debate and Soviet Policy in the
Middle East, 1967–1973," *World Politics* 38 (1986): 435–61.

13. George W. Breslauer, *Khrushchev and Brezhnev as Leaders: Building Authority in
Soviet Politics* (London: Allen & Unwin, 1982). See also T. H. Rigby, Archie Brown,
and Peter Reddaway, eds., *Authority, Power, and Policy in the USSR* (New York: St.
Martin's Press, 1980); Teresa Rakowska-Harmstone, "Toward a Theory of Soviet
Leadership Maintenance," in Cocks et al., *Dynamics of Soviet Politics*. Robert C.
Tucker, Rigby, and Stephen F. Cohen have raised a parallel challenge to the thesis
that the circular flow of power enabled the rise of Stalin, presenting him instead as
having successfully shaped opinion in the Communist Party. See Robert C. Tucker,
Stalin in Power (New York: Norton, 1990); T. H. Rigby, *Political Elites in the USSR*
(Aldershot: Edward Elgar, 1990); Stephen F. Cohen, *Bukharin and the Bolshevik Revolution: A Political Biography, 1888–1938* (New York: Knopf, 1973). Hough has also sometimes considered this view of Brezhnev (but not Stalin) admissible: *How the Soviet
Union Is Governed*, 260–74.

members depends entirely on voters' support of his or her electoral platform.

Voting may not be necessary to make a politician dependent on constituency support. A semiotician would point out that a vote is not support itself but a sign of support. Support is an attitude of approval or disapproval of the politician's conduct in office, and the attitude can exist whether or not votes signal it. In order to govern, even in dictatorships politicians may require that some members of the collectivity hold attitudes of approval. The Politburo was just ten or fifteen old men. Their arms were short, their voices did not carry. Still these few exercised the right to decide every detail of the lives of a quarter of a billion people. What magnified them into such awesome figures? They wielded the voluntary compliance of the *nomenklatura*, the massive bureaucracy whose officials they appointed directly or indirectly. This compliance must have been voluntary in the main. Of course there were penalties for noncompliance by the individual official, but the ten or fifteen in the Politburo could not penalize the millions in the nomenklatura; infliction of a penalty on any official required willing compliance by others.

As a hypothesis, one might inquire whether dependence on officials' voluntary compliance might have compelled Politburo members to compete for approval from the bureaucracy. Any Politburo member who secured approval from the bureaucrats would have contributed to the power of the Politburo as a collective. Consequently, when the Politburo decided who would occupy its seats, that member could make demands on his peers. Unless they had secured approval from other bureaucrats, they would have made no countervailing contribution to the power of the Politburo. Without their own supporters among the bureaucrats, they could not resist his demands. Individual Politburo members accordingly might have needed to build support among the bureaucracy, *even if institutional rules empowered the Politburo alone to make the actual decision regarding retention or dismissal.* Of course, this hypothesis does not require every Politburo member to have built independent support. Even a majority of the Politburo might have consisted of appointees of a minority, composed of those members who individually commanded followings among the mass of bureaucrats. In the years immediately after World War II, this may even have been a minority of one, although Stalin's monopoly of power remains disputed.

When a politician needs approval from an audience of millions, whether voters or bureaucrats, going public is a practical way to get support. Politicians can seek approval by engaging in "rational deliberation" of policy options, as Gustafson and Parrott argue, but they can also rely on what Breslauer has called "diffuse appeals"—attempts to identify themselves with potential supporters' symbolic conceptions of their own identities. In a contest no politician can afford to forgo an effective means of winning allegiances. Like political candidates in electoral polities, Politburo members would need to "stand for" their supporters by converting themselves into public symbols of grand political visions.

Going Public and the Effectiveness of Soviet Foreign Policy

What difference might going public make to the effectiveness of foreign policy? One ill-fated choice by the Brezhnev Politburo was the decision after 1969 to conduct a foreign policy of offensive détente. Jack Snyder originated the term "offensive détente" to designate the Soviet effort after 1969 to couple U.S.-Soviet détente in bilateral and European issues with interventionism in Third World conflicts, an aggressive arms buildup, and exclusion of Western influence from East Europe.[14] This policy package ultimately proved counterproductive when intervention in the Third World undermined U.S.-Soviet détente and engendered international isolation as foreign states joined the United States to balance against Soviet expansionism, when military budgets swallowed the investment resources needed to sustain economic growth, and when exclusion of Western influence from Eastern Europe compelled the payment of steadily rising subsidies that proved unsustainable as the economy slowed.

Like analyses of other countries' foreign policies, studies of offensive détente have emphasized the adaptiveness of this policy to the objective circumstances prevailing at the time of its adoption. Influenced by the argument of institutional pluralism that the Brezhnev Politburo had become increasingly dependent on and deferential to the expertise of its bureaucratic subordinates, studies of the Soviet shift to offensive détente emphasize factors that a foreign policy expert would consider important. The year 1969 marked a turning point in the objective problems facing the Politburo. Although scholars disagree about what to include in the list of advantages and disad-

14. Jack Snyder, *Myths of Empire* (Ithaca: Cornell University Press, 1991), 246–50.

vantages that shifted Soviet calculations in favor of détente over continuing the earlier antagonism toward the United States, many of
the reasons commonly cited fall into three categories: reasons why
cooperation became more urgent for the Soviet Union, reasons why
capitalist governments seemed more likely to welcome cooperative
overtures, and reasons why détente appeared unlikely to require
sacrifice of attainable ideological objectives.

Changes in foreign governments' policies and in domestic economic performance made continuing antagonism toward the United
States disadvantageous. The NATO allies responded to the invasion
of Czechoslovakia by overcoming strains that had appeared to
threaten alliance cohesion in the 1960s, committing themselves to
continued coordination of foreign and military policy. NATO's restoration of unity cast doubt on the prospects for the previous Soviet
policy of negotiating security and economic issues with West European states without the United States' participation. Open combat
along the Chinese border dramatized the urgency of the threat in
the East. After four years of rapid expansion, domestic economic
performance deteriorated in 1969, turning Soviet eyes to the world
market's capacity to inject new technology.

While the advantages of détente increased for the Soviet Union,
the capitalist powers seemed more ready to cooperate. During 1969,
for the first time, Soviet strategic forces attained nominal parity, as
measured by the number of ICBMs, with U.S. forces. The vigor of
Soviet strategic offensive programs was pressuring the United States
to enter arms-control talks and promised to impel Washington's European allies to push for U.S. concessions. President Nixon and his
new national security adviser, Henry Kissinger, were turning to
Moscow in their search for an escape from Vietnam. In Bonn the
new Social Democratic government had adopted *Ostpolitik*, a policy
signifying recognition that the solution to inter-German problems
must also be sought in Moscow.

Chances also seemed promising that East-West détente would require no sacrifice of attainable ideological goals. Defeat in Vietnam
was teaching the United States a lesson about the perils of intervention against Soviet-aided rebellions in the Third World. The demonstration of readiness to invade Czechoslovakia would discourage the
United States and the Germans from attempts to detach Eastern Europe from its allegiance and would warn East Europeans against attempts to exploit détente by balancing East against West. While embracing détente would cost less in the Third World and Eastern

Europe, refraining from détente would also gain less among foreign communists, who, under the influence of Eurocommunism, were increasingly critical of the USSR.[15]

Few observers would incorporate all the factors on this list into their explanations of the Soviet turn to détente. They disagree over the relative importance of individual factors. But most observers agree with Alexander George that détente "was the result of developments in world politics that U.S. and Soviet leaders recognized and to which they attempted to adapt."[16]

All these developments occurred, Soviet leaders knew about them, and they altered the relative advantages and disadvantages of various policy options available to the Politburo. At the same time, an explanation cast in terms of objective advantages or disadvantages conceived as exterior to the collective agent, the Politburo and its subordinate bureaucracies, omits the Politburo's problem of constituting the collectivity as an authoritative agent. When leaders resolve this problem by going public, the responsiveness of foreign policies to objective conditions becomes contingent on the competition for authority among leaders. Three contingencies can be identi-

15. This list is compiled from a broad variety of authors who disagree over the relative importance and the inclusion of the various elements. See Gelman, *Brezhnev Politburo*, 116–35; Parrott, *Politics and Technology*, 231; Erik P. Hoffman and Robbin F. Laird, *The Politics of Economic Modernization in the Soviet Union* (Ithaca: Cornell University Press, 1982), 139; Adam B. Ulam, *Dangerous Relations: The Soviet Union in World Politics, 1970–1982* (Oxford: Oxford University Press, 1983), 35–82; Lawrence T. Caldwell, "Soviet Attitudes to SALT," Adelphi Papers no. 75 (London: Institute for Strategic Studies, 1971), 5–6; A. James McAdams, *East Germany and Détente: Building Authority after the Wall* (Cambridge: Cambridge University Press, 1985), 95–96; W. E. Griffith, "The Soviets and Western Europe: An Overview," and Robert Legvold, "France and Soviet Policy," both in Herbert Ellison, ed., *Soviet Policy toward Western Europe: Implications for the Atlantic Alliance* (Seattle: University of Washington Press, 1983), 13–21 and 66–68, respectively; Gerhard Wettig, *Europäische Sicherheit: Das europäische Staatensystem in der sowjetischen Aussenpolitik, 1966–1972* (Cologne: Bertelsmann Universitätsverlag, 1972), 154–63; Coit D. Blacker, "The Kremlin and Détente: Soviet Conceptions, Hopes, and Expectations," and George W. Breslauer, "Why Détente Failed," both in Alexander George, ed., *Managing U.S.-Soviet Rivalry: Problems of Crisis Prevention* (Boulder, Colo.: Westview, 1983), 121–29, and 331–32, respectively; Samuel B. Payne, *The Soviet Union and SALT* (Cambridge: MIT Press, 1980), 20; Raymond L. Garthoff, *Détente and Confrontation: American-Soviet Relations from Nixon to Reagan* (Washington, D.C.: Brookings, 1985), 101–2; Marshall D. Shulman, "SALT and the Soviet Union," in Mason Willrich and John B. Rhinelander, eds., *SALT: The Moscow Agreements and Beyond* (New York: Free Press, 1974), 101–2; Miroslav Nincic, *Anatomy of Hostility: The U.S.-Soviet Rivalry in Perspective* (San Diego: Harcourt Brace Jovanovich, 1989), 203–7.

16. Alexander L. George, "Détente: The Search for a Constructive Relationship," in George, *Managing U.S.-Soviet Rivalry*, 19.

fied: effects of drawing nonexperts into the issue, effects of linking issues in order to claim credit before the public rather than to mirror objective interactions among issues, and effects of the emergence of a dominant leader on policy flexibility.

First, when politicians try to gain bargaining leverage by going public, not only expert opinion counts. Politicians making foreign policy in an electoral polity certainly consult experts, not least because a display of consultation with experts helps to persuade inexpert voters that the politician's policy recommendations are sound. But the attitudes of the inexpert also count. Empirical research on the United States reveals the impact of the attitudes of uninformed voters on presidents' foreign policy choices. Voters incorporate foreign policy considerations into their evaluation of presidents.[17] The tendency of the president's approval rating to spike upward after foreign crises[18] gives presidents incentives to manipulate foreign policy in order to secure popular approval. Careful statistical analyses revealing a correlation between a decline in approval of the president's performance and initiation of military action by the United States provide evidence that presidents do not overlook these incentives.[19] A clear sign of the responsiveness of foreign policy to electoral concerns is the recent discovery that electoral polities have entered wars significantly more often during the half of the electoral cycle that immediately follows an election than during the half that precedes an election.[20]

Although members of the Brezhnev Politburo did not face election

17. John H. Aldrich, John L. Sullivan, and Eugene Borgida, "Foreign Affairs and Issue Voting: Do Presidential Candidates 'Waltz before a Blind Audience'?" *American Political Science Review* 83 (1989): 122–41; Miroslav Nincic and Barbara Hinckley, "Foreign Policy and the Evaluation of Presidential Candidates," *Journal of Conflict Resolution* 35 (June 1991):333–55; Jon Hurwitz and Mark Peffley, "The Means and Ends of Foreign Policy as Determinants of Presidential Support," *American Journal of Political Science* 31 (1987): 236–58.

18. Richard Brody and Catherine Shapiro, "A Reconsideration of the Rally Phenomenon in Public Opinion," in Samuel Lang, ed., *Political Behavior Annual*, vol. 2 (Boulder, Colo.: Westview, 1989); John E. Mueller, *War, Presidents, and Public Opinion* (New York: Wiley, 1973).

19. Charles W. Ostrom and Brian Job, "The President and the Political Use of Force," *American Political Science Review* 80 (1986): 541–66; Patrick James and John R. Oneal, "The Influence of Domestic and International Politics on the President's Use of Force," *Journal of Conflict Resolution* 35 (June 1991): 307–32; Richard J. Stoll, "The Guns of November: Presidential Reelections and the Use of Force, 1947–1982," *Journal of Conflict Resolution* 28 (June 1984): 231–46.

20. Kurt Taylor Gaubatz, "Election Cycles and War," *Journal of Conflict Resolution* 35 (June 1991): 212–44; for identification of a similar cycle, see Kenneth N. Waltz, *Foreign Policy and Democratic Politics: The American and British Experience* (Boston: Little, Brown, 1967).

by inexpert mass voters, dependence on support from functionally specialized bureaucrats could have exerted similar effects on their policy choices. Influenced by a deservedly famous study of the Cuban missile crisis, foreign policy specialists often assume that bureaucrats' opinions about policy respond solely to parochial interests—that is, to the matters about which the government employs them to be experts. Yet, as Ole Holsti pointed out, Graham Allison's study of the Cuban missile crisis showed that "where you sit" was *not* "where you stand" for many of the participants in President Kennedy's executive committee.[21] No bureaucrat can be an expert on all issues, yet any bureaucrat's life chances depend at least in part on the government's performance on issues in general. Like voters, bureaucrats form opinions on issues about which they are inexpert. Moreover, in an electoral polity the bureaucrats can focus on their parochial interests because the far more numerous mass of voters swamps the effect of their opinions on broader issues. When voters are excluded from consideration, as they were in the Soviet Union, bureaucrats' views on issues beyond their parochial concerns take on added weight.

When not only informed opinion counts, not only and not all the domestic and international developments that an expert would consider relevant to policy choice actually influence policy. Symbols can displace objective circumstances as the determinants of policy choices, because evidence that an informed person would use to reach a fully considered judgment makes less difference than symbols that communicate simply to an inattentive public. Though of course experts also use symbols to communicate, a symbol useful for going public to the inexpert conveys "a range of meaning beyond itself," as Barbara Hinckley points out. "A symbolic communication need not bear any relation to what is factually true or to what people, independently of the communication, might agree to be true."[22]

Symbolic politics is evident in both the Johnson-Goldwater exchange and the Brezhnev-Kosygin exchange. Neither Johnson nor Goldwater provided enough information to permit the public to judge whether Khrushchev's ouster presaged discord or reconciliation between the USSR and China. Instead, each turned Khrushchev's ouster into a sign with meaning far beyond the event itself. In

21. Ole Holsti, "Foreign Policy Formulation Viewed Cognitively," in Robert Axelrod, ed., *Structure of Decision: The Cognitive Maps of Political Elites* (Princeton: Princeton University Press, 1976), 27–32.
22. Barbara Hinckley, *The Symbolic Presidency: How Presidents Portray Themselves* (New York: Routledge, 1990), 4–5 (emphasis deleted).

Johnson's speech, the ouster of Khrushchev was emblematic of a general proposition that the roots of discord between states must lie deeper than individual personality. Johnson's use of Khrushchev heightened the significance of the Sino-Soviet split for U.S. policy. Seeking to diminish the significance of the Sino-Soviet split for U.S. policy, Goldwater kept the symbol but inverted the symbolism, making Khrushchev's ouster into a sign of the transience of Sino-Soviet disagreements, which he said were rooted in personal "quarreling" between two "dictators." Which candidate would exert more influence in future bargaining over U.S. policy was decided by voters who reacted at least partly to the symbolism, not to the objective conditions that they lacked the information and the expertise to judge. When Brezhnev turned space into a symbol of East-West rivalry and the moral superiority of Soviet policy, Kosygin kept the symbol but inverted the symbolism, making space a sign of U.S.-Soviet cooperation. Neither even suggested that space was a reliable index of U.S-Soviet ties.

When policy decisions depend in part on appeals to nonexperts, policy may also be unresponsive to domestic and international developments because uninformed publics judge leaders by their reputations, which are acquired by adherence to symbols over time. Dependence on reputation can motivate a leader who seeks public support to repeat policy recommendations for which the leader has already become known, even when objective conditions vary widely.

Second, bargaining ensures consideration of multiple alternatives and a range of expert opinion,[23] but bargaining as a procedure may either synthesize available information and alternatives into an "integrative" policy more suited to objective circumstances than any of the initial proposals or simply combine mutually inconsistent proposals into a self-frustrating "tactical" policy adopted to maintain the cohesion of the decision-making unit.[24] When a strong broker who is able to stand aside from the bargaining is present (as in the institutional pluralists' image of the Politburo), integrative bargains become more probable. Going public to gain bargaining leverage en-

23. Alexander L. George, *Presidential Decision-Making in Foreign Policy* (Boulder, Colo.: Westview, 1980).
24. Ernst B. Haas, "Collective Learning: Some Theoretical Speculations," in George W. Breslauer and Philip E. Tetlock, eds., *Learning in U.S. and Soviet Foreign Policy* (Boulder, Colo.: Westview, 1991), 86–88; "Why Collaborate? Issue-Linkage and International Regimes," *World Politics* 32 (1980): 357–405; and *The Obsolescence of Regional Integration Theory* (Berkeley: Institute of International Studies, 1975), esp. 21–39.

courages the tactical result.[25] If the bargainers choose some synthetic policy different from the initial positions chosen for public appeal, to their supporters each bargainer may appear to have made unwarranted concessions. In order to be able to point to something gained, bargainers whose leverage comes from going public may prefer a policy reached by an "issue trade" combining adoption of each bargainer's initial policy recommendation on some issue that all bargainers agree to define as separable from other issues under consideration, regardless of the possibility of mutual interference among the policies in the final package.

While objective conditions facing the Soviet Union in late 1969 may have justified offensive détente, in the abstract this policy could equally well have resulted from tactical bargaining. Politburo members could have shared support from various Soviet publics by allowing one leader to secure détente with the United States, one détente with Europe, one advances in the Third World, one the arms buildup, and one exclusion of U.S. influence from Eastern Europe. As tactical bargains often do, offensive détente proved self-defeating. The simultaneous pursuit of all these policies engendered the U.S.-Soviet conflicts over "linkage" which ultimately derailed the détente of the 1970s.

Third, effectiveness in foreign policy notoriously demands flexibility. The central problems of foreign policy are cooperation among allies, counteraction against enemies, avoidance of escalation to war when victory would not recompense damage, and sharing gains from economic interactions. Each of these is a bargaining problem, which turns foreign policy making into a two-level game of bargaining about bargaining.[26] In the international game, policy must adjust flexibly to fluctuations in the conduct of foreign states, but when a participant in the domestic game is using policy recommendations to maintain ties to some public, each participant must resist policy shifts that omit or downgrade the proposals that the public identifies with that participant. National leaderships' flexibility in negotiating with foreign antagonists may increase if international and domestic conditions are stringently compelling, but otherwise flexibility may depend on some leader's achievement of dominance in the domestic competition. Hardly anyone would argue that the objective advan-

25. Kernell, *Going Public*, 17–25.

26. Robert Putnam, "Diplomacy and Domestic Politics: The Logic of Two-Level Games," *International Organization* 42 (1988): 427–60.

tages and disadvantages stringently compelled the Politburo to shift from antagonism to détente in U.S.-Soviet bilateral and European issues—that the Politburo *could not* continue the previous antagonism. The year 1969 marked not only a transformation of the international scene but also what Breslauer calls Brezhnev's "ascendancy" within the Politburo.[27] Did offensive détente somehow help Brezhnev achieve or hold the ascendancy that he maintained until his death in 1982?[28]

The Evidence and Alternative Interpretations

Why analyze the rhetoric of the Brezhnev Politburo? Public statements by Soviet leaders are known to be deceptive, full of bluffs and concealment or misrepresentation of facts. Rhetoric is not a reliable predictor of foreign policy actions, and there is no guarantee that Politburo members had to reveal their true beliefs or actual policy preferences when strategic deception might better have served some purpose known to them but hidden from the observer. Would not analysis of Soviet actions more reliably reveal the Politburo's intentions?

The Politburo's rhetoric merits analysis because rhetoric is the evidence needed to judge hypotheses of the theory of political competition. For example, the theory predicts that observed policies will represent compromises among the diverging policy recommendations with which the competitors have previously gone public. We cannot test that hypothesis without examining leaders' rhetoric for the presence of policy recommendations and for divergence among them. The hypothesis is consistent with observations that rhetoric will be an unreliable predictor of policy, as a compromise policy may incorporate the recommendations that the individual bargainers offer in advance but will—by the definition of compromise—differ from them. As for deceptiveness, the theory of political competition assumes that going public is a strategic behavior. It interprets public statements not as evidence of politicians' true beliefs or real policy preferences but instead as evidence for determining whether any Politburo members developed *strategies* appropriate to seeking iden-

27. Breslauer, *Khrushchev and Brezhnev as Leaders*, 179–99.
28. See Archie Brown, "The Power of the General Secretary of the CPSU," in Rigby et al., *Authority, Power, and Policy*, 148–49.

tification with outside publics. The Politburo's intentions are not at issue; whatever their intentions, its members faced problems of sustaining both the Politburo's authority to decide policy and their own participation in decisions.[29] The issue is whether they used rhetoric to solve those problems.

The evidence used to determine whether members of the Brezhnev Politburo engaged in going public comprises all *Pravda* texts of speeches, interviews, press conferences, and articles by members and candidate members of the Politburo, Central Committee secretaries, and (because of the subject matter) the ministers of defense and international affairs. *Pravda* has been chosen as a source because it used to publish the *protokol* (the official report of activities) of the Politburo,[30] including at least some text from nearly all speeches given for publication by any member of the Politburo or Secretariat. Although comparison of *Pravda*'s rescensions with those of other Soviet newspapers would have been informative, no other newspapers have been used, as the research project would have become too burdensome. As different Soviet newspapers are known to have varied the published texts of a given speech, confinement of the research to a single newspaper is a conservative strategy for investigating the hypothesis of differences among Politburo members. Because the task is to examine what Soviet audiences read at the time, evidence of leaders' public stands has never been derived from translations, from unofficial sources, or from retrospectives published under Gorbachev, although these sources have been consulted when appropriate for the analysis of bargaining.

The texts have been taken from two three-year intervals: October 15, 1964, through November 1967 and January 1970 through December 1972. The years 1968 and 1969 were omitted because during most of that period the Politburo concentrated on the question of policy toward the Czechoslovak crisis, which did not end with the intervention in 1968. That policy has been examined in two excellent

29. This is where my approach departs from "cognitive mapping." Regardless of whether rhetoric (public and private) should be taken as "representative" of true beliefs or "instrumental" in an attempt to manipulate other decision makers, the proponents of cognitive mapping argued that the causal relations expressed in rhetoric shaped policy outcomes. I agree, but the causal variable for me is not the decision makers' appreciation of causation in the external environment but their appreciation of what ideas of causality will influence domestic audiences outside the decision-making process. See Axelrod, *Structure of Decision*, 7–17, 56–60, 252–55.

30. *Materialy Plenuma Tsentral'nogo Komiteta KPSS, 19–20 sentiabria 1989 goda* (Moscow: Politizdat, 1989), 83.

full-length studies;[31] while the conclusions of this analysis differ
from theirs in some respects, the need for extensive documentation
and the complexity of the Politburo bargaining have forced exclusion
of the period here.

Because the test of the theory depends so heavily on identifying
differences over policy in Politburo members' public statements, it is
worth considering how observers can distinguish going public from
other causes that might produce apparent differences. Most students of Soviet politics will agree that the speeches of various Politburo members were not identical. Observers might, however, attribute the differences to a variety of causes other than going public,
four of which deserve consideration here: expression of personal
opinion or attitude, use of speeches to transmit international bargaining signals aimed at foreign rather than domestic audiences,
variation in the leaders' assigned public roles, and variation in domestic audiences.

Personal Opinion or Attitude

Many observers take differences in public speeches by Politburo
members as the natural variation to be expected when diverse individuals conduct a discussion. If Politburo members were freed by
the circular flow of power from the need for public support, they,
unlike electoral candidates, would not have faced pressures to conceal opinions likely to alienate voters. As personalities of Politburo
members varied, in this model the opinions they expressed about
policy would have varied also.

Although personality differences manifest themselves in the rhetoric of electoral candidates and presumably also affected the public
positions taken by Politburo members, some Soviet evidence casts
doubt on how much personality was allowed to show through. An
Izvestiia correspondent who interviewed former staff assistants to
members of the Brezhnev Politburo comments that the members'
speeches were "identical, not so much in the ideas, but in the way
thoughts were expressed. . . . They were people of varied education, intellect, temperament, but everything they said, everything
signed with their names was like two drops of water. This phenom-

31. Jiri Valenta, *Soviet Intervention in Czechoslovakia, 1968: Anatomy of a Decision* (Baltimore: Johns Hopkins University Press, 1979); Karen Dawisha, *The Kremlin and the
Prague Spring* (Berkeley: University of California Press, 1984).

enon is explained to some extent by the words I heard from a former assistant to the General Secretary . . . 'we were supposed to put every phrase on *shock absorbers.' "*[32] Formal analyses by linguists confirm adherence of the Brezhnev Politburo's speeches to rigid stylistic conventions.[33] The emphasis on "shock absorbers" suggests that Politburo members took care not to display personality.

Moreover, results of psychological research indicate that a finding of policy outcomes typical of bargaining would disconfirm the interpretation of differences in public speeches as a result of personality. The notion that variation in personal opinion explains differences in public speeches rests on an analogy between Politburo members and any group of individuals. Cross-cultural studies of individuals discussing joint decisions in small groups have shown that the consensus reached by the group "polarizes" toward one of the extremes advocated during the discussion. Irving Janis was too hasty in labeling this polarization a "risky shift," as later research showed that the shift could as well be toward the cautious extreme as toward the risky one.[34] Bargaining, in contrast, produces either (*a*) the choice located at the power-weighted median when policy alternatives range along a single issue dimension or (*b*) a combination of choices located along different issue dimensions. In no case can bargaining among multiple powerful participants produce polarization to a single extreme, as persuasion does in small groups. Consequently, observation of the results expected from bargaining would discredit the interpretation that variation in personal opinion alone shaped the public stands of Politburo members.

Relying on newspaper texts of public speeches, I also refrain from interpreting statements as evidence of Politburo members' cognitive processes at work. All the irrationalities discussed by the foreign policy literature that draws on cognitive psychology will be found in these texts: excess consistency, excessive readiness to learn from sa-

32. Leonid Shinkarev, "Koridory vlasti—Na polputi k kabinetam, gde prinimaiut resheniia," *Izvestiia*, April 25, 1990. Accounts of the composing of several speeches by Brezhnev can be found in G. A. Arbatov, *Zatianuvsheesia vyzdorovlenie, 1953–1985: Svidetel'stvo sovremennika* (Moscow: Mezhdunarodnye Otnosheniia, 1991), 135–41.

33. Patrick Seriot, *Analyse du discours politique soviétique* (Paris: Institut d'Etudes Slaves, 1985); A. N. Vasil'eva, *Gazetno-publitsisticheskii stil' rechi* (Moscow: Russkii Iazyk, 1982); Michael E. Urban, "Political Language and Political Change in the USSR: Notes on the Gorbachev Leadership," in Peter J. Potichny, ed., *The Soviet Union: Party and Society* (Cambridge: Cambridge University Press, 1988), 87–106.

34. Hermann Brandstatter, J. H. Davis, and G. Stocker-Kreichgauer, eds., *Group Decision Making* (New York: Academic Press, 1982).

lient historical examples, resistance to discrepant information, wishful thinking, cognitive dissonance, oversimplification, attribution of excessive cohesion to enemies and excessive importance to the self.[35] One may wonder, however, how representative these texts are of individual cognition. Politburo speeches were group products—composed by speechwriting teams according to directions from individual leaders and at least sometimes subjected to the scrutiny of Politburo peers—not just the leaders' personal utterances, and the texts used in this study were further edited by *Pravda*. Moreover, a question arises about why the texts oversimplify the international situation. Does the speaker choose the text by processing information about the international situation or about the audience? If the latter, the speaker may oversimplify because oversimplifications help to communicate to an inexpert audience.[36]

International Bargaining Signals

Many observers have interpreted public statements by members of the Brezhnev Politburo as international bargaining signals directed not at domestic audiences but at foreign ones. Often Politburo members formulated their public statements in language that rendered such an interpretation highly plausible. In June 1971, for example, commenting publicly on the strategic arms negotiations, Brezhnev said,

> Even Washington recognizes the principle of equal security in words. In deeds, however, the American side can in no way make itself implement this principle consistently. . . . The question arises on what basis can Washington expect us to renounce programs already adopted if in

35. This list is drawn from the classic book by Robert Jervis, *Perception and Misperception in International Politics* (Princeton: Princeton University Press, 1976). See also Michael Brecher, *Decisions in Crisis: Israel, 1967 and 1973* (Berkeley: University of California Press, 1980); Glenn H. Snyder and Paul Diesing, *Conflict among Nations: Bargaining, Decision Making, and System Structure in International Crises* (Princeton: Princeton University Press, 1977); Debra Welch Larson, *Origins of Containment: A Psychological Explanation* (Princeton: Princeton University Press, 1985); Robert Jervis, Janice Gross Stein, and Richard Ned Lebow, eds., *Psychology and Deterrence* (Baltimore: Johns Hopkins University Press, 1985); Axelrod, *Structure of Decision*.

36. For further discussion of cognitive theories of foreign policy, see Richard D. Anderson, Jr., "Why Competitive Politics Inhibits Learning in Soviet Foreign Policy," in George W. Breslauer and Philip E. Tetlock, eds., *Learning in U.S. and Soviet Foreign Policy* (Boulder, Colo.: Westview, 1991), 100–134; see also Snyder, *Myths of Empire*, 26–31.

the course of the talks the American government itself has adopted several very major decisions on augmenting its strategic forces? It is long past time to renounce a double measure, a double standard in evaluating one's own actions and those of others.[37]

This passage does indeed read very like an international bargaining signal demanding a concession in SALT from the United States.

On further examination, however, the merits of such a reading are less apparent. The "principle of equal security" (to be discussed at more length later) justified an agreement that exchanged Soviet advantages in some types of weapons for U.S. advantages in other types. Brezhnev's "programs already adopted" referred to Soviet plans to retain heavy strategic missiles and replace medium ones. The United States side had been demanding the Soviet side cancel these plans. When Brezhnev issued this ostensible international bargaining signal in mid-June 1971, he knew that in May 1971 Kissinger had already agreed to drop the U.S. demand. As the agreement had been reached in the "back channel" through Ambassador Anatolii Dobrynin,[38] Brezhnev was privy to this information when his Soviet audiences were not. The pose of demanding something that has already been privately conceded exploits domestic audiences' lack of information to gain the leader credit for extracting concessions from the foreign government when the agreement reached privately is later announced.

Such instances cannot be generalized to the conclusion that all apparent international bargaining signals are poses for the benefit of domestic audiences. At the same time, the more such cases that are found, the less plausible the interpretation of Politburo statements as international bargaining signals. Unfortunately, most cases are hard to judge. Observers usually lack detailed reconstructions of secret international negotiations comparable to Raymond Garthoff's magisterial study of U.S.-Soviet negotiations, and without such a record one can never judge in any given instance whether a statement is an intended signal or merely a pose. Given the rewards of posing, observers have no reason to suppose that any particular statement is directed at a foreign audience alone. A thoughtful analysis of international signaling by the Soviet Union points out that public statements by leaders are ill suited to this task. The key ele-

37. June 12, 1971.
38. Garthoff, *Détente and Confrontation*, 157–58, 162.

ment in signaling is the credibility of the commitment communicated to the foreign government. Signals become more credible as
their cost to the sender rises, but talk is cheap. Military and naval
deployments, economic sanctions, tightening of border controls and
customs, and diplomatic moves make more effective international
signals than do public declarations. Politburo statements have the
further disadvantage that the brevity of a public speech often makes
cryptic a message that can be clarified when it is delivered in more
detail through confidential channels, when the recipient has the advantage of being able to interrogate the diplomatic messenger concerning any ambiguities. If ambiguity advantages the sender, the
diplomat need not answer questions.[39]

Any leader whose influence in foreign policy bargaining depends
on public support actively wants foreign governments to adopt behaviors that confirm, in the eyes of the leader's domestic public, the
validity of the leader's vision of the world situation. Consequently,
leaders should use their public statements to try to send international bargaining signals, even though they cannot expect foreign
governments to interpret them accurately. The leader's problem is
that domestic audiences receive these signals, too. The leader needs
to make sure that international bargaining signals are consistent
with the image the leader seeks to project to the domestic audience.

An account by a former speechwriter for Brezhnev provides direct
testimony that speeches signaled both domestic and foreign audiences and that domestic audiences were crucial. The speechwriter
describes his efforts to persuade Brezhnev to reject a draft of a November 1966 speech in Georgia written by others who had filled it
with encomiums to Stalin. He "decided . . . that not abstract discussions about the harmfulness of the cult of personality . . . but maxi-
mally substantive arguments about the harmful practical consequences of such a speech by the new leader for himself, the party,
and the country" would persuade Brezhnev. The arguments concerned the reaction of domestic and foreign audiences to the speech.
Reading to Brezhnev a series of anti-Stalin statements by other Politburo members, the speechwriter asked Brezhnev, "How would they
. . . look in the eyes of the party, the broad Soviet and international
attentive public, after such a speech by the new General Secretary?
. . . Or did Comrade Brezhnev specially want to discredit them in

39. Thomas M. Cynkin, *Soviet and American Signalling in the Polish Crisis* (London:
Macmillan, 1988), 5–13.

order then to get rid of them?" Moreover, even though the final speech contained extensive commentary on East-West relations, the only foreign audiences that the speechwriter mentioned to Brezhnev were East European and Western communists.[40]

Two general empirical tests can distinguish whether Soviet leaders' statements should be interpreted as signals to international audiences or as signals to a domestic audience that may also be addressed to an international one. Of course, one test is whether *Pravda* published the statement in Russian. When Politburo members wanted to reach foreign audiences only, they could always give interviews not distributed to the Soviet public, as Kosygin did when he was interviewed by Senator Frank Church in 1971.[41] The intended recipients of anything published in Russian by the Communist Party's own newspaper must have included domestic audiences.

The other test relies on internal features of the rhetoric itself. The Soviet leaders might use lexical items or semantic codes understandable to domestic audiences but confusing to foreign audiences. When the Soviet leaders disagreed over their response to U.S. escalation in Vietnam in 1965, for example, the proponents of counterescalation consistently called the U.S. escalation an "adventure," whereas the opponents of counterescalation called it a "provocation." To the foreign audience the term "provocation" sounds like a justification for Soviet counteraction, but in Russian *provokatsiia* happens to mean "an incitement to some action that could entail grave consequences."[42] "Provocation," by drawing attention to the "grave consequences" of counterescalation, cued the audience to hear an argument against it. Semantic codes aim at readers with specialized linguistic knowledge. According to a Soviet linguist, an "informed" audience read speeches differently from the mass audience. The informed reader was attentive to the "importance of every detail," such as who appeared in lists of public figures.[43] Accordingly, Brezhnev's former speechwriter recounts as a significant accomplishment his success in limiting mention of Stalin in Brezhnev's speech to a single instance in a list of Georgian revolutionaries—

40. Arbatov, *Zatianuvsheesia vyzdorovlenie*, 135–36.
41. *Interview with Kosygin* (Washington, D.C.: U.S. Government Printing Office, 1971).
42. S. N. Ozhegov, *Slovar' russkogo iazyka* (Moscow: Sovietskaia Entsiklopediia, 1968), 597.
43. Vasil'eva, *Gazetno-publitsisticheskii stil' rechi*, 45–51.

"and then in alphabetical order (i.e., closer to the end of the list)."[44] Attentive domestic publics paid attention to these signals; foreign governments ignored them.

Assigned Public Roles

It is possible that public statements of Politburo members vary only because they were assigned to play different official roles. In order to improve its performance as a broker, the Politburo might have divided the labor of following particular issues, and this division of labor might have diversified public statements by individuals. Garthoff noted, for example, that the head of state, N. V. Podgorny, was "assigned particular responsibility in the Politburo for African affairs."[45] The rhetoric of Politburo speeches encouraged the belief that its members, like their appointees to subordinate offices, retained their posts not by competing for public support but by impersonal assignment. Brezhnev himself spoke of "the responsible work . . . that the party has assigned me at the present time."[46] Speeches occasionally opened with variants on the formulaic "The Politburo assigned me . . ." or "The Politburo asked me . . ."[47] Before a member of the Brezhnev Politburo gave a speech, its content sometimes (and perhaps routinely) had to be reviewed by other members.[48]

Specialization of responsibilities by assignment is not inconsistent with the hypothesis of individualistic competition among Politburo members. Members of Congress maneuver for assignments to committees in which their constituents can see them deliberating on legislation of special interest to them. Committee assignment covaries with the topics that senators and representatives address in public statements. David Mayhew argues that when elected politicians specialize in particular issues each can claim credit for a policy achievement on a different issue.[49] For the same reason, competing mem-

44. Arbatov, *Zatianuvsheesia vyzdorovlenie*, 137.
45. Garthoff, *Détente and Confrontation*, 531.
46. December 20, 1966.
47. January 8, 1966; January 20, July 25, October 4, 1971.
48. Eduard A. Shevardnadze, *Moi vybor: V zashchitu demokratii i svobody* (Moscow: Novosti, 1991), 93; Fedor Burlatskii, "Brezhnev i krushenie ottepeli: Razmyshlenie o prirode politicheskogo liderstva," *Literaturnaia Gazeta*, 1988, no. 37 (September 14), 13–14.
49. David R. Mayhew, *Congress: The Electoral Connection* (New Haven: Yale University Press, 1974), 85–94.

bers of the Politburo might have agreed to divide public roles and to devote their public comments mainly to their particular issues.[50]

Specialization by role is also consistent with the competitive hypothesis because it enables politicians to reinforce verbal appeals with tangible rewards. Especially in the Soviet Union under Brezhnev, where income and status were so tightly tied to rank, the power of appointment associated with an official role provided an occupant with opportunities to reward supporters and to retaliate against foes. A typical Soviet phenomenon was the practice among newcomers to an office of appointing their subordinates from previous assignments to key jobs in the new hierarchy. Because one's official role held such promise for reinforcing verbal appeals with tangible rewards and penalties, a Politburo member's public statements should have emphasized those public recommendations that he could reinforce with the powers of his office; where Politburo members sat should have been where they stood.

Despite these resemblances to a division of labor by expertise, a competitive division of labor will differ in two respects. One is instability. A division of labor established by expertise increases in value to a decision-making group the longer each member of the group pursues a specialty. The distribution of roles in a competitive division of labor shifts as participants succeed or fail in their efforts to gain control of more issues. A division of labor established by expertise should feature neither sudden irruptions by one leader into others' specialties nor a general role expansion by any single leader.

The other is variation of individual statements within and across roles. Competitors gain by recruiting not only the supporters accessible within the exercise of their official roles but also any other available supporters. Role assignment is insufficient to explain differences if Politburo members did not always stand only where they sat; that is, if two sequential occupants of the same role made different statements, if two simultaneous occupants of the same collective role made different statements, if an occupant of any role made distinctive statements on issues beyond his formal competence, if an individual's statements remained consistent across a transfer from one role to another, or if a continuing occupant of a role suddenly

50. For evidence of this mutual deference in the Central Committee Secretariat, see Leon Onikov, "Ia obviniaiu apparatnykh mechenostsev Stalina v tragedii KPSS," October 7, 1991.

expanded the range of issues on which he developed distinctive public stands.

Variation in Audiences

Differences in public speeches are sometimes attributed to variation in audiences. According to this interpretation, the Politburo adopted a sophisticated propaganda policy that recognized that the contents of its members' speeches should depend on the group being addressed. The contents of speeches certainly did vary noticeably with the audience. The statements made by a Politburo member addressing guests at a dinner for a visiting French official differed from those made by a colleague, or even from those he made himself when he addressed a public rally for a visiting East European communist.

When a leader goes public, the content of a speech varies with the audience because that audience *is part of the message to the broader audience that the leader hopes to mobilize.* Any statement that appeared in *Pravda* reached a far larger audience than the people present on the immediate occasion of its delivery. By telling the broader audience what immediate audience the leader was facing, *Pravda* formed expectations about the speech's content. Regular readers of *Pravda* should have come to expect that speeches to French officials would differ from speeches to East European communists. Consequently, Politburo members could alert their broader audiences to the content of their public stands by picking immediate audiences appropriate for the messages they wanted to send.

Variations in audiences could not explain all differences in Politburo statements if two leaders addressing comparable audiences on occasions near in time made differing statements on the same issue or if some Politburo member repeated statements to diverse audiences.

Outline of the Book

This book consists of twelve chapters. Chapters 2 and 3 present further theoretical arguments. Chapters 4 through 11 present empirical evidence of going public by Politburo members in the early Brezhnev years. Chapter 12 offers concluding reflections on the interaction between Soviet domestic politics and foreign policy.

Chapter 2 concerns the meaning of constituency in a nonelectoral polity such as the Soviet Union. It explains how cross-pressures acting on Soviet bureaucrats would make them responsive to Breslauer's diffuse appeals as well as to appeals aimed at their parochial interests, how bureaucrats unable to vote could nevertheless register their approval or disapproval of Politburo rivals, and why Politburo members chosen by their peers had nevertheless to compete for bureaucratic support.

Chapter 3 explores the abstract relationship between constituency competition and foreign policy. It argues that political rivals compete for support by going public with contrasting visions of how to sustain a domestic social order. The domestic visions must incorporate symbolic appeals in order to overcome doubts about the credibility of promises of material benefit. Trying to maintain the domestic audience's awareness of the differences among them, the competitors replicate the contrasts among their domestic visions in opposing grand strategies, which tell how to sustain the state in international affairs. In order to replicate contrasting domestic visions in international strategies, each leader chooses a grand strategy symbolically coherent with that leader's domestic vision.

Whenever leaders' grand strategies imply different international courses of action, they must choose policy by bargaining. In the process each leader seeks to ensure that the enacted policy conforms no more closely to any rival's grand strategy than to the leader's own. The policy chosen in the bargaining then encounters world conditions, which may either reinforce or erode the persuasiveness of the leaders' strategies to constituents. Since the policies are compromises that mix intentionally incompatible strategies, policies normally prove self-frustrating, and all leaders' persuasiveness to constituents generally erodes over time. Because not all leaders' persuasiveness need erode at the same rate, however, in the course of time some leader may be left with a stronger hold on constituents' loyalties. This stronger base affords the leader an opportunity to expand the constituency by enunciating a new vision that recruits disaffected former followers of rivals. If some leader engages in constituency expansion, bargaining over foreign policy will begin to manifest the spread of that leader's novel grand strategy across more issues.

Chapters 4 through 11 present empirical evidence on which we may judge whether this model, compiled from literature on electoral polities, describes the behavior and foreign policy choices of members of the Politburo from October 1964 through November 1967 and from January 1970 through December 1972. Chapter 4 investigates whether Breslauer's contrasts between the domestic political visions of Brezhnev and Kosygin from 1964 through 1967 extended to any other members of the Politburo. We find that both Podgorny and Mikhail Suslov developed distinctive visions of socialism; with one exception discussed below, lesser Politburo members offered distinctive policy recommendations on particular issues but did not generate an overall vision that would compete with the four seniors. Chapters 5 through 8 investigate whether these four senior members of the post-Khrushchev Politburo replicated their domestic political visions in contrasting grand strategies in international affairs, whether the different grand strategies produced public advocacy of opposed policies on specific issues, and whether the Politburo resolved public disagreements by choosing policies that compromised among their various strategies.

The organization of Chapters 5 through 8 mirrors the tendency of political competition to produce specialization among rival leaders. The four senior members of the Politburo resolved their competition by allowing each of them to take a dominant but not exclusive role in a different regional or functional issue. Chapter 5, on Eastern Europe, is mainly about Brezhnev; Chapter 6, on China and world communism, describes how Suslov frustrated Brezhnev's attempt to seize issue leadership; Chapter 7, on East-West relations, describes how U.S. escalation in Vietnam cost Kosygin control of policy; and Chapter 8 describes how Kosygin responded by intruding on the Third World issues that otherwise would have been allotted to Podgorny.

Chapter 9 exploits an opportunity, unexpectedly discovered in the documents, to test directly whether going public affected policy compromises by the Brezhnev Politburo. In the spring of 1966 a fifth Politburo member, Aleksandr Shelepin, went public with a sectarian grand strategy. If going public was useless or harmful to a Politburo member, neither the public stances of the four senior members nor the policy compromises need have changed in response to Shelepin's initiative. But if going public provided bargaining leverage, to prevent Shelepin's entry into the inner circle of the Politburo the four senior members would have needed to alter their public stands and the compromise policy in order to demonstrate to Soviet officials that Shelepin's sectarianism could not direct foreign policy. Chapter 9 describes Shelepin's innovative grand strategy and the four senior members' reactions to it during 1966 and 1967.

Chapters 10 and 11 assess the impact of Brezhnev's ascendancy, which Breslauer's study of domestic politics dates to December 1969, on the transition to détente in policy toward the United States. Chapter 10 presents evidence of Brezhnev's new grand strategy for international affairs from 1970 through 1972. The chapter examines whether the new strategy combined the objectives of preserving his former appeals while selectively incorporating appeals formerly associated with rivals whose constituencies might have become disaffected. It also presents evidence of continuity in the public stands of the other three leaders, as a means for judging whether the new grand strategy was Brezhnev's or a consensual reaction to changed international circumstances. Chapter 11 investigates the contribution of bargaining within the Politburo to the two principal U.S.-Soviet agreements of the period: the breakthrough on linking East-West issues in May 1971 and the holding of the Moscow summit in May 1972.

Chapter 12 returns to the question whether Politburo members during the Brezhnev years acted as brokers, infighters, or advocates who formed a ruling coalition by representing different constituencies of bureaucrats. It examines the evidence for a relationship between going public and the Brezhnev Politburo's enactment of self-defeating foreign policies. It ends with a commentary on the relevance of the perspective adopted here to politics and foreign policy in the very different domestic institutions that Gorbachev introduced and Yeltsin took over.

Chapter 2

Constituencies in
Soviet Politics

The idea that members of the Brezhnev Politburo went public
to gain support from constituencies in much the same way that electoral politicians seek voter approval often encounters understandable skepticism. There is reason to question a metaphor comparing
Politburo members with electoral candidates. Until Gorbachev's final
years, Soviet institutions excluded the contested elections that ordi-
narily are supposed to motivate politicians to go public.

Even when doubts about the validity of an underlying metaphor
are plausible, they cannot properly be used as criteria for evaluating
a theory. Darwin rooted his theory of evolution in a metaphor comparing competitive reproduction in nature with an artificial breeder's
improvement of domesticated animal and plant species.[1] Even though
all evolutionists have recognized that nature lacks a breeder, evolu-
tionary biology remains a valid theory because the metaphor of the
nonexistent breeder draws the observer's eye to natural phenomena
whose significance would otherwise go unrecognized. The merits of
using a theory of competitive politics to explain Soviet foreign policy
deserve to be judged by whether the phenomena predicted by the
theory are found in the empirical investigation, not by whether the
metaphor seems appropriate in advance of the observations. Every
theory is rooted in some metaphor, and metaphors, which by their

1. Charles Darwin, *The Origin of Species* (New York: New American Library, 1958),
31–57.

34

very nature compare things that are in some respects unlike, are always doubtful.

Even though the theory deserves to be judged by the empirical test, it may nevertheless be worthwhile to speculate in advance how competitive politics could work in the absence of contested elections. If members of the Brezhnev Politburo sought constituent support, they looked for it not among the general population, excluded by Soviet institutions from politics, but among the bureaucrats appointed through the system of nomenklatura. The issue of how competition for support from Soviet bureaucrats could have worked breaks down into three subordinate questions.

First, competing politicians in an electoral polity gain from going public only if voters' choices are uncertain or at least labile. In contrast to voters, bureaucrats are often supposed to evaluate a politician's platform solely by consulting their parochial interests. Rooted in fixed organizational affiliations, parochial interests are both known and unchanging. If bureaucrats are strictly parochial in their response to policy proposals, a Politburo member considering an appeal to Soviet bureaucrats should have recognized that argument would have no effect. What are the possible sources of uncertainty or lability in the attitudes of Soviet bureaucrats that might have made going public attractive to a Politburo member?

Second, even if Politburo members could alter the attitudes of bureaucratic constituencies, how could Soviet bureaucrats express their approval or disapproval of a Politburo member when they had no opportunity to vote and were forbidden even to utter an opinion concerning the personal suitability of Politburo members for office?

Third, why would Politburo members, chosen for and removed from office by their peers, whose decisions routinely received approval by unanimous vote of the Central Committee, have felt their tenure in office to be dependent on support from bureaucrats?

The answer to the first question is that Soviet bureaucrats were severely cross-pressured among organizational interests, career advancement, and personal attitudes. Generating uncertainty about the responses of bureaucrats to political appeals, these cross-pressures presented Politburo members with opportunities to compete for the allegiance of bureaucrats by advancing a variety of symbolic appeals.

Second, Soviet bureaucrats could express their opinions indirectly, by a combination of private lobbying, public commentary about policy lines associated with various Politburo members, and variation in the enthusiasm with which they executed policy decisions. Their performance of bureaucratic functions constituted a kind of continuing referendum on the Politburo.

Third, loyalty from bureaucrats helped Politburo members to ensure their own tenure in office. Because the Politburo as a whole was powerful only insofar as bureaucrats voluntarily imposed its decisions on society, any Politburo member who commanded the confidence of the bureaucracy augmented the powers of the Politburo as a whole. Other members who did not command the confidence of bureaucrats would have found themselves dependent on him for their powers. Without making any countervailing contribution to his powers, they would have found themselves unable to challenge his decisions about their own retention of office. Any Politburo member who sought the allegiance of the bureaucracy compelled others to match his efforts in their own self-interest, regardless of formal electoral rules that provided for election and dismissal of Politburo members solely by the Central Committee.

Cross-Cleavages within the Soviet Bureaucracy

Soviet bureaucrats evaluating policy proposals by a Politburo member would have been responsive to more than the parochial interests of their organization. Their attitudes toward a Politburo member would have been sensitive to their parochial interests dictated by their distribution in competing economic sectors, but also to the competition among them for promotion, to their placement in bureaucracies with distinctive missions but overlapping responsibilities (particularly their multiple subordination to organizations with functional and territorial responsibilities), and to their personal values and opinions. Because the pressures resulting from these organizational and attitudinal affiliations could push the individual bureaucrat in opposite directions, no single cleavage appears capable of determining how Soviet bureaucratic opinion would have responded to a policy line advocated by a given Politburo member, and consequently how the bureaucrats would have viewed that member's retention in or removal from the Politburo. If bureaucratic opinion depended on the way issues were posed, Politburo members faced opportunities to shape bureaucratic allegiances by competing to define the issues.

Distribution in economic sectors should have exerted a significant pull on the allegiances of Soviet bureaucrats. Any government taxes some people and issues subsidies to others. Governments collect revenues and expend them on goods and services; those who produce the goods and services demanded by a given policy profit, while others' income diminishes because it is taxed to pay for the goods and services in demand. Economic sectors are composed of people who share a common competence. Everyone in a sector receives an opportunity to gain income when demand increases for the product of the people in that sector. Consequently, common membership in a sector provides an incentive for individuals to evaluate government policies in a uniform way.[2]

Sectoral incentives would have influenced policy making in the Soviet Union differently from the way they influence policies in mass democracies. In the latter, wage earners in a given sector can vote for or against candidates whose policies benefit or harm that sector. In the Soviet Union, too, wage earners gained or lost by policies that increased or reduced the state's demand for their services, but the ban on independent association and the absence of institutionalized consultation with the mass public in the form of contested elections limited the influence of wage earners on decisions.

At the same time, expansion of demand for the services of people employed in a particular sector benefited not only the wage earners within that sector but also their supervisors within the bureaucracy. In any bureaucracy, the number and rank of supervisory positions must be related, at least loosely, to the number of supervisees. Accordingly, expansion of the Soviet state's demand for the product of a sector would increase the number and the rank of supervisory posts in that sector. Therefore the sectoral distribution of the labor force can serve as a proxy for the distribution of bureaucrats among economic sectors (information that has not been published for the Brezhnev period). Table 1, which shows the sectoral distribution of Soviet wage earners in 1970, confirms the familiar impression that Soviet employment combined a large agricultural sector with a nonagricultural labor force divided between one enormous sector and a number of smaller ones. Workers in machinery production alone accounted for 17 percent of manual workers. In addition, they pro-

2. Gary Becker, "A Theory of Competition among Pressure Groups for Political Influence," *Quarterly Journal of Economics* 98 (August 1983): 371–400; Jeffry A. Frieden, *Debt, Development, and Democracy: Modern Political Economy and Latin America, 1965–1985* (Princeton: Princeton University Press, 1991), 15–29.

Table 1. Sectoral distribution of Soviet manual workers and cultural employees, 1970
(in thousands)

Sector	Number of workers
Heavy industry	19,121
Agriculture and fisheries	22,815
Light industry	4,403
Retail, cleaning, and child care	5,180
Services	5,433
Construction	5,432
Wood products and printing	2,220
Intercity transport and postal service	3,459
Urban transport	6,244
Warehousing and inspection	3,050
Miscellaneous	3,666
All manual workers	83,759
Cultural employees	9,631

Source: Tsentral'noe Statisticheskoe Upravlenie pri Sovete Ministrov SSSR, *Itogi vsesoiuznoi perepisi naseleniia 1970 goda*, vol. 6, *Raspredelenie naseleniia SSSR po zaniatiiam* (Moscow: Statistika, 1973), Table 2.
Note: After rounding, the categories of manual workers add to 81,023,000, not to 83,759,000. The discrepancy is present in the source table. Chances are that the missing 2.7 million manual workers are either military conscripts or prisoners, but the source provides no explanation.

cessed nearly all products of metallurgy and used most energy output and fuel supplies. When these sectors are included, heavy industry accounted for about a quarter of the Soviet labor force.

This sector's share of bureaucrats exceeded its proportion of the work force. Bureaucrats in the Soviet Union consisted of two categories: "leading personnel" and "engineering-technical personnel." Agriculture employed more than a quarter of the Soviet labor force but only 13 percent of leading personnel and 7 percent of engineering-technical personnel. On the (very conservative) assumption that the remaining bureaucrats were distributed evenly among the industrial sectors, heavy industry provided jobs for about three times as many bureaucrats as agriculture. The very small consumer industry sector would have justified offices for even fewer bureaucrats than agriculture. The retail and services sectors were close in size to consumer industry. The ability of officials in these sectors to exert influence on Politburo calculations is further reduced by the subordination of many of their enterprises to local rather than national authorities. More remote from the top than the heavy industry officials whose ministers, located in Moscow, enjoyed direct access to the Politburo, officials in light industry, retailing, and services would have faced greater difficulties in making their opinions known.

The remaining sector, culture, was probably more densely bureaucratized than any other. The cultural sector included categories of persons with very diverse status. Ninety percent of the employment in this sector fell into two categories, medicine and education, in which the status of most persons was low (doctors, teachers, nurses, librarians). In this part of the cultural sector, the proportion of supervisors would presumably have been similar to the ratio in industry. On the other hand, such occupations as journalism, research, and art and literature were politically salient in the Soviet Union, and a large Party and government bureaucracy developed to supervise the activities of the relatively few persons employed in these occupations. Researchers, writers, and artists sometimes reached Central Committee rank without any supervisory responsibilities. While the politically empowered portion of people working in this part of the cultural sector was very large in relation to their number, this part of the sector was small enough that its bureaucrats would still have been outnumbered by those in the heavy industry sector.

The preponderance of heavy industry in Soviet employment suggests that if sectoral considerations alone dictated the alignment of bureaucrats, only a coalition of all other sectors would have been capable of counterbalancing the influence of heavy industry. A sectoral model of Soviet constituencies draws credibility from the association between the preponderance of heavy industry officials in the bureaucracy and the historical success of politicians who defended heavy industrial interests. Both Khrushchev and Brezhnev, like Stalin before them, achieved dominance in the Politburo while publicly advocating expansion of heavy industry at the expense of other sectors. They both defeated rivals—Malenkov and Kosygin—who publicly pleaded for an increase in the priority of light industry.

Although the association between Khrushchev's and Brezhnev's public stands in favor of heavy industry and their dominance within the Politburo speaks in favor of a sectoral model of Soviet politics, it would still be premature to conclude that sectoral considerations were in fact all-powerful. Such a view would overlook the reasons why Stalin succeeded with a program of expanding heavy industry at a time when this sector was woefully weak. This view also does nothing to explain why Malenkov or Kosygin tried to compete against Khrushchev or Brezhnev with any program other than continuation of the priority for heavy industry. Finally, support for heavy industry is not the only possible explanation for the success of Khrushchev and Brezhnev, who differed from their opponents on a variety of other issues, too. Both men were also advocates of new policies in the agricultural sector, and Brezhnev in particular framed his advocacy of heavy industry in terms of a summons to an expansion of investment in agricultural machinery—a policy that expanded demand for harvesters, combines, and trucks, and for the investment goods that went into their production, but offered little to producers of other lines of machinery.

Explicit evidence has become available that at least some of the time, sectoral considerations actually did not override Soviet bureaucrats' other concerns. Iurii Prokof'ev, then first secretary of the Moscow city committee, noted in a speech to the Central Committee in February 1990 that Gorbachev's reform program was receiving especially strong endorsements from the Party committees of the defense industry.[3] In an interview in October 1990, Iurii Denisov, former ideology secretary of the Leningrad province committee, independently reported that in the Leningrad Party organization, support for perestroika was also concentrated among defense industry employees. Denisov then said that the leadership of the Leningrad committee had warned the defense industry Communists that Gorbachev's reform program, with its cuts in the defense budget, would jeopardize their jobs—but to no avail. Evidently support for perestroika among these Communists was not motivated by sectoral considerations.

Why might Soviet bureaucrats reward Politburo members with support in return for policy proposals that, if adopted, would levy an implicit tax on the bureaucrats' sector to subsidize other sectors? An equation of officials' interests with expansion of their sector would neglect the reality that individuals within an economic sector are simultaneously potential beneficiaries of an expansion of that sector and competitors for the division of the benefits of that expansion. Moreover, reduction of all interests to economic gain ignores the possibility that individual officials may define their interests in quite different ways. There are three possible reasons why sectoral interests may not have solely determined Soviet bureaucrats' response to policy proposals by Politburo members: competition for career advancement, subordination to multiple organizations with overlapping responsibilities, and personal values and attitudes.

---

3. *Materialy Plenuma Tsentral'nogo Komiteta KPSS, 5–7 fevralia 1990 goda* (Moscow: Politizdat, 1990), 46.

First, competition for career advancement should have encouraged subordinate officials within any Soviet bureaucracy to scout the ranks of Communist Party leaders for potential patrons whose policy orientations promoted something other than advancement of the narrow sectoral interest. In any economy, employees within a sector are not only common beneficiaries of subsidies to that sector but also close competitors for division of the spoils. In the Soviet bureaucracy, competition among bureaucrats within a sector operated with special intensity. Competition for promotion was intense because the government's monopoly of virtually all economic activity deprived bureaucrats of alternative employment possibilities. As all rewards—both official compensation and opportunities for bribe-taking and other illegal remuneration—were tied strictly to rank, promotion was virtually the only means for officials to increase their incomes.

During the Brezhnev years, official careers became increasingly specialized. As bureaucracies with sectoral responsibilities promoted more often from within, officials became less likely to advance their careers by lateral moves across bureaucratic boundaries. As the new career pattern emerged, advancement came increasingly to require displacement of superiors. The notorious "stability of cadres" policy, which accorded lifetime tenure to many holders of Party jobs, should not conceal the continuous turnover among industrial managers and other specialized officials.[4] To the extent that the existing leadership of a bureaucracy controlling a sector of economic activity was able to increase that sector's entitlement to centrally allocated resources, the existing leaders' job performance was likely to improve, and consequently they were more likely to avoid removal from office. Conversely, proposals from outsiders to reduce the resources available to a given sector, demanding more efficient performance of its task, would increase the prospect that deteriorating task performance resulting from budget cuts would discredit existing leaders and open opportunities for advancement of subordinates in their place.

Because all positions were on the nomenklatura of some Communist Party committee, career advancement depended on the favor of some Communist Party patron. Accordingly, competition for promotions within a sector presented subordinate bureaucrats with incentives to welcome Party leaders' policy proposals even when they ran counter to the sectoral interest. An official could hope to ad-

4. V. V. Zhuravlev, ed., *Na poroge krizisa: Narastanie zastoinykh iavlenii v partii i obshchestve* (Moscow: Politizdat, 1990), 106.

vance either through the patronage of bureaucratic superiors or through the patronage of critics of their performance outside the functional bureaucracy. Junior officials might therefore welcome either policies that would make more resources available to their sector or policies that, by diminishing the availability of resources, might encourage turnover of their superiors. Observers should expect a mixed pattern in which some officials aligned along the lines of sectoral interests while others aligned athwart sectoral lines.

Second, subordination to multiple overlapping bureaucracies would have subjected Soviet bureaucrats to competing demands on their loyalties, while at the same time making available to them diverse strategies for promotion. After joining the Communist Party, the Soviet bureaucrat was simultaneously an official, subordinate to a ministry or state committee with functional responsibilities, and a Party member, under the discipline of a committee with territorial responsibilities. As Sidney Tarrow points out, in any modern polity the territorial division of authority enables local elites to protect themselves against the prospect of displacement by functionally organized interests located in the national capital and relying on technological expertise as their main political resource.[5] In the Soviet polity, local elites centered on Party committees wielded a variety of resources that enabled them to contest the dominance of the Moscow ministries and state committees.

These resources included the local first secretary's control of promotions within the province, the ability of provincial Party committees to colonize central ministries, and the opportunities for Party committee staffs to intervene in the allocation of raw materials and (especially) transport. Even before Brezhnev's accession to the post of general secretary, the Central Committee's cadre department had virtually stopped intervening in appointments to posts below the province level in the Russian republic or below the republic level in the other republics.[6] The Central Committee's hands-off policy increased the discretion of the province or republic first secretary. By influencing careers below the province level, the first secretaries were able to shape the composition of the class of officials who were eligible for promotion to the ministries by reason of professional ex-

5. Sidney Tarrow, "Introduction," in Tarrow, Peter J. Katzenstein, and Luigi Graziani, eds., *Territorial Politics in Industrial Nations* (New York: Praeger, 1978).
6. John Miller, "*Nomenklatura*: Check on Localism?" in T. H. Rigby and Bohdan Harasymiw, eds., *Leadership Selection and Patron-Client Relations in the USSR and Yugoslavia* (London: Allen & Unwin, 1983), 87–88.

perience in the industrial and other organizations subordinate to the Moscow ministries but located in the provinces. Since the ministries drew their staffs from large factories and other organizations located in particular provinces, provincial Party organizations were able to colonize particular ministries in Moscow by filling senior offices with their appointees. Rostov province, for example, with its large agricultural machinery plant Rostsel'mash, was able to place a series of appointees in high offices in the Ministry of Agricultural Machine Building.[7] The transformation of province committee staffs into "dispatchers," who responded to urgent requests from factories and other organizations for railroad cars and for raw materials and parts allocated but not delivered in time for fulfillment of production quotas, was criticized for eroding the distinction between Party and economic officials, but this transformation also supplied province first secretaries with tools for disciplining officials formally subordinate to the ministries who might otherwise have resisted a first secretary's recommendations for appointments within their organizations.

Given the provincial first secretaries' dominance of low-level careers and the resulting pattern of mutual obligations between Moscow ministry officials and local Party leaders, Soviet bureaucrats faced a choice between their ties to their ministerial superiors and their ties to the Party organization of their province of origin. Often policies that rewarded the ministry might also benefit the province, but provincial officials' claims on resources in the hands of central authorities might also compete with the ministry's efforts to advance its organizational goals by seeking allocations from those same authorities. Bureaucrats within the ministry might gain by aligning themselves on either side of such a dispute, creating opportunities for Politburo members to recruit among them by their policy advocacy.

Third, sectoral interests did not necessarily correlate with officials' personal values and attitudes. A reduction of Soviet officials' interests to their sectoral interests would exemplify what Nelson Polsby condemned as "a substitution of analysts' choices for actors' choices."[8] Observers know that Soviet officials had many noneconomic inter-

7. Joel C. Moses, "Regionalism in Soviet Politics: Continuity as a Source of Change, 1953–1982," *Soviet Studies* 37 (1985): 184–211.

8. Nelson W. Polsby, *Community Power and Political Theory: A Further Look at Problems of Evidence and Inference* (New Haven: Yale University Press, 1980), 224.

ests. The people who staffed Soviet bureaucracies in the late 1960s and 1970s were veterans of the disputes among university students within the Komsomol in the 1950s, which culminated in public condemnation of "demagogic statements counterposing the Komsomol to the Party."[9] These *shestidesiatniki*—"men of the sixties"—suffered defeat in 1962, but the university graduates staffing the bureaucracy remained the passive audience for both dissident *samizdat* and the liberal literature published in the "thick" journals, especially in *Novyi Mir*.

Not only closet liberals might be found in the ranks of the bureaucracy. The 1950s and 1960s also witnessed the flourishing of the *derevenshchiki*, the "village prose" writers. Their attribution of all social ills to technological progress could be read as a plea to safeguard traditional rural life from excessive reliance on mechanization, chemical fertilizers, and irrigation projects, but their lamentation of the destruction of the Russian village also served in part as advocacy for the redirection of resources into the agricultural sector. Some Politburo members' welcoming attitude toward the activities of the derevenshchiki may also be attributable to these writers' condemnations of sympathizers of the capitalist West. One of them, I. Shevtsov, was particularly active in condemning artists who deviated from the canon of socialist realism.[10] Among their Politburo protectors was Brezhnev, who in early 1973 forced their critic Aleksandr Iakovlev into diplomatic exile as ambassador to Canada for having published an attack on village prose in *Literaturnaia Gazeta*. While welcomed by some Politburo members, the derevenshchiki also encountered opposition within the Politburo for espousing Russian nationalism in preference to a Soviet allegiance stripped of ethnic content and for their barely concealed denunciations of collective farming. The audience for the derevenshchiki also included educated intellectuals in the bureaucracy.

A third ideological group emerged after Khrushchev's ouster—the Stalinists, who held that his program of de-Stalinization had gone too far. During 1966 they staged a campaign to restore Stalin's reputation. The participants in this campaign, according to Roy Medvedev, included "leading ideologists, prominent military men and

---

9. Boris Kagarlitskii, *The Thinking Reed: Intellectuals and the Soviet State from 1917 to the Present* (London: Verso, 1988), 144–48.
10. Ibid., 168.

some writers."[11] The campaign took the form of an effort to restore Stalin's works to the curricula of Party and other schools, attacks on writers and historians for "obscuring the heroic struggle of the Soviet people" by writing too much about Stalin's "mistakes,"[12] and memoirs by wartime commanders making "the necessary corrections" to efforts to blame Stalin for the Soviet army's early defeat and to deprive him of credit for the victories at Stalingrad and Kursk.[13] These officials organized an ideological conference held in Moscow in October 1966, at which the Georgian ideological secretary D. G. Sturua proclaimed openly, "I am a Stalinist,"[14] and their activities formed the social base for a push to celebrate the centennial of Stalin's birth in December 1969. This push encountered overt resistance from prominent members of the scientific and cultural communities.[15]

While observers know that Soviet bureaucrats included shestidesiatniki, readers of village prose, and Stalinists, outsiders lack any means of estimating the distribution of these ideological orientations among economic sectors. One might reasonably suppose that Stalinists were more common in the heavy industrial and defense ministries, which had been the beneficiaries of Stalin's policies, that village prose was more appealing to collective farm chairmen, and that shestidesiatniki were more common in consumer industry and the service sector. But this analysis would be merely a presumption, and the converse might be argued just as plausibly. Better educated

11. Roy Medvedev, "Stalinism after the Twentieth Congress of the CPSU as the Reflection of Internal and International Problems of the USSR," in Medvedev, ed., *The Samizdat Register*, vol. 2 (New York: Norton, 1981), 8.

12. S. Trapeznikov, "Marksizm-Leninizm—nezyblemaia osnova razvitiia obshchestvennykh nauk," October 8, 1965. Trapeznikov argues for restoring Stalin's works to the Party schools' curriculum by criticizing the "so-called problematic course" of Party history, "which in essence reduces this science to the study only of the last decade." On his role in the Stalinist campaign, see Medvedev, *Samizdat Register*, 9.

13. V. Morozov, "O voennykh memuarakh," January 4, 1967. Another military Stalinist was Aleksandr Epishev, head of the Soviet armed forces' Main Political Directorate; see his speech to the XXIII Congress, April 5, 1966, particularly his attack on "petty bourgeois licentiousness . . . under the pretext of struggle against the consequences of the cult of personality . . . in the guise of 'champions' of historical truth and credibility."

14. D. G. Sturua, "I Am a Stalinist: A Meeting of Party Officials," in Stephen F. Cohen, ed., *An End to Silence* (New York: Norton, 1982), 158–61. Drawn from Roy Medvedev's *Political Diary*, this material is represented as notes taken by a participant in a conference of ideological officials, described in *Pravda*, October 12, 18, 26, 1966.

15. Medvedev, *Samizdat Register*, 11–12, 20; S. I. Ploss, "Soviet Politics on the Eve of the 24th Party Congress," *World Politics* 23 (October 1970): 72–73.

than either the agricultural or the consumer and services officials, the heavy industry officials were likely to read any of the literary schools and to have partitioned themselves accordingly among the intellectual currents swirling through the educated milieu.

The cross-pressures acting on bureaucrats in the Soviet Union imply that policy disputes would transcend organizational boundaries. Indeed, division within occupational and institutional groups is just what a series of observers have found. Vernon Aspaturian discerned "six principal groups [able] to exert pressure" on the Politburo (party officials, ministry officials, economic managers, the intelligentsia, the police, and the armed forces); yet "these major groups are by no means organized as cohesively united bodies, speaking with a single authoritative voice, but rather themselves are made up of rival personal and policy cliques, gripped by internal jealousies, and often in constant collision and friction with one another in combination or alliance with similarly oriented cliques in other social groups."[16] Tatiana Zaslavskaia noted that even the proposal for economic reform, which with its promise to transfer resources from heavy industry to consumer industry and services had a clear-cut sectoral bias, drew a divided response. It split managers in both sectors between the "more qualified, energetic and active" personnel who felt the existing command economy demanded too little of their abilities and "the more apathetic, the more elderly, and the less qualified" who preferred the centralized decision making that reform would limit. The "social necessity" for reform could "not find a clear and precise echo in the interests of many social groups."[17]

The same conclusion runs throughout the literature on interest groups in Soviet politics. In the debate over hydraulic versus thermal generation of electrical power, Gustafson discovered, specialists working in different organizations formed opinion coalitions across institutional boundaries rather than "support only their organizations' 'line.'"[18] David Lane concluded that it was "difficult to find evidence of the articulation and aggregation of a *managerial* interest; rather the findings seem to point to fragmentation and particulariza-

16. Vernon V. Aspaturian, ed., *Process and Power in Soviet Foreign Policy* (Boston: Little, Brown, 1971), 572–75.

17. Murray Yanowitch, ed., *A Voice of Reform: Essays by Tatiana Zaslavskaia* (Armonk, N.Y.: M. E. Sharpe, 1989), 172. See also Erik P. Hoffman and Robbin F. Laird, *The Politics of Economic Modernization in the Soviet Union* (Ithaca: Cornell University Press, 1982), 40–41.

18. Thane Gustafson, *Reform in Soviet Politics* (Cambridge: Cambridge University Press, 1981), 60.

tion of managerial concern."[19] Noting differences within the Party officialdom between ideologues and organizers, between generalists and specialists, and between specialists in industry and agriculture, Georg Brünner confirmed Hough's earlier finding that "functional differentiation can surely summon forth interest divergences on particular issues within the party apparatus." Brünner found the military split between traditionalists and technocrats, and while the security police "form[ed] a caste-like consciousness of identity," even their solidarity was weakened by exchange of personnel with Party officialdom.[20] Roman Kolkowicz found evidence that regional groupings of generals and admirals took opposing sides in Politburo rivalries.[21] Theodore Friedgut found that kolkhoz chairmen expressed solidarity on some issues, were divided on others, and tended to encounter criticism from employees of the Stalin-era machine tractor stations. Donald R. Kelley found that an informal coalition of environmentally minded officials helped to block ministerial projects that would have polluted Lake Baikal.[22]

In short, no single principle appears capable of determining how Soviet officials would react to policy ideas voiced by Politburo members. Soviet bureaucrats had parochial interests, but they also had personal interests and attitudes; the parochial and the personal did not necessarily converge. Cross-pressured by occupational interests, promotion prospects, multiple subordination to functionally specialized ministries and to territorially organized Party committees, and personal attitudes and values, any individual Soviet bureaucrat is likely to have been susceptible to the appeal of a wide variety of political arguments, varying in their relative emphasis on any of his or her multiple interests and attitudes. Empirical studies confirm the impossibility of predicting Soviet bureaucrats' opinions from organi-

19. David Lane, *State and Politics in the USSR* (New York: New York University Press), 241.
20. Georg Brünner, *Politische Soziologie der UdSSR*, pt. 2 (Wiesbaden: Akademische Verlagsgesellschaft, 1977), 161–65. See also Jerry Hough, "The Party *Apparatchiki*," in H. Gordon Skilling and Franklyn Griffiths, eds., *Interest Groups in Soviet Politics* (Princeton: Princeton University Press, 1971), 47–92.
21. Roman Kolkowicz, *The Soviet Military and the Communist Party* (Princeton: Princeton University Press, 1967). See also Timothy Colton, "Perspectives," in Colton and Thane Gustafson, eds., *Soldiers and the Soviet State: Civil-Military Relations from Brezhnev to Gorbachev* (Princeton: Princeton University Press, 1990), 13; Jiri Valenta, *Soviet Intervention in Czechoslovakia, 1968* (Baltimore: Johns Hopkins University Press, 1979), 21–23; Richard D. Anderson, Jr., "Soviet Decision-Making and Poland," *Problems of Communism*, March–April 1982.
22. These studies are reviewed in H. Gordon Skilling, "Interest Groups and Communist Politics Revisited," *World Politics* 36 (October 1983): 1–27.

zational affiliation or occupational specialty. The cross-cleavages within the bureaucracy created the uncertainty that rival politicians could exploit to attract broad-based bureaucratic support by competing to attract officials' attention to their respective projects.

Modes of Expression of Bureaucratic Opinion

Soviet bureaucrats should have been susceptible to persuasion, but how could they communicate to the Politburo the opinions they formed in response to persuasive messages? In electoral polities public opinion about leaders communicates itself through votes for rival candidates and through surveys that ask voters to rate politicians by name, but Soviet institutions specificially excluded any opportunity to vote for or against Politburo members in a contested election. Far from conducting surveys, the Politburo prohibited even passive listening to spoken comment about its members' personal suitability for office. The Central Committee secretary in charge of cadres summoned V. E. Semichastnyi, former director of the KGB, told him that the Politburo knew of his failure to object to criticisms voiced in his office against "the leadership of the Central Committee," and "warned him that if he behaved that way in the future they would severely punish him."[23] Sergei·Nikitich Khrushchev, himself a ranking missile engineer, recounts that whenever he tried to discuss other Politburo members with his father, Nikita Khrushchev would reprimand him for interfering in matters that were none of his business.[24]

Deprived of vote or voice, Soviet bureaucrats nevertheless could express their attitudes toward Politburo members in at least three behaviors: individual lobbying and private advice, public comment on policy, and varied execution of policy decisions by the Politburo. As long as an individual Politburo member identified himself publicly with a preference for a particular policy line, bureaucrats' reactions to a policy enactment implied an evaluation of a Politburo member who recommended that policy.

Two channels were open to Soviet bureaucrats for the private expression of their opinion in the ordinary course of their duties. First, the Politburo actively solicited their advice on policy decisions. In an interview a former chief of the General Staff, S. F. Akhromeev, indi-

23. A. N. Shelepin, "Istoriia—Uchitel' surovyi," *Trud*, March 15, 1991.
24. Sergei N. Khrushchev, *Khrushchev on Khrushchev: An Inside Account of the Man and His Era*, ed. and trans. William Taubman (Boston: Little, Brown, 1990), 14.

cated how this opportunity could be used to express support or opposition for Politburo decisions. He explained that in his view the invasion of Afghanistan had been a "mistake." Asked whether he had resisted the decision, Akhromeev dismissed the possibility of opposing Politburo decisions. Arguing against the Politburo would have resulted in his removal from office. Nevertheless, he said, "No arguments, but a report, taking a stand for our position, was possible. That is how it was in the Afghanistan situation. The leadership of the General Staff reported that with those present forces that had been allocated for Afghanistan, it was impossible to accomplish military missions. The leadership heard that out, but acted according to its own view." Despite the Politburo's decision, the General Staff continued to advise that a military solution was unachievable.[25]

Akhromeev was taking a stand on an issue within the purview of his responsibilities, but bureaucrats also enjoyed opportunities to object to decisions beyond their own spheres. As Communists they enjoyed the formal right to correspond with Politburo members on any topic under consideration. At least sometimes they used this right. In 1966, when the Politburo was considering a "direct or indirect rehabilitation of Stalin," twenty-five scientists and cultural figures signed a joint letter to Brezhnev opposing any such step.[26]

Private advice and lobbying were supplemented by public comment. Soviet newspapers and journals solicited articles from bureaucrats of various ranks discussing the execution of policy decisions, and the system of political education invited them to lecture to public audiences. These activities provided very imperfect forums for the expression of bureaucratic opinion. The norms guiding composition of articles and speeches compelled authors to incorporate a positive endorsement of any Politburo decision they discussed. Authors sometimes found themselves credited with views opposite to their own. After a factory director published an enthusiastic endorsement of the 1965 economic reform, the minister to whom he reported admitted that ministry officials had pressured the director into revising his real opinion.[27]

Despite the rules requiring that all articles endorse official policy and the pressures for inauthenticity, Soviet bureaucrats devised inventive techniques to infiltrate their real attitudes into the press. The

25. Andrei Karaulov, *Vokrug Kremlia: Kniga politicheskikh dialogov* (Moscow: Novosti, 1990), 223.
26. Zhuravlev, *Na poroge krizisa*, 56.
27. K. N. Rudnev, "Effekt reformy," July 5, 1967.

expectation that endorsements of policy would segue into discussions of problems of implementation offered authors opportunities to minimize or emphasize the obstacles facing a given policy, depending on whether they favored or opposed it. They could also signal subordinates that excess zeal in implementing a policy might adversely affect their career opportunities. In 1976, for example, the Politburo appointed a new defense minister and charged him with improving military discipline by reinvigorating the inspectorate function of the political officer corps. Military officers commenting on the new policy noted that its improper application had caused a deterioration of some officers' performance evaluations, to the detriment of their prospects for promotion. By highlighting a few cases of perverse consequences of the new policy, the commentators warned the officer corps that the policy was contrary to their career interests. The commentators then reinterpreted the policy with glosses that discouraged political officers from reporting negative findings of their inspections. A year later, bureaucratic opposition expressed in this manner had persuaded the defense minister to abandon his advocacy of the new policy.[28]

The rules guiding the press generally restricted bureaucrats to publishing articles concerning their own functional specialties, a restriction that made it difficult to comment on policy in general. Nevertheless, Soviet bureaucrats exhibited creativity in linking topics within their functional responsibilities to broader issues. Détente with the United States was a question of foreign policy lying outside the duties of the armed forces' branch for political indoctrination, yet a major general writing in the branch's professional journal was able to link détente to the topic of troop indoctrination and thereby express an evaluation of the policy: "Soviet soldiers, like our whole people, unanimously support [détente]. However, if corresponding work is not done, the aforementioned détente may be subject to one-sided understanding by some people, without consideration of active opposition to it on the part of aggressive forces, the more so that today even the most inveterate militarists do their black deeds under the cover of conversations about peace."[29]

Even while upholding rules that limited expression of opinion and forced bureaucrats to resort to a variety of subterfuges to communi-

---

28. Richard D. Anderson, Jr., "Neotraditionalism and the Question of the Political Quiescence of the Soviet Military," 1984, typescript.

29. Maj. Gen. S. Ilin, "Sovremennoe razvitie Vooruzhennykh Sil i nekotorye voprosy voinskogo vospitaniia," *Kommunist Vooruzhennykh Sil*, 1976, no. 18 (September), 35.

cate, Politburo members actively sought press coverage favorable to their visions of Soviet society. In December 1964 Kosygin gave the speech that launched his campaign for economic reforms. He ended the section on economic reform by welcoming "the proposals for further improvement of the management of the economy" which "many scholars and officials of industry and economic and planning organs have recently published in our press." Evidently seeking to encourage the writers, Kosygin promised that "the Central Committee of the Party and the government will examine these proposals and approve the necessary measures."[30]

Another forum for public comment on Politburo proposals (as Bruce Parrott has emphasized) were meetings referred to as "conferences" or "seminars," to which selected officials were invited.[31] The practice of applying academic terms to gatherings where bureaucrats could articulate their interests was part and parcel of the extended metaphor that presented politics as a "scientific" activity involving not the pragmatic resolution of conflicts of interest but the "correct solution" of political "assignments." The political significance of these seminars can be seen in a rebuke directed at the Politburo member in charge of ideology during the Gorbachev years by a regional official who accused him of "self-isolation from the leadership of ideological activity." He had found time, she said, to "meet journalists, religious leaders, and other categories of officials, but had found an opportunity to consult with the Party's province committee secretaries responsible for ideological work only once in the last two years at a one-day seminar." As a result, not only had he developed no coherent ideological strategy; he had also failed "to make the ideologists his allies."[32]

So likely were publications to be taken as the expression of attitudes toward the Politburo member responsible for advocating a policy that officials often avoided newspapers' invitations to submit articles. A former Politburo member recalls how Khrushchev stripped a bureaucrat of his medals for publishing an article that made recommendations for improvement of grain production that diverged from Khrushchev's own.[33] When asked why officials of research institutes paid attention to Politburo members' speeches, a junior staffer re-

30. December 10, 1964.
31. Reports of these seminars are one of the principal forms of documentation for Bruce Parrott, *Politics and Technology in the Soviet Union* (Cambridge: MIT Press, 1983).
32. "A. V. Shutyleva," June 7, 1990.
33. G. I. Voronov, "Nemnogo vospominanii," *Druzhba Narodov*, 1989, no. 1 (January), 200.

called having submitted a draft for publication under a supervisor's name. Even though the draft was strictly factual, the supervisor warned the staffer against showing it to anyone else, explaining that it diverged too far from recent Politburo descriptions of the international scene.[34] The former head of *Pravda's* "Party work" department recalls that in the Brezhnev years, secretaries of province committees routinely refused requests to submit articles, even when *Pravda's* editor persuaded the Politburo to instruct them to publish more.[35] The reluctance of many officials to commit themselves in print combines with other factors—the inauthenticity of the opinions expressed in many articles, the prohibition against publications by whole categories of officials (such as KGB officers and defense industry personnel), and the nonrandomness of the selection of authors—to render infeasible any effort by an outside observer to estimate from a survey of the press the distribution of bureaucratic support for particular Politburo members.

Besides private advice and lobbying and public comment, bureaucrats could also express their views of policy by varying the execution of policy—by enthusiasm when they welcomed a decision and foot-dragging when they did not.[36] "Were there cases when the execution of decisions, which were undoubtedly correct, was sabotaged?" the former Politburo member Gennadii Voronov wrote. "There were. For example, the broad-scale implementation of the . . . brigade contract was intentionally obstructed in agriculture and in construction and especially in industry . . . because the then leadership of agriculture consisted almost entirely of furious opponents of the '*beznariadka.*'" He noted that "cases of open sabotage" were encouraged when "the press (*Sel'skaia zhizn'* was especially zealous in this respect) spoke out against this system of organization and compensation."[37] In the Gorbachev years, print and broadcast journalists freed by *glasnost'* began to increase the frequency of reports of bureaucratic obstruction of Gorbachev's decisions. "What Blocked the Needle: How an Ordinary Bureaucrat Canceled a Decision of the President of the USSR" was the title of one report, which explained how a minor Council of Ministers staffer had failed to forward Gor-

34. Personal communication.
35. V. Kozhemiako, "Chto tam, v obkome?" April 16, 1990.
36. Stephen White, "Elites, Power, and the Exercise of Political Authority in the USSR," in David Lane, ed., *Elites and Political Power in the USSR* (Aldershot: Edward Elgar, 1988), 276–78.
37. Voronov, "Nemnogo vospominanii," 199.

bachev's instruction to increase production of needles for medical injections.[38]

Bureaucratic obstruction of unwelcome Politburo decisions is believed to have been a principal reason for the failure of the 1965 economic reform. The reform would have reduced the powers of the industrial ministries reestablished by the Politburo decision authorizing the reform. Ed A. Hewett writes: "The ministries, and the *glavki* under them, were in the front lines, relying on a combination . . . of procrastination, assimilation, complication and regulation." Ministry officials delayed introduction of the reform whenever possible, "'assimilated' new procedures into old" prereform bureaucratic rules, added "complexity" by converting general rules intended to provide common guidelines for all enterprises into separate deals tailored for individual enterprises, and engaged in arbitrary interventions, contrary to the statute, that imposed decisions on the management of subordinate enterprises.[39]

Soviet commentators took these behaviors as evidence of bureaucratic opinion. As one minister wrote, his subordinates responded to the reform by what Hewett calls "assimilation"; they engaged in double bookkeeping, one set of books according to the reform instructions and one set according to the old instructions. The minister interpreted their conduct as evidence of "a reserved attitude" toward the reform.[40] A semiofficial Soviet history of the Brezhnev years tied bureaucratic obstruction to awareness of the public stances of Politburo members. "The former administrators and the partisans of command administration noted definite signs of disagreement between L. I. Brezhnev and A. N. Kosygin as early as 1965. . . . As Brezhnev consolidated his leadership of the Party, the chairman of the Council of Ministers encountered difficulties. Many officials in the increasingly numerous ministries and departments responded to the decline in Kosygin's influence by altering their conduct."[41]

The implementation of the reform responded not only to evidence of its effectiveness but also to decisions that were substantively (if

38. *Izvestiia*, July 5, 1990; for other examples, see Timothy Colton, "Approaches to the Politics of Systemic Economic Reform in the Soviet Union," *Soviet Economy* 3 (April–June 1987): 159–60; "Zakliuchitel'noe slovo M. S. Gorbacheva na Plenume TsK KPSS, 25 aprelia 1989 goda," April 27, 1989.

39. Ed A. Hewett, *Reforming the Soviet Economy: Equality vs. Efficiency* (Washington, D.C.: Brookings, 1988), 237–38.

40. Rudnev, "Effekt reformy."

41. Zhuravlev, *Na poroge krizisa*, 177.

not politically) unconnected. According to the same Soviet history, "The Czechoslovak events of 1968 further stimulated the partisans of the administrative command system of management. The very posing of the issue of market relations again became dangerous, punishable."[42] When the Politburo approved the invasion of Czechoslovakia, which Kosygin publicly opposed and Brezhnev favored, the bureaucratic backers of both men took the invasion as an indicator of the two leaders' relative strength. Like voters backing a winner, bureaucrats who resisted the reforms intensified their pressure while those who favored the reforms lost heart.

Of course Soviet bureaucrats would fear to obstruct the implementation of policy decisions if they expected the Politburo to retaliate by removing them from office in favor of more energetic executants of the Politburo's will. But those bureaucrats who obstructed a policy known to be opposed by some Politburo member could expect that member to shield them against retribution, while other bureaucrats who energetically enforced a policy could expect protection and advancement from a Politburo member who favored the policy. Accordingly, the existence of bureacratic obstruction and enthusiasm in the execution of policy depended on two conditions: the bureaucrats' awareness of policy disputes among Politburo members and their ability to estimate Politburo members' prospects in the contest for power. Bureaucratic obstruction and enthusiasm were responses to going public by Politburo members in their efforts to gain advantage in the policy bargaining, and the outcomes served as indicators to the bureaucracy of their relative strength in the leadership.

In sum, Soviet bureaucrats' daily performance of their duties constituted something like a continuing referendum on the members of the Politburo. Of course, private advice and lobbying, limited public commentary, and obstruction or enthusiasm in execution of policy supplied a very clumsy measure of bureaucratic opinion. Elections do not tell what the voting public thinks about policy, but at least they supply a clear indication whether a majority of voters wants an incumbent to remain in office.[43] The Politburo, lacking any simple numerical indicator of bureaucratic attitudes, would have needed to reach a far more tentative judgment.

42. Ibid., 198.
43. Marjorie Randon Hershey, "Campaign Learning, Congressional Behavior, and Policy Change," in Gerald C. Wright, Jr., Leroy N. Rieselbach, and Lawrence C. Dodd, eds., *Congress and Policy Change* (New York: Agathon, 1986), 156–59; William H. Riker, *Liberalism vs. Populism: A Confrontation between the Theory of Democracy and the Theory of Social Choice* (San Francisco: W. H. Freeman, 1982).

If the Politburo experienced difficulty gauging the distribution of bureaucratic support among its members, an observer should expect that the Politburo would have taken much time to conclude that any of its members had lost the allegiance of his bureaucratic supporters. Indeed, one finds that some Politburo members dragged on in office long after they had apparently suffered full defeat. Shelepin recounts that he suffered his decisive setback in 1967, but he remained in the Politburo until 1975.[44] Podgorny lost on the issues in 1972 but clung to his position for five more years—and reportedly expressed surprise when a Central Committee member proposed that Brezhnev take over his duties.[45] Voronov took two years after his removal from the office of head of the Russian Republic to conclude that he should request retirement from the Politburo.[46] Brezhnev began feeling out the Central Committee members about his move against Khrushchev as early as February 1964, yet he waited eight months to move, and when he finally did, Mikhail Suslov thought Khrushchev still enjoyed so much support that "civil war" seemed imminent.[47]

Of course the use of obstruction or enthusiasm in execution of policy to register bureaucratic opinion is also an expensive way to decide who should hold national office. It may be a principal advantage of electoral democracy that the result of elections can affect the conduct of public business so strongly with such slight interference in the performance of official duties.

Bureaucratic Influence on Politburo Tenure

Why should Politburo members have cared about bureaucratic opinion when they decided their peers' tenure in office? The formal rules for election to the Politburo provided for no input from the bureaucracy. Individuals gained or lost membership in the Politburo by decision of their peers. While the general secretary seems to have taken the initiative in proposing both nominations to and expulsions from the Politburo, accounts of these actions make clear that after consulting with other members, he would propose these actions for

44. *Trud*, March 14, 15, 19, 1991.
45. Karaulov, *Vokrug Kremlia*, 150 (interview with Petro Shelest).
46. Voronov, "Nemnogo vospominanii," 200.
47. Werner Hahn, "Who Ousted Nikita Sergeyevich?" *Problems of Communism*, May–June 1991, 109–15.

consideration by the Politburo as a whole.[48] The Politburo's recommendation was then submitted to the next meeting of the Central Committee for decision by simple majority vote. In practice, the Central Committee consistently approved Politburo recommendations, the only known exception being its rejection of a recommendation by a majority of the Politburo (then known as the Presidium) to remove Nikita Khrushchev in 1957. Doubtless the general secretary and the Politburo considered the Central Committee's anticipated reaction when they decided whether to issue a recommendation for inclusion into or expulsion from the Politburo; thus whether the Politburo's or the Central Committee's opinion was decisive remains open to question. The Central Committee in turn was elected by the delegates to the Party congress from nominees chosen by the Politburo. Again, post-Stalin Party congresses always approved all the Politburo's nominees for the Central Committee. The practice of selection of delegates by Central Committee members who led territorial Party committees, themselves acting under the supervision of the senior Politburo member who was also the Central Committee secretary overseeing the staff department for Party personnel, and of election of the delegates without opposition at Party conferences ensured the delegates' approval of the Politburo's slate.

Despite institutional rules freeing Politburo members from challenge from below, individual Politburo members' tenure in office might nevertheless have been dependent on bureaucratic opinion. Numbering only ten to fifteen members, the Politburo wielded the right to decide any question of Soviet life. Of course, in practice such a small group could not find time to decide all matters, but they enjoyed the opportunity to intervene in any matter and could expect their intervention to prove decisive. They were able to intervene because they commanded the loyalty of the bureaucracy, which by the end of the Brezhnev years numbered some eighteen million officials, who were prepared to enforce the Politburo's decisions on the rest of Soviet society and, to the extent possible, on the outside world.

Either of two abstract models could explain why the Soviet bureaucracy would obey commands from the Politburo. Any large or-

48. Voronov, "Nemnogo vospominanii," 200; Shelepin in *Trud*, March 19, 1991; Karaulov, *Vokrug Kremlia*, 150–52; Petr Shelest, "Kak eto bylo," *Sovershenno Sekretno*, 1990, no. 6, 20–22; Boris N. Yeltsin, *Ispoved' na zadannuiu temu* (Leningrad: Chas Pik, 1990), 83–84; Eduard A. Shevardnadze, *Moi vybor: V zashchitu demokratii i svobody* (Moscow: Novosti, 1991), 79–81.

ganization consisting of many members experiences difficulties in coordinating their actions, and the organization is more efficient if its members bind themselves to obey the instructions of some smaller number of central coordinators.[49] Thus the bureaucracy as a whole stood to benefit by complying with Politburo orders. Indeed, this is the explanation that Lenin originally gave when the Central Committee was first established and again later when the smaller Politburo was formed from the members of the larger Central Committee.

The other model argues that compliance originates not only in the nomenklatura officials' appreciation of the efficiency gains of central coordination but also in the bureaucrats' approval of the content of Politburo policy choices. The Politburo's ability to rule depended on voluntary compliance by Soviet bureaucrats. Individual members of the Politburo who could generate the approval of bureaucrats made a contribution to the authority of the Politburo as a whole, while Politburo members who did not enjoy bureaucratic confidence made no such contribution. Consequently, when Politburo members considered their recommendation concerning their peers' tenure in office, the members able to muster bureaucratic approval could make demands that the other members could not effectively oppose. In these circumstances, any Politburo member who sought to preserve himself in office or to improve his standing in the leadership should have gone public in an attempt to acquire bureaucratic supporters, whose eagerness to execute his policy recommendations the Politburo member could trade to his peers for tenure in office.

These two abstract models of the Politburo's authority within the bureaucracy are subject to a pair of simple tests. First, if the Politburo derived its authority from its services as a coordinating center that improved the efficiency of the Soviet bureaucracy, its members should indeed have acted like arbiters of bureaucratic controversies. They had no reason to go public. They might make public statements for the purpose of performing their coordinating function, but if these statements were to provide a focal point for bureaucratic coordination, they should have been uniform. On the other hand, if individual Politburo members' reputations among bureaucrats could

49. For reviews of the literature on this model, see Randall L. Calvert, "Leadership and Its Basis in Problems of Social Coordination," *International Political Science Review* 13 (1992): 7–24; Terry M. Moe, "The New Economics of Organization," *American Journal of Political Science* 28 (1984): 739–77, and "Political Institutions: The Neglected Side of the Story," *Journal of Law, Economics, and Organization* 6 (1990): 213–66.

contribute to the authority of the Politburo as a whole, then the Politburo should have decided individuals' tenure in office by the weight of their contributions. Politburo members would have had every reason to go public.

Second, if the Politburo gained authority by maximizing the efficiency of the bureaucracy, it should never have made decisions by logrolling. Logrolls consisting of mutually interfering policies are always less efficient than decisions that set clear priorities. On the other hand, if Politburo members' tenure in office depended on their individual reputations among bureaucrats, they had every reason to logroll, because decisions that combine the distinctive policy recommendations of rival politicians enable the rivals to share a reputation among attentive publics for influence on policy, whether or not the combination is sustainable.

Thus the twin phenomena of going public and logrolling enable the observer to decide whether the authority of the Politburo, like that of an elected government, depended on its members' individual authority among the politically enfranchised portion of those over whom they ruled. Note the radical inadequacy for Politburo members of directing their policy recommendations to the three hundred or so Central Committee members, despite the Central Committee's right to vote up or down on tenure in the Politburo. Even as the ten to fifteen Politburo members were too few to impose their will on Soviet society, so were the hundreds of members of the Central Committee. The audiences that counted were the masses of bureaucrats, who were not too few.

* Chapter 3

Political Competition
and Foreign Policy

An investigation of the possibility that Soviet foreign policy owed its maladaptation to competitive politics needs to begin with a theory that links domestic politics to foreign policy. The objective of the theory is dual: to specify the observations to be expected if competitive politics is found in the Soviet Union and to explain how those observations diminish the adaptiveness of foreign policy to objective world conditions.

Existing work on foreign policy offers little guidance on how to construct the needed theory. As recently as 1989, two authors commented, "Not much successful theorizing about the effects of domestic politics has been accomplished in international relations—simply because domestic factors add complications that are currently impossible to deal with."[1] Although much theoretical work identifies

1. Christopher H. Achen and Duncan Snidal, "Rational Deterrence Theory and Comparative Case Studies," *World Politics* 51 (January 1989): 155; see also Jack S. Levy, "Domestic Politics and War," *Journal of Interdisciplinary History* 18 (1988): 653–73. Since their comment, Jack Snyder has published *Myths of Empire* (Ithaca: Cornell University Press, 1991), which successfully confronts many of these complications. Despite its merits, however, Snyder's work does not address the problem presented here. He attributes foreign policy decisions by coalitions within national leaderships to the interplay of sectoral economic interests, but as I argued in chap. 2, fixed interests defined in economic terms seem unable to account for competitive behavior by Soviet leaders. For a variety of attempts, see Bruce Bueno de Mesquita and David Lalman, "Domestic Opposition and Foreign War," *American Political Science Review* 84 (1990): 747–65; Michael Barnett, "High Politics Is Low Politics: The Domestic and Sys-

a range of domestic variables that may affect foreign policy and explores their interaction with international conditions, contests for office are rarely among the variables given consideration.

While the foreign policy literature provides little guidance, one can draw on a rich literature concerned with competition for office in electoral polities, and particularly in the United States. In this literature, the state coheres as a collective agent because leaders engage in activities along two dimensions, vertical and horizontal. Along the vertical, leaders recruit constituents by going public. Along the horizontal, leaders organize their constituencies into a cohesive state by bargaining with one another.

Foreign policy may be understood as the product of actions along both dimensions of this model. Foreign policy emerges in a process consisting of four activities. The first two activities construct leaders' vertical ties to their constituencies. Contenders for national office build constituencies by going public with distinctive *visions of social order at home* that tell how to preserve the state by describing the main domestic problems facing society and recommending policies to solve those problems. Leaders then cement their ties to constituencies by going public with distinctive *grand strategies* that tell how to sustain the state in world politics by describing the main international problems and recommending appropriate foreign policies.

The third activity coheres the state by constructing horizontal ties among leaders. Competitors who have won constituencies adequate to secure participation in policy making resolve the differences among their policy recommendations by *bargaining* (in the broad sense of strategic interaction, not merely in the narrow sense of face-to-face negotiation). The fourth activity is the compromise policy's *encounter with actual world conditions*. The compromise policy responds to world events that erode the persuasiveness to constituents of some contestants' domestic visions or associated grand strategies and enable their rivals to demand concessions in the bargaining over policy.

temic Sources of Israeli Security Policy, 1967–1977," *World Politics* 42 (1990): 529–62; B. Thomas Trout, "Rhetoric Revisited: Political Legitimation and the Cold War," *International Studies Quarterly* 19 (1975): 251–84; Alexander L. George, "Domestic Constraints on Regime Change in U.S. Foreign Policy: The Need for Policy Legitimacy," in Ole R. Holsti, Randolph M. Siverson, and Alexander L. George, eds., *Change in the International System* (Boulder, Colo.: Westview, 1980); Bruce W. Jentleson, "From Consensus to Conflict," *International Organization* 44 (1984): 667–704.

In this four-part model, foreign policy will generally be maladaptive to world conditions because leaders making foreign policy respond to concerns other than effectiveness alone. Political competitors want effective foreign policies. As in classic theories of international politics, competitors generally seek to protect the state and to enrich it. By protecting the state, they safeguard their own hold on office against competition from foreigners. By enriching the state, they augment the benefits they can dispense to constituents as rewards for allegiance. At the same time, the effectiveness of foreign policy in pursuing the protection and enrichment of the state is limited by two behaviors in which competitors must engage: symbolism and logrolling.

Symbolism builds constituencies; logrolling combines them. By transforming selected international situations into symbols of larger objective problems, political competitors can communicate intelligibly to constituents whose inattention and lack of information about world affairs preclude their comprehending synoptic analyses of complex problems. Because a competitor's foreign policy stance is intended to retain the allegiance of constituents recruited by the domestic vision, the symbolism of the grand strategy must replicate the symbolism of the domestic vision. Constrained by the need to replicate a vision that explains a domestic social order to its inhabitants and by the need to communicate intelligibly to domestic audiences ill informed about world affairs, the grand strategies of political competitors are unlikely to match the optimal response to objective international conditions. Logrolling introduces a further source of maladaptiveness to world conditions, as political rivals combine various policy recommendations with an eye to easing the search for compromise rather than solely to the likely interaction of the policies with world events.

The theory also explains how foreign policy changes. Foreign policy adapts continuously to world events, but the effects of events are contingent on what the contestants for leadership have included in their grand strategies. Much of the time, national leaders can simply ignore constituents in making foreign policy, because the constituents are not paying attention. When world events fail to affect constituents' evaluations of leaders, leaders can adjust foreign policy directly to events. But the inattentiveness of constituencies is double-edged. Political competitors' first concern is to get anyone to pay attention. To do so they must etch sharply the policy differences among themselves; as Lenin wrote, "We must from the very start demarcate between ourselves and all others."[2] Looking for any means of persuading potential constituents that the choice between political candidates makes a difference, would-be leaders search the international situation for issues on which they can take opposing positions. Some foreign policy choices become issues in political contests, others do not; it depends on what the competitors think will attract constituents' attention.

When world events do influence the contest for leadership, they produce two kinds of change in the compromise policy: oscillating and directional.

As long as the competitors' grand strategies remain fixed, foreign policy *oscillates* within the range of policy recommendations. Grand strategies generally do remain fixed, because the leader is using them to build a reputation among constituents, and building reputation requires repetition of symbols over time. The effect of world events on policy is to select among the range of grand strategies. Events can persuade constituents that a competitor's policy recommendations have become more or less urgent or more or less feasible. Events that diminish the persuasiveness of any competitor's grand strategy force that competitor to make concessions in the bargaining, while events that enhance a competitor's persuasiveness enable him or her to demand concessions from rivals. As long as unfolding events are as likely to favor one competitor as another, over time foreign policy will move back and forth among the recommendations of the various competitors.

Directional change occurs when some competitor receives an opportunity to alter the grand strategy. World events tend to erode the persuasiveness of all competitors' grand strategies, but not necessarily at the same rate. Over time some competitor may begin to stand out among the rivals for promoting policies more persuasive to constituents. That "ascendant" competitor (the term is Breslauer's) now has a unique opportunity to expand his or her constituency. He or she can change his or her grand stategy, incorporating variants of policy recommendations formerly identified with rivals in order to recruit their disaffected former constituents. By shrewd choice of new policy recommendations, a leader with an expanded following may also be able to dominate bargaining by occupying the

2. V. I. Lenin, *Polnoe sobranie sochinenii*, 55 vols., 5th ed., vol. 6 (Moscow: Politicheskoi Literatury, 1967), 256.

median along a variety of the issue dimensions defined by rivals' opposing policy recommendations. A foreign policy controlled by an ascendant leader remains more stable over time. If world conditions change, however, stability may not be adaptive.

Why Visions Differ and Why They Are Symbolic

Political competitors recruit constituents by going public with contrasting visions of social order. A vision of social order is an explanation that tells how support for the leader will preserve the society among whose members the leader seeks constituents. The vision defines the objective problems urgently demanding social action and the feasible policies—actions by the state—that address those problems. The vision builds authority for the leader by supplying potential constituents with reasons to identify a candidate for leadership with their personal attitudes and values.

To serve competitive purposes, visions must display three traits. First, all visions will converge on a promise to preserve the social fabric, but the visions will diverge in their descriptions of objective problems facing society and in their distinctive policy recommendations. Second, in order to build their reputations, competitors will keep their differences consistent over time. Third, visions will incorporate not only material appeals but also symbolic ones. Each competitor not only will promise that policies will benefit supporters but also will try to become a symbolic personification of the supporters.

First, the combination of convergence on the goal of preserving the social fabric with divergence on techniques[3] characterizes the visions of political competitors because they all face a dilemma identified by Anthony Downs. He remarks that electoral candidates "are caught in the classic dilemma of all competitive advertisers. Each firm must differentiate its product from all near substitutes, yet it must also prove this product has every virtue that any of the substitutes possesses."[4] Although too often misremembered (by me, too) for having argued that electoral candidates "quickly converge on the

3. Murray Edelman, *Constructing the Political Spectacle* (Chicago: University of Chicago Press, 1988), 49–54.

4. Anthony Downs, *An Economic Theory of Democracy* (New York: Harper & Row, 1957), 97–98.

median voter with their proposals,"[5] actually Downs grounded his argument on the observation that voters would support candidates only if they believed that it would make a difference who held office. Inclusion of this condition among the assumptions of the median voter theorem is known to separate the expected ideological positions of candidates.[6] Differentiation is necessary to make constituents care which competitor wins, but convergence is necessary to appeal to as many constituents as possible. In the United States, presidential candidates diverge on techniques to attain converging promises of "peace and prosperity." Members of the Brezhnev Politburo converged on promises to attain "peace and socialism."

Second, the differences among political competitors' visions remain consistent over time because each candidate's hold on supporters depends on the candidate's reputation for adhering to certain policy recommendations and to descriptions of the objective situation that justify those recommendations. Reputation supplies inattentive and ill-informed constituents, who are unsure how to judge their interest in any given circumstance, with a "cheap summary indicator" to decide whether a leader is faithful to them.[7] By cultivating a reputation for fidelity to certain principles, leaders also avoid the appearance of inconstancy, which would undermine their persuasiveness to constituents whose experience teaches them that success demands persistence. Building reputation requires political candidates to repeat themselves over time. The importance of reputation is the reason candidates in the United States typically rely on "stump speeches," outlines or texts to which they revert again and again with only minor modifications appropriate to the varying occasions for their remarks.

At the same time, the need for reputation does not require a political competitor to remain absolutely consistent over time in every

5. Bryan D. Jones, "Causation, Constraint, and Political Leadership," in Jones, ed., *Leadership and Politics: New Perspectives in Political Science* (Lawrence: University Press of Kansas, 1989), 11. For my repetition of this mistake, see my "Why Competitive Politics Inhibits Learning in Soviet Foreign Policy," in George W. Breslauer and Philip E. Tetlock, eds., *Learning in U.S. and Soviet Foreign Policy* (Boulder, Colo.: Westview, 1991), 105.

6. Gary W. Cox, "Centripetal and Centrifugal Incentives in Electoral Systems," *American Journal of Political Science* 34 (1990), 903–35.

7. Sam Peltzman, "Constituent Interest and Congressional Voting," *Journal of Law and Economics* 27 (1984): 181–210; John R. Lott, Jr., "The Effect of Non-transferable Property Rights on the Efficiency of Political Markets," *Journal of Public Economics* 32 (1987): 231–46; Joseph P. Kalt and Mark A. Zupan, "Capture and Ideology in the Economic Theory of Politics," *American Economic Review* 74 (1984): 279–300.

detail of the vision. Political competitors know that any potential supporter monitors not only their statements but also objective conditions. As objective conditions change, formerly persuasive descriptions become unpersuasive. Consequently leaders face a dilemma between consistency and persuasiveness. They resolve this dilemma in part by finding arguments that interpret changing events as consistent with their former descriptions; Lyndon Johnson, for instance, interpreted Khrushchev's successors as his picked men, experienced and realistic enough to continue the good sense shown by Khrushchev in cooperating with Johnson's policy of negotiations. Competitors seek identification with overall themes while varying their stands on particular issues.

Another solution to the dilemma between consistency and persuasiveness is a tendency to maintain not absolute consistency with all previous stands but positioning in relation to rivals.[8] Political competitors differ in their policy recommendations and descriptions of objective conditions because they are trying to give potential constituents a choice—a choice that will motivate the constituents to take an interest in the contest between candidates. As long as a contestant voices policy recommendations closer to the preferences of constituents than any rival's stand, the contestant can sustain a reputation for responsiveness to the constituents' wants.

The distinctions between themes and issues and between absolute and relative positioning are crucial to the competitive model. They make it possible for leaders to maintain continuity in their visions and grand strategies while compromising on particular issues.

Third, while political competitors promise material benefits to constituents (such as "prosperity"), they must couple material appeals with "symbolic politics." Promises of material benefit appeal to a potential constituent's rational self-interest. Analysis of rational grounds for acceptance of the truth of statements has demonstrated that acceptance is justified to the degree that the preferences of the person uttering the statement converge with the preferences of the

8. Henry E. Brady and Stephen Ansolabehere, "The Nature of Utility Functions in Mass Publics," *American Political Science Review* 83 (1989): 143–63; Henry E. Brady and Paul Sniderman, "Attitude Attribution: A Group Basis for Political Reasoning," ibid. 79 (1985): 1061–78; Donald Philip Green, "On the Dimensionality of Public Sentiment toward Partisan and Ideological Groups," *American Journal of Political Science* 32 (1988): 758–80.

person or persons hearing the statement.[9] Listeners know a speaker's preferences by comparing the sum of the speaker's past choices with the best alternatives known to have been available to the speaker.[10] Constituents, however, are commonly thought to be "rationally ignorant." Knowing that no one constituent's support can determine the success or failure of a candidate, all constituents lack motivation to discover whether a candidate's past choices coincide with their own preferences. If constituents lack the information to evaluate the convergence of preferences, no candidate can rationally expect constituents to believe promises of material benefits alone.

Would-be leaders must overcome potential constituents' inattentiveness by associating themselves with symbols that identify the leader and the constituents as members of a common collective agent. The purpose of symbolic politics is to transcend the rational individualism that corrodes belief in the promises of leaders—to cause constituents to base their decisions whether to confer support on consideration of costs and benefits not to themselves alone but to the collectivity as a whole. The method of symbolic politics is the leader's personification of the constituency, a self-presentation that transforms the leader's policy recommendations into symbols that designate actions by the constituency in the minds of its members. Symbolic politics circumvents attention to potential conflicts of interest between leaders and followers by encouraging followers to see the leader as identical with themselves.

Can symbolic politics transcend the calculus of individual interest? Research on public opinion and voting in the United States converges from a variety of methodological perspectives—surveys, aggregate analysis of returns, experiments—on paradoxical findings that seem inexplicable except by the assumption that symbolic politics works. Presidents discuss the benefits of their economic policies for the nation as a whole, not the distributional consequences to individuals.[11] Surveys show that voters respond by evaluating a president's performance in economic policy not by their personal gains or losses but by the performance of the economy as a whole.[12]

9. This analysis is ably summarized in David Austen-Smith, "Strategic Models of Talk in Political Decision Making," *International Political Science Review* 13 (1992): 45–58.
10. David M. Kreps, *Notes on the Theory of Choice* (Boulder, Colo.: Westview, 1988), 11–16.
11. Barbara Hinckley, *The Symbolic Presidency* (New York: Routledge, 1990), 49–50.
12. Samuel Kernell, *Going Public* (Washington, D.C.: Congressional Quarterly Press, 1986), chap. 7.

The degree to which economic performance affects voters' evaluation of the president depends on whether the president's rhetoric emphasizes economic performance as a goal.[13] Analysis of presidential election returns indicates that "the similarity of symbols posed by the policy issue [in a presidential campaign] to those of [voters'] long-standing predispositions" outweighs material self-interest in determining choices among candidates for office.[14] Experimental evidence shows that voters are more likely to judge a president favorably when he appears in association with policy accomplishments than when the policy accomplishments—which determine the president's impact on the voter's material interest—are presented in isolation.[15]

While leaders find many symbols other than rhetoric to engage the attention of their constituencies, rhetoric is an especially important vehicle. The characteristic mode of rhetorical personification of constituencies is synecdoche. A synecdoche is a metaphor in which a whole is symbolized by a part.[16] The very concept of political representation is itself a synecdoche in which the leader "stands for" the constituency.[17] In the rhetoric of modern United States presidents, regardless of party or personality, the most common sentence subject referring to an actor is "we"—a pronoun interchangeable in their speeches with "the nation" and "the American people." The

13. M. Stephen Weatherford, "The Interplay of Ideology and Advice in Economic Policy-Making: The Case of Political Business Cycles," *Journal of Politics* 49 (1987): 926–28.

14. David O. Sears, Richard R. Lau, Tom R. Tyler, and Harris M. Allen, Jr., "Self-interest vs. Symbolic Politics in Policy Attitudes and Presidential Voting," *American Political Science Review* 74 (1980): 670–84; see also M. Stephen Weatherford, "Economic Voting and the 'Symbolic Politics' Argument: A Reinterpretation and Synthesis," ibid. 77 (1983): 158–74.

15. Shanto Iyengar and Donald R. Kinder, "More than Meets the Eye: TV News, Priming, and Public Evaluations of the President," *Public Communications and Behavior* 1 (1986): 135–71.

16. George Lakoff and Mark Johnson, *Metaphors We Live By* (Chicago: University of Chicago Press, 1980), 35–40. Synecdoche is a special case of enthymeme (a syllogism whose major premise is determined by appeal to "the reputable beliefs of the audience") and metonymy (the representation a thing by something related to it). On enthymeme and metonymy in political rhetoric, see Robert Paine, ed., *Politically Speaking: Cross-cultural Studies of Rhetoric* (Philadelphia: Institute for the Study of Human Issues, 1981); Forrest McDonald, "The Rhetoric of Alexander Hamilton," in Glen E. Thurow and Jeffrey D. Wallin, eds., *Rhetoric and American Statesmanship* (Durham, N.C.: Carolina Academic Press, 1984). McDonald's definition of enthymeme is on p. 78.

17. Hanna Fenichel Pitkin, *The Concept of Representation* (Berkeley: University of California Press, 1967).

national "we" often precedes action verbs referring to performances instigated by the president himself; that is, presidential rhetoric conflates the person of the president with the nation as a whole.[18] Common parlance does the same; it makes as much sense in ordinary speech to say "President Reagan reduced inflation" or "President Bush increased unemployment" as it does to say "the nation overcame inflation" or "we lost more jobs."

Leaders build identification by using synecdoches in which concrete situations—often very minor—stand for larger objective problems facing the polity, while particular policies stand for progress toward solving those objective problems. A mother on welfare stands for poverty, a rape by Willie Horton has stood for crime, Boston Harbor has stood for the environment. A liberal political commentator singled out Ronald Reagan for his tendency to "reduce complications to simple symbols and images of good and bad,"[19] but in fact substitution of simple symbols for complex problems characterizes the rhetoric of all modern presidents and presidential candidates, regardless of party. Both Johnson and Goldwater reduced the complexity of the Sino-Soviet split to the personality of Khrushchev; Johnson assigned him the good quality of sober judgment and Goldwater assigned him the bad qualities of deceit and quarrelsomeness.

Synecdoches that replace larger problems with concrete instances build identification by placing the president in the same rhetorical spot vis-à-vis the problem that the voter occupies. Synecdoche enables the president to make his interpretation of objective complexities readily intelligible to a public uninformed about social problems, inexperienced with them, and therefore unable to comprehend them when they are presented in the abstract, synoptic terms that alone permit objective analysis.[20] By "framing the issue"—reducing its information content to a vivid example or two—synecdoche makes the issue more memorable to voters. Experiments show that citizens' recall of information about national problems increases when it is presented as concrete stories about individuals' experience and decreases when it is presented as abstract generalizations.[21] The president portrays himself as acting on the same limited infor-

18. Hinckley, *Symbolic Presidency*, 38–59, 85.
19. Leslie H. Gelb, "The Mind of the President," *New York Times Magazine*, October 6, 1985, 112–13.
20. See Jeffrey Tulis, *The Rhetorical Presidency* (Princeton: Princeton University Press, 1987), chap. 5.
21. Shanto Iyengar, "The Accessibility Bias in Politics: Television News and Public Opinion," *International Journal of Public Opinion Research* 2 (1990): 1–15.

mation presented to the voter and as acting as the voter would given that information. The president then names the specific policies addressing a particular situation, but he never analyzes the adequacy of specific actions for resolving the larger problem, because that analysis would require abandonment of the synecdoche in favor of synoptic, abstract concepts that inexpert voters find hard to remember and that do not build identification.

How does standing for "the people" as a whole mesh with the competitive requirement that rivals differentiate their visions? Political competitors *express opposition in the political sense by constructing oppositions in the semiotic sense.* The most obvious kind of semiotic opposition is inversion of the incumbents' symbolism. When the king is styled "His Most Christian Majesty," the revolutionaries can turn to pre-Christian symbolism by portraying themselves as Romans of classical antiquity.[22] When the king constructs himself as father of the people, the revolutionaries can call themselves the Sons of Liberty.[23] When the tsar is God's annointed, the revolutionaries can become scientific atheists. When one party stands for government regulation to redress social inequality, the opposition can stand for redressing inequality by deregulating the market. Because symbolic differentiation is necessary to compete, an effective tactic for winning political contests should be to identify with symbols so popular that rivals dare not identify with opposed symbols. When the rival's surname sounds foreign, a candidate can recite the Pledge of Allegiance—and the rival lacks any effective answer, because any semiotic opposite to a nationalist symbol merely underlines how alien the rival seems to many voters.

Political competitors' choice of symbols depends on what is familiar to their potential supporters. "The central elements in political belief systems may be strong affective commitments to certain symbols, which remain constant for many years due to long histories of reinforcement."[24] Because the symbols that work are drawn from the past experience of voters, political symbols display continuity over time. Even so, continuity is by no means absolute, because competition continuously generates inversions that perpetuate old symbols in the process of rebutting them.

The visions of political competitors portray them as standing not

22. Karl Marx, "The Eighteenth Brumaire of Louis Bonaparte," in Robert C. Tucker, ed., *The Marx-Engels Reader* (New York: Norton, 1972), 436.
23. Carole Pateman, *The Sexual Contract* (Stanford: Stanford University Press, 1988).
24. Sears et al., "Self-interest vs. Symbolic Politics."

only for a larger political collectivity but for a distinctive symbolic conception of that collectivity's identity. Although all presidents stand for all "the people," they differ in the symbolic identities they attribute to the people, in the actions that the people are said to want, and in the views of objective problems that the people are said to hold.

Domestic Origins of Grand Strategies in World Politics

Ideally, political competitors would prefer to insulate foreign policy from the domestic contest. They would pursue office and influence by going public with their visions of domestic social order. Once in office, they would decide foreign policy by seeking the most effective solutions to objective domestic and international problems facing them and their constituents. In practice, however, competitors who look down the decision tree cannot divorce foreign policy from the competition for support. They expect to justify to their constituents a domestic policy chosen by bargaining in which each side has made concessions. Because bargaining among multiple competitors produces a domestic policy different from that recommended by any of them, their public espousal of the compromise policy erodes the differences among them that have motivated constituents to pay attention to the contest. The expectation of concluding bargains on existing domestic issues impels political competitors to engage in an ongoing search for new issues on which they can reconstruct their mutual opposition; they extend their contest to foreign policy because the world scene supplies additional issues.

Extended to world politics, the visions of social order by which political competitors recruit support at home become "grand strategies." A grand strategy tells how to advance the state's interest in international affairs. It defines the threats and opportunities presented to the state by the international order, identifies likely enemies and potential allies, and specifies a general orientation for foreign policy.

The inattentiveness of constituents impels each political competitor to seek a reputation for advocating a *global* grand strategy, said to be applicable in relations with all foreign states. In principle, the most effective foreign policy strategy might discriminate finely among foreign states and among international issues. But voters, who lack information to distinguish among the policies of the many foreign states composing the world system, form judgments instead by proceeding from "core values" (e.g., ethnocentrism, antiwar sentiment) to preferences concerning the general orientation of policy (e.g., isolationism, militarism, anticommunism).[25] When a leader advocates a foreign policy fine-tuned to subtle variations in the policies of foreign states, among which constituents cannot discriminate, the constituents are likely to perceive the leader as merely inconstant and therefore unreliable.

Political competitors' grand strategies in foreign policy bear a relation to visions of domestic order that might be described as *symbolic coherence:* whatever competitors stand for in domestic politics, they try to stand for it again in world politics. Political competitors cannot simply repeat their domestic visions in international politics: because of the difference between the domestic and world scenes, a vision that is persuasive against the domestic backdrop will be unpersuasive against the international one. U.S. voters organize their opinions of candidates' domestic visions along dimensions (liberal vs. conservative, rich vs. poor) that do not coincide with the general preferences they use to evaluate foreign policies.[26] Reagan's speechwriter provides a vivid example of symbolic coherence between a vision of social order and a grand strategy: Reagan stood for "a man who got upset because the feds were taking all his money. . . . There he was, finally making the big money regularly, and he's looking at the check and seeing the bite Washington's taking. . . . And he figured that the Soviets, the biggest confiscators of all, were the exact expression of how bad it could get."[27] A vision of minimal government interference in the economy at home could be replicated in a grand strategy of antagonism to state socialism abroad. Symbolic coherence, however, is a relationship of implication rather than entailment; no vision of social order bears any one-to-one relation of necessity to any grand strategy. The domestic vision informs a leader's choice of grand strategy but does not compel it.

Because the grand strategy is intended to accomplish the same pair of goals served by the domestic vision—to promise material

25. Jon Hurwitz and Mark Peffley, "How Are Foreign Policy Attitudes Structured? A Hierarchical Model," *American Political Science Review* 81 (1987): 1098–1120, and "The Means and Ends of Foreign Policy as Determinants of Presidential Support," *American Journal of Political Science* 31 (1987): 236–58.

26. Hurwitz and Peffley, "How Are Foreign Policy Attitudes Structured?"

27. Peggy Noonan, *What I Saw at the Revolution: A Political Life in the Reagan Era* (New York: Ballantine, 1990), 278.

benefits to the constituency and to engender symbolic identification—the symbolism of a grand strategy replicates the reliance of a
domestic vision on synecdoche. The leader's public activities (speeches
given during foreign trips, talks with foreign delegations) stand for
the state actions prescribed by the grand strategy. By giving speeches
during foreign trips, U.S. presidents can reinforce the effects of
those world events that enhance their popular approval and counteract the effects of events that diminish it.[28] Particular events stand
for larger international problems, as the ouster of Khrushchev stood
for the condition of the Sino-Soviet split and the severity of the communist threat to the United States. Particular foreign countries stand
for the class of foreign states designated as either enemies or allies
by the grand strategy. Particular foreign policy acts—treaties, declarations of war, threats of military action, trade and financial exchanges, arms deliveries, economic aid—stand for progress toward
resolving larger problems, as the invasion of Grenada stood for
progress toward winning the global contest between communism
and capitalism.

As Khrushchev's ouster and the invasion of Grenada show, incidents chosen as symbols of larger problems and of progress toward
their solution *need not be valid objective indicators of the condition of the
overall problem or of its solution.*[29] The reason symbolic politics exists is
that constituents are too inexpert to analyze the larger problem reliably. If the constituents cannot tell whether the synecdoche is a
valid indicator, they give the politician no incentive to confine the
incidents chosen to stand for the larger problem or the actions chosen to stand for its solution to objectively valid indicators. Instead
the constituency rewards the politician for choosing incidents dramatic enough to seize its wandering attention and simple enough to
render complexities intelligible.

Bargaining over Policy

For a political competitor, policy coalitions are inseparable from
constituency building. Coalitions among politicians form around

28. Dennis M. Simon and Charles W. Ostrom, Jr., "Impact of Speeches and Travel
on Presidential Approval," *Public Opinion Quarterly* 53 (1989): 58–82.
29. Hinckley, *Symbolic Presidency*, 5; Edelman, *Constructing the Political Spectacle*, 12–
25.

policy bargains because, and to the extent that, policy bargains help them retain the allegiances of their constituents. When constituents grant their allegiance to a leader on the ground that the leader's policy recommendations symbolize actions that the constituents would take themselves in the state's place, they will withdraw allegiance from a leader whose recommendations fail to shape observable actions by the state. As competitors' policy recommendations differ, no individual leader can expect that policy enactments will conform to his or her recommendations in every instance. To retain constituents' loyalties, a leader must join coalitions that either distribute opportunities to "claim credit" for shaping policy or at least prevent policy from conforming more consistently to any rival's recommendations than to the leader's own.

While political competitors must represent the international situation to public audiences in symbols chosen for intelligibility and dramatic effect, in the abstract they presumably would prefer to divorce their choice of foreign policy from the symbolism that attracts constituents. The observation that political competitors go to great lengths to gain and keep office implies that they should preserve the institution comprising the offices they hold—that is, the state. Enrichment of the state increases the material benefits available to them for distribution to constituencies. Political competition should therefore produce an interest in foreign policies objectively well designed to protect the security of the state and to increase its wealth. Presumably national leaders do choose many foreign policies by ignoring the public and heeding objective analyses prepared by foreign policy experts, especially as the public is not paying close attention to the actions of the state.

But when political leaders turn a concrete international situation into a symbol for a larger global problem and a particular course of action into a symbol for its solution, they do so in the hope that the situation will attract public attention and that the action will earn them credit from the public for progress toward remedying the problem. Having created expectations among constituents about state action in selected international situations, political competitors would defeat their own purpose if they made no effort to conform foreign policy in those situations to the prescriptions of their grand strategies. Therefore they cannot decide policy without contemplating its suitability for building coalitions that help them retain constituents' allegiances.

Because political competitors' grand strategies differ, they must choose a foreign policy by bargaining. To the extent possible, political competitors should avoid compromises, because public defense of the compromise policy erodes their distinctiveness. They can avoid compromises by engaging in issue specialization, in which each competitor focuses public attention on a different issue. But no grand strategy qualifies as global if its policy recommendations are confined to a single world region or a single functional issue. Consequently, some international situations become test cases for several of the grand strategies. In these situations mutual persuasion is not available to political competitors as a means to reconcile their conflicting policy recommendations. Persuasion works by informational influence,[30] but the competitors differ not over the facts but over the symbolism of the international situation. With mutual persuasion ruled out, the competitors must reconcile their conflicting policy recommendations by bargaining.

The bargaining game that results may be represented abstractly as follows. Each competitor for national leadership wants his or her grand strategy to control policy on as many issues as possible. Each competitor with enough supporters to demand entry into the national leadership is assumed to have two choices of action: the leader can either insist on his or her own policy proposal or accept some other policy proposal. If every leader but one accepts some other policy proposal when the remaining leader insists on his or her own, the policy is assumed to be the insistent leader's own proposal; if all accept some proposal other than their own, the policy is assumed to be some intermediate compromise. Any other outcome produces disagreement and no policy choice. This set of assumptions produces the game matrix shown in Figure 1 for the case of bargaining between two leaders.

If each leader's constituents support that leader for gaining enactment of his or her own policy recommendation, for disagreeing in preference to enactment of rivals' recommendations, and for enacting a mutually acceptable policy in preference to disagreement, this game is the familiar prisoner's dilemma. It is iterated over indefinitely many policy decisions over time. No leader can precommit to

30. Eugene Burnstein and Amiram Vinokur, "Testing Two Classes of Theories about Group-Induced Shifts in Individual Choice," *Journal of Experimental Social Psychology* 9 (1973): 123–37, and "Persuasive Argumentation and Social Comparison as Determinants of Attitude Polarization," ibid. 13 (1977): 313–22; Eugene Burnstein, "Persuasion as Argument Processing," in Hermann Brandstatter, J. H. Davis, and G. Stocker-Kreichgauer, eds., *Group Decision Making* (New York: Academic Press, 1982).

	Leader 2	
	Accept other proposal	Insist on own proposal
Leader 1 Accept other proposal	Mutually acceptable policy	Leader 2's policy
Leader 1 Insist on own proposal	Leader 1's policy	Disagreement: no policy

Figure 1. A foreign policy bargaining game

any strategy. Precommitment depends on the existence of an enforcer of commitments external to the game, but the leaders are the ultimate enforcers of all commitments in their polity. The game has the additional feature of uncertainty about who has the last move. Elected leaders do not know for certain who will win the next election; Politburo members in the Brezhnev years could die in office, fall ill and retire, or be removed by the Central Committee. As the uncertainty over the last move precludes backward induction from the expectation of disagreement on the last move, this prisoner's dilemma belongs to a class of noncooperative bargaining games known to feature multiple equilibria.[31]

While there is an equilibrium in the cell that produces continuing postponement of policy decisions, competing leaders can avoid it by turning to two kinds of equilibria that produce policy choices. One kind of equilibrium, located in the "mutually acceptable" cell, involves *convergent concessions* by all leaders; the other kind of equilibrium is a *sequential exchange*, in which each leader alternates between insisting on his or her own recommendation and accepting a rival's recommendation on the next policy issue.[32] The sequential exchange can occur among any number of leaders, as long as two conditions prevail: (*a*) policy decisions must be numerous enough to allow each leader an expectation of future turns and (*b*) the leaders must be few enough that they face negligible costs of keeping track of whose turn it is to insist.

Policies chosen by convergent concessions and sequential ex-

31. George Tsebelis, *Nested Games: Rational Choice in Comparative Politics* (Berkeley: University of California Press, 1990).

32. Russell Hardin, *Collective Action* (Baltimore: Johns Hopkins University Press, 1982).

change differ observably: compromises by convergent concession depend on *issue separation*, while compromises by sequential exchange depend on *issue linkage*.

To separate issues is to treat policy choices as irrelevant to each other, whether or not mutual interference exists among the policies' substantive consequences. Before separating issues, policy makers presumably scout the objective situation to assess the consequences of deciding an issue in isolation. But political competitors must trade off any drawbacks of isolating an issue against the gain, measured in constituency support, of easing their search for compromises. Convergent concessions can produce bargains only when the participants can find a compromise located at the median of their preferences. The medians of the same group of participants on different issues are located at a single point only under very unusual conditions.[33] To reach bargains by convergent concessions, leaders usually must separate issues in the hope that the policy consequences will be desirable. For example, majorities in the U.S. Congress have often favored both a balanced budget and a combination of reduced taxes and increased federal spending. For Congress to compromise at the median on all three issues, it had to vote on balancing the budget separately from its votes on taxation and on federal spending. It is not impossible for the combination of a tax cut and increased spending to stimulate the economy sufficiently to permit rising revenues to bring the budget into balance.

To link issues is to treat policy choices as mutually interdependent whether or not the policies' substantive consequences will display any mutual interaction. Issue linkage is a response to the infrequency of the conditions that permit bargains by convergent concession. I. William Zartman confirms the expectation of formal theories that compromise by convergent concessions will rarely be possible when he remarks that "negotiations in the real world are generally not matters of incremental convergence." Instead, the negotiators first agree on a "formula," specifying the issues to be included in a package agreement, and then define the final bargain by trading off those issues.[34] When political competitors cannot reach bargains by convergent concession, they can resort to the alternative of sequen-

33. For a plain-language presentation of this point, see Nicholas R. Miller, Bernard Grofman, and Scott L. Feld, "The Geometry of Majority Rule," *Journal of Theoretical Politics* 1 (1989): 379–406.
34. I. William Zartman, "Negotiation as a Joint Decision-Making Process," in Zartman, *The Negotiating Process: Theories and Applications* (Beverly Hills, Calif.: Sage, 1978), 76.

tial exchange by linking acceptance of one competitor's policy recommendation on some issue to acceptance of other competitors' recommendations on other issues. (A classic example is the distribution
of ministerial portfolios to form a coalition cabinet in a parliamentary
democracy.)[35] As in the case of issue separation, when bargainers
contemplate an issue linkage they search the policy environment to
find information that the substantive consequences of the policy will
be mutually compatible, but they trade off their gains from finding
mutually acceptable compromises against the losses of packaging
unrelated issues. Issue linkage may be explicit—that is, policy documents begin to connect issues formerly discussed in isolation from
one another. Alternatively, leaders may prefer tacit linkages, which
may be observed from simultaneous or concurrent changes in foreign policy behaviors which formerly moved independently.

Compromises by sequential exchange offer a competitive advantage. These compromises allow rival leaders to share opportunities
to claim credit to their constituencies for having achieved enactment
of their policy recommendations on some issue. If competitors anticipate that they will compromise by sequential exchange, it makes
sense to prepare in advance by engaging in *issue specialization*. Each
competitor devotes the bulk of symbolic statements in the vision and
grand strategy to one or a few issues, anticipating that rivals will
limit their commentary on that issue in return for the competitor's
restraint on their issues. As David Mayhew comments about Congress, "Whatever else it may be, the quest for specialization in Congress is a quest for credit. Every member can acquire a piece of policy turf small enough so that he can claim personal responsibility for
some of the things that happen on it."[36]

When foreign policy is chosen by political competitors, their practice of compromising by sequential exchange produces linkages not
only among various international issues but also across the domestic-international divide. Exchanges of one leader's recommendation
on foreign policy for another's on domestic policy produces interactions between domestic and foreign policy that cannot be predicted
from study of objective domestic and international conditions alone.
The same is true of interactions between regional or functional issues. The division of labor natural among scholars has understand-

35. David Austen-Smith and Jeffrey Banks, "Stable Governments and the Allocation of Policy Portfolios," *American Political Science Review* 84 (1990): 891–906.
36. David R. Mayhew, *Congress: The Electoral Connection* (New Haven: Yale University Press, 1974), 85–94.

ably led to the separation of the study of domestic politics from the study of foreign policy, and to the separation of specialized studies on policies toward particular regional or functional issues from the global context. Although this division of labor is necessary and productive, a focus limited to objective problems within specialized areas constantly risks neglect of the consequences of any national leadership's concern with finding compromises. Objective developments within regional and functional issue areas can interact with policy not only because the developments are substantively interconnected but also because sequential exchanges chosen for easing the process of compromise, not for mirroring real-world interactions between policies and events, help national leaders solve their problem of finding compromises that enable them to share authority among constituents.

Consequences of the Encounter with World Conditions

Descriptions that reduce international problems to symbols simple and dramatic enough to communicate with uninformed and inattentive constituents are unlikely to be confirmed by unfolding international developments. Policies chosen by linkage or separation of issues for reasons other than substantive interactions are unlikely to produce the promised results. Constituents evaluate leaders retrospectively, using new information about international conditions to decide whether the leaders' grand strategies continue to identify urgent problems and to offer feasible solutions. The discrepancy between unfolding international events and policies chosen by compromise among leaders' grand strategies causes constituents to lose confidence in leaders over time, generating continuing change in foreign policy as bargains shift in line with concessions registering shifts in constituent support and as leaders introduce new policy recommendations to take advantage of opportunities to capture rivals' disaffected constituents. Two kinds of policy change occur: frequent short-term oscillations among the options presented by rivals for leadership and infrequent longer-term directional change.

One kind of change produced by the misfit between unfolding events and leaders' descriptions of international problems is a short-term oscillation of policy among the leaders' grand strategies. In order to make their grand strategies more convincing to constituents, leaders supply select bits of information about the international scene. They select the information for its ability to buttress the apparent wisdom of their own policy recommendations and to challenge the expediency of rivals' strategies, not for its descriptive accuracy or predictive reliability.[37] The limited information supplied by Johnson about Khrushchev's successors made them appear eager to continue cooperating with the United States, while Goldwater's information made Khrushchev appear never to have sincerely sought cooperation and made his successors appear likely to revert to open confrontation. Information supplied by political contestants serves as what Murray Edelman calls a benchmark by which constituents can evaluate leaders.[38] Benchmarks set a personal agenda for each leader, defining some events or trends as decisive for the constituents' expectations that the leader's policy recommendations will produce progress toward resolving objective problems.

These benchmarks enable an observer to estimate the direction (if not the magnitude) of the impact of events on political contestants' public support, even in the absence of direct evidence in the form of opinion surveys or election returns—an important consideration for a study of Soviet politics during the Brezhnev era, for which this direct evidence is entirely unavailable. As Samuel Kernell comments, "events and conditions which intuitively seem to be important determinants of a president's popularity are in fact the primary explanatory variables."[39] Robert Shapiro and Benjamin Page concur that in the United States public opinion on foreign policy "respond[s] reasonably to foreign and domestic events as political leaders, other elites, and the mass media report and interpret them."[40] A study of West European public opinion about NATO reaches the same conclusions.[41] Constituents react not directly to international developments but to the relative success of competing political leaders in finding interpretations of the changing international scene that sus-

37. B. Thomas Trout, "Rhetoric Revisited: Political Legitimation and the Cold War," *International Studies Quarterly* 19 (1975): 255–56.

38. Edelman, *Constructing the Political Spectacle*, 40–42.

39. Samuel Kernell, "Explaining Presidential Popularity: How Ad Hoc Theorizing, Misplaced Emphasis, and Insufficient Care in Measuring One's Variables Refuted Common Sense and Led Conventional Wisdom Down the Path of Anomalies," *American Political Science Review* 72 (1978): 519 (emphasis deleted).

40. Robert Y. Shapiro and Benjamin I. Page, "Foreign Policy and the Rational Public," *Journal of Conflict Resolution* 32 (1988): 211–47; see also John E. Mueller, *War, Presidents, and Public Opinion* (New York: Wiley, 1973), 267.

41. William K. Domke, Richard K. Eichenberg, and Catherine M. Kelleher, "Consensus Lost? Domestic Politics and the 'Crisis' in NATO," *World Politics* 39 (1987): 382–407.

tain the urgency and feasibility of their grand strategies. Each leader's description of the situation identifies the information that constituents will use to evaluate that leader's proposals.[42]

Unfolding events can reinforce or erode a leader's persuasiveness to constituents. Leaders who gain persuasiveness can insist on their policy recommendations. The leader whose persuasiveness erodes may try to devise new policy recommendations, but because those recommendations are new, the leader has built no reputation for commitment to them and therefore will need time to generate public support. In the interval, therefore, the only alternative facing a leader whose persuasiveness erodes is to accept policies agreeable to rivals. Consequently the pattern of policy enactments shifts toward the rivals' grand strategies.

Oscillating policy change is likely to be relatively frequent but temporary. Because competitors try to build reputations, they keep their grand strategies relatively fixed over time. As all the contestants choose their benchmarks for symbolic appeal rather than for accuracy in describing international conditions, the sequence of international events over time is likely to include some that erode the persuasiveness of all contestants' images of international problems. Consequently, the immediate effect of the sequence of events is to move the compromise back and forth within the range of existing policy options offered by the various contestants.

Directional policy change is much less frequent but can be more enduring. It has its origins in the counterproductive policies that result from issue linkage and separation. When policies are chosen by the criterion of easing the search for compromises as well as in contemplation of substantive interactions among issues, the policies can be expected to prove generally maladaptive to domestic and international conditions, even if favorable circumstances occasionally allow such policies to succeed. As constituents observe the discrepancy between promised effects of policy and actual achievements, they lose confidence in the leader's vision. Every postwar U.S. president's approval rating has declined over his time in office.[43]

Self-frustrations attendant upon competitive bargaining over policy create an opportunity for some contestant to embark on what

42. Richard Brody, "Public Evaluations and Expectations and the Future of the Presidency," presented at the Conference on the Future of the Presidency, 1980; cited in Weatherford, "Economic Voting," 171.

43. Kernell, "Explaining Presidential Popularity," 518–19; Mueller, *War, Presidents, and Public Opinion*; Hinckley, *Symbolic Presidency*, 26–30.

Richard Fenno calls *constituency expansion*.[44] The decline of confidence in leaders over their time in office develops a pool of disaffected constituents. The effect of deteriorating performance by U.S. presidents is not to cause voters to switch parties but to move the president's loyalists into the camp of independents and to shift the independents into the opposing party.[45] The constituents disaffected from their former leaders become available as new recruits for expansion of a rival's constituency. Some competitor is normally in a position to use this opportunity for constituency expansion, because though every leader's persuasiveness tends to erode over time, not all leaders' persuasiveness necessarily declines at the same rate.

When one competitor loses persuasiveness less rapidly than do rivals, over time that competitor gains more opportunity to insist on his or her own policy recommendations in the bargaining. As one leader begins to look more successful in bargaining over policy, constituents perceive that leader increasingly winning the political contest—in Breslauer's term, becoming "ascendant" within the leadership. In the United States, constituents react to the imminence of political victories by realigning themselves on the side of winning candidates. The first poll taken after a presidential inauguration—before the new president has been able to take any official action—consistently shows popular approval of the new president's conduct in office to be ten to twenty points higher than the new president's share of the popular vote.[46] Fenno notes that congressional candidates typically enter the phase of constituency expansion after victories in the party primaries. Victories in presidential primaries change American voters' estimates of a candidate's prospects for election independently of their approval of the same candidate and alter election results accordingly.[47]

In order to recruit new constituents, the ascendant leader revises the vision and associated grand strategy. As Fenno comments, con-

44. Richard F. Fenno, *Home Style: House Members in Their Districts* (Boston: Little, Brown, 1978).

45. Nelson W. Polsby and Aaron Wildavsky, *Presidential Elections: Strategies of American Electoral Politics*, 6th ed. (New York: Scribner's, 1984), 19.

46. Hinckley, *Symbolic Presidency*, 26–30.

47. Paul R. Abrahamson, John H. Aldrich, Phil Paolino, and David W. Rohde, "'Sophisticated' Voting in the 1988 Presidential Primaries," *American Political Science Review* 86 (March 1992): 55–69; Larry M. Bartels, "Candidate Choice and the Dynamics of the Presidential Nominating Process," *American Journal of Political Science* 31 (1987): 1–30.

stituency expansion involves "reaching out for additional elements of support."[48] Persistence in the original vision cannot win over rivals' disaffected constituents; if those people had ever found the ascendant leader's original vision attractive, presumably they would have supported that leader in the first place. Confirming the expectation that ascendant competitors will try to change their political identities, a study of roll calls in the House of Representatives found that members running for election to the Senate changed their voting records significantly more than did members running for reelection. The "ideological and population differences" between their House constituency and the statewide Senate constituency were "reasonably accurate predictors" of the "direction and size of change."[49]

In order to recruit from the pool of disaffected supporters, the ascendant leader engages in what Breslauer calls "selective incorporation" of variants of rivals' policy recommendations and descriptions of objective problems.[50] By incorporating variants of the policy recommendations that rivals formerly used to attract those same constituents, the ascendant leader increases his or her appeal to them; but because the recommendations are *variants*, the ascendant leader maintains differentiation from rivals. A record of success in bargaining supplies evidence to constituents disaffected by the rivals' records of failure that the ascendant leader's variants have more promise of controlling policy than the rivals' original recommendations. If the contestants have previously specialized by issue, the ascendant leader's incorporation of variants of rivals' policy recommendations will produce a "role expansion" as he or she begins to comment on issues formerly reserved to rivals.

Selective incorporation and role expansion present an ascendant leader with a strategic dilemma that shapes the rhetoric marking constituency expansion. Change in the vision is inconsistent with maintaining the leader's reputation among original constituents. As Fenno notes, leaders who engage in constituency expansion risk "losing touch" if responsiveness to the desires of new supporters prevents them from devoting adequate attention to their original

48. Fenno, *Home Style,* 172–73.
49. John R. Hibbing, "Ambition in the House: Behavioral Consequences of Higher Office Goals among U.S. Representatives," *American Journal of Political Science* 30 (1986): 651–65.
50. George W. Breslauer, *Khrushchev and Brezhnev as Leaders* (London: Allen & Unwin, 1982), chaps. 5 and 11.

constituency.[51] An ascendant leader typically resolves this dilemma by telling the original constituents that policy successes earned by their support for the original recommendations have created new objective circumstances justifying a shift to a new set of policy recommendations at home and abroad. Anticipating his landslide victory in 1984, President Reagan began to assure conservatives that the military buildup won by his election in 1980 had compelled Soviet leaders to understand that they had no alternative but to cooperate with the United States.

The ascendant leader's attentiveness to new international conditions when revising the grand strategy combines with an increase in that leader's influence on bargaining to stabilize a new direction of foreign policy. The ascendant leader is temporarily less dependent on the constancy of his or her reputation for adherence to certain policy recommendations. The need to find new objective conditions that justify revision of the grand strategy motivates the ascendant leader to reevaluate international circumstances. Consequently the ascendant leader should use the opportunity to adjust policy recommendations to international conditions prevailing at the time of constituency expansion.

More realistic in terms of contemporary international circumstances, the ascendant leader's revised policy recommendations are also more likely to be enacted, for two reasons. First, by adding disaffected former constituents of rivals, the ascendant leader controls a larger proportion of the available political support. Second, when several rivals are competing for leadership, differences among rivals' grand strategies provide the ascendant leader with an opportunity to control policy bargaining by *strategic position*.

Consider the bargaining game analyzed earlier. In the two-leader variant presented in Figure 1, neither leader gains any competitive advantage if both agree on a policy located in the "mutually acceptable" cell. When more than two rivals are bargaining, though, any leader who begins with a policy recommendation close enough to what the others would find mutually acceptable can successfully insist on adoption of his or her policy. In that case, to the constituents of all the rivals, the leader who has proposed the mutually acceptable policy recommendation appears more successful in bargaining than rivals. The opportunity to revise the grand strategy offers an ascendant leader the chance to exploit this possibility. When select-

51. Fenno, *Home Style*, 182–83.

ing variants of rivals' policy recommendations for incorporation into the revised grand strategy, the ascendant leader can pick policy recommendations intermediate between the alternatives favored by rivals. These recommendations occupy the median on issue dimensions defined by rivals' contrasting recommendations.[52] By choosing policy recommendations that occupy a median, the ascendant leader can ensure that his or her recommendations become the collective preference on those issues, and reap the competitive benefits of constituents' perception that the leader's policy recommendations are controlling policy enactments.

Rivals are unable to dislodge an ascendant leader who seizes the median. Their old recommendations define the issue dimension, creating a median for the ascendant leader to occupy. Therefore rivals could, in the abstract, eliminate the median by changing their issue positions. But they will not. If they did, they would sacrifice the allegiance of the remaining constituents who back them precisely because of their reputations for consistent advocacy of those policies. When the ascendant leader occupies the median, the rivals are trapped between their need to adhere to their past policy recommendations and their need to display success in bargaining.

The ascendant leader's ability to control policy on many more issues increases the flexibility of foreign policy. When foreign states act in a manner that enhances the persuasiveness of the ascendant leader's grand strategy, that leader gains constituents. When foreign states act in a manner that erodes the persuasiveness of the grand strategy on some issues, the ascendant leader can separate those issues from other policies, granting control of policies on those issues to rivals as a side payment for agreeing to his or her control of policy on remaining issues. Either way the ascendant leader stays in charge, as long as foreign states do not act in a manner that discredits the leader's strategy on all issues.

Credit earned for adaptiveness to new international conditions, a record of continuing success in bargaining built on an expanded constituency and strategic occupancy of the median, and greater flexibility of policy combine to perpetuate a leader's ascendancy over time. The ascendant leader's policies appear to constituents to work better. This leader's constituents gain confidence in his or her ability

52. On the concept of the median, see Peter C. Ordeshook, *Game Theory and Political Theory: An Introduction* (Cambridge: Cambridge University Press, 1986), 160–75; Miller et al., "Geometry of Majority Rule," 383–86.

to win policy conflicts, while rivals' constituents lose hope. International events unfavorable to a given policy course do less to discredit an ascendant leader whose centrist positioning provides more flexibility in response.

At the same time, these competitive advantages equate to no more than a provisional enhancement in the effectiveness of foreign policy. The ascendant leader's innovative domestic vision remains a symbolic expression of objective problems, not a synoptic analysis. The revised grand strategy remains a symbolic replica of the new vision, not a differentiated response to international circumstances varying by region or issue. Bargaining continues to produce a policy marked by tactical issue linkage and separation, not by substantive integration of issues mirroring the interaction between policies and real conditions. As the domestic and international conditions prevalent at the time of the ascendant leader's incorporation of new policy recommendations give way to new circumstances, the competitive advantages to the leader of adhering to policy recommendations tailored to earlier conditions limit the responsiveness of the policy the leader controls.

Competitive Politics and Soviet Foreign Policy

Is a theory of political competition drawn from the experience of electoral polities also a theory of Soviet foreign policy? It is if an observer of Soviet politics can observe the developments predicted by the theory.

First, at least some leaders in the Soviet Union should go public with different visions of social order at home. Second, at least some of these leaders should recapitulate the symbolism of their domestic visions in grand strategies for international politics. Third, both domestic visions and grand strategies should display consistency over time. Fourth, the leaders should use synecdoche to communicate both the domestic visions and the accompanying grand strategies. Fifth, the leaders should specialize by issue in order to avoid competition when possible. Sixth, when a foreign situation overlaps the issue specialties, rivals should recommend contrasting policies toward that situation. Seventh, when they do, foreign policy should be a bargain characterized either by convergent concessions or by sequential issue trading. Eighth, policy bargains should cross the domestic-international divide. Ninth, leaders should define benchmarks for evaluation of their grand strategies. Tenth, when events occur that an observer would judge to erode the persuasiveness of a leader's grand strategy, that leader should make concessions in the bargaining. Eleventh, if an ascendant leader emerges—one who engages in selective incorporation of variants of policy recommendations formerly associated with rivals—this leader will tell constituents that changes in the world scene accomplished by their support for the original policy recommendations justify the leader's shift to the new ones. Twelfth, if the ascendant leader picks the new policy recommendations to occupy medians between rivals' stands on contested issues, on those issues bargaining by convergent concessions should displace bargaining by sequential issue trading.

Let us see if we can observe these twelve processes at work in the early years of the Brezhnev Politburo.

Chapter 4

Contrasting Visions
of Socialism, 1964–1967

Political competitors recruit constituents by going public with contrasting visions of social order. A vision of social order explains how support for the leader will preserve the society in which the leader seeks constituents. If leaders are competing, their visions converge on the goal of sustaining the social fabric but diverge on methods for achieving the goal. Each competitor's vision defines as crucial a different objective problem and a different set of policies to address that problem. Each set of recommended policies defines a social task that stands as a synecdoche for accomplishment of the goal of sustaining the social order. The vision builds authority for the leader by supplying potential constituents with reasons to identify one contender, in preference to rivals, with their personal attitudes and values.

After Khrushchev's forced resignation in October 1964, four of the eleven Politburo members developed contrasting visions of socialism: Leonid Brezhnev, Aleksei Kosygin, Mikhail Suslov, and Nikolai Podgorny. Their visions converged on the goal of preserving socialism but diverged in presenting alternative conceptions of why the Soviet populace would continue to accept socialism and in recommending different sets of policies to sustain popular acceptance. Each leader idealized a particular bureaucratic role whose occupants were said to be the chief instruments in moving Soviet society toward that leader's vision of socialism.[1]

---

1. My discussion of Brezhnev and Kosygin accords, in the main, with the inter-

Brezhnev and Suslov agreed that the survival of socialism demanded development of a particular set of popular attitudes, but Brezhnev argued that heroic accomplishments would inspire people to accept socialism, while Suslov recommended indoctrination to persuade people of socialism's merits. Brezhnev's symbols of heroic accomplishment were the modernization of Soviet agriculture, which he described as a project comparable to the industrialization achieved under Stalin, and the continuing accumulation of military power. He would achieve both goals by continuing to expand heavy industry while redirecting its output. Arguing that minds would change in response to indoctrination, Suslov subordinated questions of resource allocation to the goal of ensuring a receptive social environment. He advocated expansion of industry to increase employment in factories, whose workers he depicted as the social stratum most susceptible to inculcation of socialist values; he denigrated consumer production as corrosive of those values while advocating defense spending as symbolic of readiness to sacrifice for internationalism.

Podgorny and Kosygin argued that working people would judge socialism by its performance in providing material rewards. Kosygin said the people would accept socialism if it improved the availability of industrial consumer goods, and he proposed measures to make the economy more efficient. Podgorny said that the socialist worker differed from the capitalist employee in being motivated by collective rewards, not private gain. Consumerism was a vice of capitalism; under socialism people preferred to take their rewards in the form of access to education, medical care, and subsidized housing.

The differences over whether workers would accept socialism for attitudinal or material reasons produced disagreement over principles of administrative organization of the bureaucracy. The issue was what should replace the regional economic councils (*sovnarkhozy*) introduced by Khrushchev. As advocates of channeling resources into consumer production or social services, both Kosygin and Podgorny opposed restoration of the centralized economic administration, which they blamed for short-changing the Soviet consumer. Their proposed solution was to place economic decisions in the hands of factory managers. As defenders of industrial expansion, Brezhnev and Suslov favored a restoration of the old central-

---

pretation presented by George W. Breslauer, *Khrushchev and Brezhnev as Leaders* (London: Allen & Unwin, 1982), 137–78, but is based on review of the original documents.

ized institutions, which could concentrate resources on their priority targets.

Differences in visions also produced contrasting stands on the key issue of defense spending. Brezhnev depicted the augmentation of military power as a positive accomplishment that would maintain the inspiration of working people. Suslov presented defense spending as a sacrifice that workers indoctrinated with socialist values would bear willingly. Kosygin called it a sacrifice necessary to protect the Soviet Union but argued that a stronger defense depended on a more efficient economy. Podgorny said that the Soviet people should no longer be asked to sacrifice social welfare for defense.

Presenting four different conceptions of the main social problem facing Soviet officialdom and recommending four different sets of policies, the four Soviet leaders emphasized the contributions of four different kinds of officials. For Brezhnev the Party cadres were the main instruments of change, the people other officials should emulate. Kosygin portrayed the manager as a symbol of efficiency who should be freed from the demands of Party cadres. Suslov drew attention to the "ideological worker" (a specialist in indoctrination), while Podgorny stressed the importance of the work of officials of national, republic, and local soviets. While each leader held up a particular social role as the epitome of the Soviet bureaucrat, none tried to appeal to all its occupants or confined his appeals to the occupants of that role alone. Instead each leader advanced diffuse appeals capable of attracting support across the breadth of Soviet officialdom.

The other six active members of the October 1964 Politburo did not attempt to compete publicly with the four leaders by advancing overall visions; instead they confined their speeches mainly (not exclusively) to building reputations on relatively narrow issues. Gennadii Voronov and Dmitrii Polianskii concentrated on agriculture, Anastas Mikoian on foreign policy toward the Third World, Petro Shelest on Ukrainian autonomy, Andrei Kirilenko on industrial management, and Aleksandr Shelepin on social discipline. (The eleventh member, the aged Nikolai Shvernik, seldom appeared in public and seemed inactive.) As compromises blurred the differences among the four core leaders and failures in foreign policy diminished the persuasiveness of Brezhnev's and Kosygin's visions during 1964–1965, one of the junior members, Shelepin, expanded his discussion of particular issues into a comprehensive vision with which he vied for membership in the inner circle of the Politburo. Shelepin's challenge and his failure are the topic of a later chapter.

The Construction of Opposition

Converging on promises to preserve socialism, the four competitors constructed mutual opposition by contrasting their descriptions of Soviet working people and by recommending different policies to maintain popular acceptance of the Soviet regime. Brezhnev said that heroic accomplishments would inspire allegiance to socialism. Suslov said that indoctrination would persuade people to accept it. Kosygin said that efficiency in producing consumer goods would motivate allegiance. Podgorny said that satisfaction of basic human needs would cause the populace to regard socialism as just. Presenting different definitions of the objective problem facing socialism, the leaders disagreed over the administrative arrangements that would replace Khrushchev's sovnarkhozy and direct resources to the accomplishment of different projects.

Brezhnev said that heroic accomplishments had and would inspire loyalty to socialism. Steel was his synecdoche. For the workers, he said, the attainment of the goal of 18 million metric tons annually on the eve of World War II had been convincing proof of the merits of socialism. The postwar target of 60 million metric tons had been so far overfulfilled that production was now 100 million metric tons yearly, "and even this cannot satisfy us. Already we see new horizons, mark new prospects. And thus it is in all branches of the economy, in all spheres of public life. Forward and only forward—only thus can socialist society develop."[2] Whether the economy could make effective use of more steel was for Brezhnev of secondary importance. The point was to identify big projects that workers could understand and that would give them reasons for pride, and to design economic and political institutions suitable for carrying out those projects.

Brezhnev identified two inspirational projects: the modernization of Soviet agriculture and the accumulation of military might. In both cases his theme was emulation of the heroic past. In the 1930s and 1940s the centralization of economic administration had been harnessed first to the goals of industrialization and defense and then to

2. May 13, 1967.

postwar reconstruction. Brezhnev said Soviet industry was now second to none and capable of achieving new objectives. One such objective was to overcome the traditional backwardness of Russian and Soviet agriculture, a project whose urgency for the 1960s he placed on a par with industrialization in the 1930s.[3] Brezhnev called for a vast increase in the supply of farm machinery and fertilizer, for construction of more farm buildings, for extension of electric power to the 12 percent of collective farms that still lacked it, and in May 1966 for a huge project of drainage and irrigation. Brezhnev lent urgency to his agricultural program—which simultaneously defined a priority task for industry—by calling it an "all-people's task" and "a first-order, all-state task."[4]

Brezhnev's other project was the strengthening of the armed forces. To his three rivals, budget allocations to defense represented a sacrifice: for Suslov a worthy one, for Kosygin a necessary one, for Podgorny an unnecessary one. To Brezhnev the consequences of defense spending were all positive. "Heroic feats" in the Civil War and in World War II had earned the armed forces "the great love and respect of our whole people." Feeling "legitimate pride" in the power of the armed forces, the Soviet people backed the Politburo's decisions to allocate additional resources to defense. Not only would these decisions give the "special attention to nuclear missile weaponry" which produced a deployment program of 200 intercontinental missiles yearly throughout the 1966–1970 plan; as Brezhnev said, "we do not forget the large role that, as before, conventional types of armaments retain."[5] This promise represented Brezhnev's break with Khrushchev's preference for nuclear weapons over conventional forces;[6] it responded to a call issued in February 1965 by the defense minister, Marshal Rodion Malinovskii, for "due attention" to improvement of "all" weapons types.[7]

Brezhnev's discussions of administrative reorganization favored restoration of institutions for centralized planning,[8] which provided

3. In a speech to the Komsomol, May 18, 1966, he called the radical transformation of agriculture the task of the new generation. And see November 4, 1967.

4. March 27, 1965; November 21, 1964. See also June 11, October 16, 1964.

5. July 4 and May 9, 1965. See also March 30, June 11, July 2, 1966.

6. See Harry Gelman, *The Brezhnev Politburo and the Decline of Détente* (Ithaca: Cornell University Press, 1984), 79–83.

7. February 23, 1965.

8. Cf. Suslov's discussions of the September 1965 Plenum reforms (January 27 and June 8, 1966) with Brezhnev's (September 30, October 24, 1965; January 16, March 30,

industry with detailed targets measured in volume of output, to be achieved by factories that received centralized allocations of raw materials and intermediate goods. The standard model of Soviet economic administration, this set of institutional arrangements was understood to be effective in channeling inputs to a few high-priority goals, such as Brezhnev's agricultural and defense projects.

Suslov shared Brezhnev's preference for centralized administration of the economy but gave different reasons. Suslov's vision of socialism could be characterized as indoctrinational. Whereas Brezhnev emphasized the Party's capacity to inspire workers by heroic deeds, Suslov emphasized the Party's capacity to persuade by virtue of its knowledge of objective truth. Thus Suslov took issue with an excessive concern for economic progress while highlighting the contributions of Communist intellectuals:

> The problem of building communism is not fully resolved by the creation of an abundance of material goods. We must also establish communist societal relations in all areas of life, and this is connected with the establishment of communist views, with mastery of the scientific world view and the riches of human culture, with assurance of the development of all sides of the personality, physical and spiritual. The role of the intelligentsia in the accomplishment of these tasks is exceptionally great.[9]

Centralized administration of the economy was desirable because it would steer resources to industry and to defense, but these material objectives were less important in themselves than as signs of the Party's success in transforming workers' preoccupations from consumption to socialist values. Suslov said that because the strengthening of defense entailed "no small material sacrifices by Soviet people," it symbolized the development of an "internationalist" consciousness.[10]

May 20, 1966). Both emphasize the reforms' restoration of centralized branch ministries and refinement of central planning in the context of overall approbation of the September Plenum decisions. See Breslauer, *Khrushchev and Brezhnev as Leaders*, 160–65.

9. June 5, 1965. Note Suslov's comments on "objective laws of the development of society" and the importance of reversing "neglect of ideological influence on the masses"; the "movement for the communist attitude toward labor" as the key to raising productivity; the necessity for internal struggle against bourgeois ideas; and the preservation of the workers' "combat traditions" as the Party's main task (June 8, 1966).

10. June 5, 1965.

In Kosygin's view, workers would judge socialism less by inspirational accomplishments or by the Party's persuasive efforts than by the satisfaction of their material wants. If Brezhnev's theme was emulation of the heroic past and Suslov's was persuasion, Kosygin's theme was efficiency. He repeatedly argued that workers' loyalty depended on their "confidence" that "development of productive forces . . . will become the basis for further growth of [their] material welfare."[11] The sign of this improvement, Kosygin claimed, would be the saturation of the market with industrial consumer goods, which stood with technological advances and quality control as the symbols of economic efficiency. Kosygin reasoned that an increase in production of consumer goods would spur efficiency by rewarding hard workers for achieving higher productivity.[12]

Kosygin's espousal of efficiency led him to argue for institutional arrangements that would transfer administrative responsibility from central control to the individual plant or association of plants—depending on the industry—and would use profitability rather than volume of output as the critical planning target. Combined with reform of prices to express relative scarcity, this change would give managers a means to measure whether they were making most efficient use of resources. To afford managers an opportunity to become more efficient, Kosygin proposed to relieve the center of the responsibility for allocating many types of raw materials and semifabricates and to replace centralized allocations with wholesale commodity markets. He advocated increases in wages and formation of special incentive funds under the control of enterprise managers, so that they could give bonuses to more productive workers and reward all employees in proportion to the factory's profits.[13]

Kosygin defended his reforms by advancing one synecdoche and denying another. Avoiding rivals' reductionist definitions of socialism, he offered his own. Brezhnev had said socialism was "the movement of the popular masses themselves, the result of their labor, their creativity."[14] Suslov had said socialism was "the establishment of communist views." Although in July 1965 Kosygin accepted Suslov's definition, in September he reduced socialism to a question

11. July 19, 1965. See also February 9, April 8, 1965; June 9, 1966.
12. Relevant speeches by Kosygin include October 20, December 10, 1964; July 11 and 18, September 28, 1965; April 5 and 8, June 9, August 4, November 3, 1966; March 7, October 3, November 7, 1967.
13. December 10, 1964; September 28, 1965; April 5, August 4, 1966.
14. October 24, 1965.

of property: "whose hands hold the state power and the means and tools of production, in whose class interest production develops and profit is distributed." At the same time that he equated one element of socialism with the whole, he rejected claims that equated the introduction of aspects of capitalism—profitability, markets, commodity exchange—with a wholesale reversion to capitalism. These claims were the "vain hopes" of "our enemies."[15]

Kosygin's statements on defense spending conformed to his theme of economic efficiency. Responding to U.S. escalation in Vietnam, in July 1965 Kosygin would admit that strengthening the military had become the "very first task."[16] But even in the worsening international situation, he also noted the "advantages" of reducing military expenditures, and he would later affirm that the way to build defense was "by developing our economy."[17]

Like Kosygin, Podgorny was a strong advocate of the decentralizing economic reforms adopted at the September 1965 Central Committee Plenum,[18] and he agreed with Kosygin's view that working people would judge socialism by its satisfaction of their material wants. But Podgorny disagreed with Kosygin's image of what the people wanted. Instead of private consumption, Podgorny said, Soviet working people wanted the satisfaction of basic human needs: "housing construction, urban amenities, health care, and services for the daily needs of the population." In this speech Podgorny never mentioned expanding the production of consumer goods.[19]

Depending on Podgorny's audience, he might choose one or another of these "social funds of consumption" as his synecdoche. In a speech in June 1966, he singled out housing as more important to Soviet workers than Kosygin's consumer goods: "Now, when you travel around the country, meet with the toilers, analyze their letters, you more and more rarely encounter complaints about the shortage of goods, although here too not everything is done. Requests connected with inadequate housing still arrive in great numbers."[20] In a speech to the Sechenov medical institute, however, Podgorny chose medical care for his example.[21]

15. September 28, 1965.
16. July 25, 1965.
17. July 11, 1965; April 5, 1966.
18. May 9 and 22, July 25, 1965; April 1, June 1 and 10, 1966; March 4 and 10, 1967.
19. May 22, 1965. See also July 25, 1965; June 10, 1966.
20. March 10, 1967. See also December 11, 1965; April 1, June 1 and 10, 1966.
21. December 11, 1965.

Podgorny's vision of socialism positioned him between Kosygin on the one hand and Brezhnev and Suslov on the other. He agreed with Kosygin and disagreed with Brezhnev and Suslov in portraying the population as judging socialism by their personal circumstances, but he agreed with Brezhnev and Suslov and disagreed with Kosygin in stressing the ideological distinctiveness of Soviet society. Podgorny even directly criticized a version of Kosygin's argument, contrasting "capitalism, which sets the human being apart from society and cultivates individualism," with socialism's characteristic "strengthening and development of the feeling of collectivism."[22]

Though a moderate on the dimension of ideology versus material conditions as the motivator of popular allegiance to socialism, Podgorny was the extremist along the dimension of support for defense spending. When he, Kosygin, and Brezhnev gave speeches at ceremonies commemorating victory in World War II, Podgorny alone failed to call for strengthening defense.[23] At the end of May 1965, Podgorny denied that it was still necessary, as it had been in the 1930s, to sacrifice the Soviet populace's material welfare to industrialization and defense.[24] Even in July, when the others had committed themselves to an increase in military outlays, Podgorny attributed the victory over Germany not, as the other leaders did, to prewar measures for preparedness (which in fact had not been decisive) but to the Soviet Union's having been "ideologically stronger."[25]

The rhetoric of the four leaders confirms the surmise that they sought constituents not among the populace as a whole but within the bureaucracy. Constituents are those with whom the leader seeks to identify himself or herself as members of a common collective agent. The leader builds identification by placing himself or herself in the same rhetorical stance vis-à-vis the objective problem that the constituent occupies. By defining popular attitudes as the objective problem facing their audience, the four Politburo members rhetorically distanced themselves from the population while taking their stance together with officials variously assigned to manipulate, guide, control, or serve the population. Although each Politburo member identified some bureaucrats as problems, no Politburo member defined the behavior of bureaucrats as the problem while taking a rhe-

22. June 10, 1966.
23. May 8 and 9, 1965.
24. May 22, 1965.
25. July 25, 1965.

torical stance with the people. No one tried to represent the populace.

Idealization of Bureaucratic Roles

Each of the four leaders idealized a particular bureaucratic role, summoning all Soviet bureaucrats to emulate the occupants of that role. Brezhnev idealized the Party cadre, Kosygin the manager, Suslov the "ideological worker" (not an ideologue, but an official charged with educating and indoctrinating), and Podgorny the official of a soviet. While each leader held up an occupant of some bureaucratic role as a model for officials in general, none sought to represent only the occupants of that role or all its occupants.

Brezhnev ascribed to the Party the "leading role" in Soviet society. Kosygin typically avoided this stock phrase, preferring instead to refer to the Party's responsibility "to organize and to mobilize."[26] Neither explicitly defined the difference between "leading" and "organizing and mobilizing" (although generally "to lead" meant to decide policy, while "to organize" meant to select personnel and "to mobilize" meant to conduct mass propaganda). But the consistency of the difference in their respective usages indicated that their views of the Party differed in *some* respect. And Kosygin clearly ascribed less importance to the Party hierarchy. Where Brezhnev sought to draw his audiences' attention to the Party's past accomplishments by lengthy citations of named individuals and concrete events, before like audiences at like ceremonies Kosygin's references to the Party's contributions were cursory and abstract.[27] In contrast to Brezhnev's heroic image of the Party as the driving force in the dynamics of socialism, Kosygin portrayed the Party as an auxiliary to economic administrators. In Kosygin's view the Party bureaucrats

26. May 17, 1966; for other references, see November 26, 1964; July 11 and 18, 1965. When he did ascribe a "leading role" to the Party at the September 1965 Plenum, Kosygin redefined "leading" to mean "organizing and mobilizing." In a speech published November 7, 1967, Kosygin finally referred to the "leadership of the Communist Party."

27. Cf. the treatments of the Party's contribution in Brezhnev's speech on the fortieth anniversary of the Uzbek Republic and in Kosygin's speech on the fortieth anniversary of the Turkmen Republic, November 21 and 26, 1964; in Brezhnev's speech at a ceremony for returning cosmonauts and in Kosygin's speech at a reception for them, March 23 and 24, 1965; in speeches at Leningrad and Volgograd commemorating the two cities' wartime heroism, July 11, 1965.

should monitor the administration to guard against mismanagement, insubordination, or corruption and should instill a sense of responsibility among workers for conscientious job performance.[28]

The obverse of Brezhnev's and Kosygin's differences over the Party bureaucracy was their disagreement about the role of managers (*khoziastvenniki*). Just as Kosygin was inattentive to the roles of Party bureaucrats, Brezhnev avoided talking about managers. But while endorsing the call for managers to be competent specialists, Brezhnev stressed that the manager was also a Party *vozhak*: literally, "leader of a social movement," a "guide to the blind."[29] The manager should be an inspirational leader who persuaded his workers that they were a team of labor comrades engaged in a great undertaking. By his reference to the manager as vozhak, Brezhnev identified himself with those who thought that an ideal manager would spend a significant part of his time on the shop floor explaining to his workers the social significance of their labor.[30] Kosygin identified with the opposite view: "A resolute struggle must be waged against those who conceive economic leadership as didacticism [*mentorstvo*], who supplant real businesslike leadership with high-handed tutoring. . . . Lengthy and unnecessary sessions that waste the time of qualified officials have to stop."[31]

While Brezhnev upheld the Party cadre and Kosygin the manager as a model, Suslov exalted the indoctrination specialist, or "ideological worker." Just as Brezhnev and Kosygin accompanied their apotheoses of one type of cadre or manager with criticisms of other types, Suslov did not seek to identify with all occupants of the role he idealized. He opposed those ideologists, led by his subordinate V. I. Stepakov, who attempted to subordinate the work of ideologists to Kosygin's call for increasing the economic literacy of managers and other industrial employees.[32] Suslov instead urged "com-

---

28. Breslauer, *Khrushchev and Brezhner as Leaders*, 150; Kosygin: July 11 and 18, 1965; April 8, June 9, 1966.

29. October 24, 1965. See also November 2, 1966, and the summary of what he emphasized during a private meeting with Party and managerial officials at the Gorky obkom, January 8, 1967. For the definition of *vozhak*, see S. N. Ozhegov, *Slovar' russkogo iazyka* (Moscow: Sovietskaia Entsiklopediia, 1968), 86.

30. E.g., "Rukovodit'—znachit' i vospityvat'," February 20, 1965; Iu. Polukarov, "Partiinost' khoziaistvennika," March 2, 1966; V. Churpita, "Avtoritet rukovoditelia," October 12, 1966.

31. December 10, 1964. See also September 28, 1965

32. V. Stepakov, "Ovladevat' velikim ucheniem marksizma-leninizma," August 4, 1965; "Prochnaia sviaz' s massami," July 27, 1966; "Revoliutsionnaia teoriia i partiinaia

munist indoctrination of the toilers" and "more autonomy in the examination of economic issues . . . assurance of more precise division
of the functions of Party and state organs."[33]

Podgorny idealized officials of the soviets, which bore the responsibility for allocating housing and the other administratively distributed goods and services that Podgorny defined as the main wants of
the population. "The Party sees its most important task as developing the activity of the laboring people . . . ," he said. "The soviets of
people's deputies play a special role in this." While emphasizing the
soviets' "special role," however, like the other leaders Podgorny criticized some occupants of that role. Noting the tendency of local
Party cadres to usurp functions assigned to the soviets, Podgorny
said, "It is possible that this suits some officials of soviets, since it
relieves them of the responsibility for carrying out their duties."[34]

Symbols and Policies

As political competition theory leads one to expect, some members of the Politburo advanced diverging visions of social order consisting of contrasting images of the problems involved in the preservation of socialism and recommending corresponding policies to
address those problems. Brezhnev's vision was of inspirational socialism, Suslov's of indoctrinational socialism, Kosygin's of efficient
socialism, and Podgorny's of collectivist socialism. While each leader's
vision implied a different allocation of resources across economic
sectors, each built the vision around diffuse symbolic appeals that
could have been expected to draw support across sectors. Brezhnev's vision steered resources to agriculture, defense, and the parts
of heavy industry that produced end products for those sectors, but
the heroic past from which he drew inspiration was common to officials of all sectors. Suslov's vision perpetuated the existing bias of
resource allocations in favor of heavy industry and defense, but ef-

propaganda," January 30, 1967; and "Chelovek, sozydaiushchii novyi mir," September 12, 1967; V. Tolstikov, "Novye usloviia, vozrosshie trebovaniia," October 23, 1965;
A. Botvin, "Vooruzhaem kadry ekonomicheskimi znaniiami," November 22, 1965; N.
Golovko, "Shkola ideinoi zakalki," June 18, 1966; G. Romanov, "Krugozor spetsi-
alista," July 7, 1966; M. Sergeev, "Stupeni rosta," July 9, 1966; N. Musina, "Propa-
gande—nauchnye osnovy," June 6, 1967. For Kosygin's call, see September 28, 1965.
33. June 5, 1965.
34. April 1, 1966.

forts to persuade working people to adopt a "communist attitude toward labor" would have eased the supervisory tasks facing officials throughout the bureaucracy. Kosygin's vision steered resources into the consumer goods sector, but his proposals for increasing efficiency held appeal for ambitious subordinates throughout the economy. As he said, "There are leaders who . . . continue to conduct business according to the old way. One cannot tolerate this. And such economic officials must be replaced."[35] Threats to replace managers who failed to adjust to the economic reform were simultaneously promises of promotion opportunities to their juniors. Podgorny's vision steered resources into the housing sector, but at the same time it promised to relieve complaints addressed by working people to hard-pressed officials in every sector.

None of the leaders engaged in synoptic deliberation of the objective circumstances facing the Soviet Union as a whole. Instead each rival singled out a particular element of socialism as crucial and recommended policies that focused on that element of the overall situation. What Herbert Simon called suboptimization was a conscious choice by the Politburo members to communicate more effectively by simplifying the complexity of the circumstances facing officials. If leaders after Khrushchev designed policies that combined massive new investment in agriculture and defense with economic reforms aimed at efficiency, new efforts in housing construction, and tighter control of political indoctrination, they did so because each of these policy lines had its own champion among the four contenders for leadership of the Politburo.

35. December 10, 1964.

Chapter 5

Brezhnev and Eastern Europe,
October 1964–April 1966

Issue specialization lets political competitors share opportunities to claim credit. Anticipating that they will choose policy by sequential issue trading, political competitors may decide to focus their descriptions of the world scene and their policy recommendations on a restricted range of issues. Each competitor can approve a policy package that incorporates that competitor's recommendations on his or her own issues with rivals' recommendations on their issues. Then all the competitors can persuasively tell their respective constituents that they have succeeded in gaining the assent of rivals to the policy proposals that each has offered as a benchmark for constituents' evaluation of his or her ability to control the policy of the state.

After the ouster of Khrushchev, Brezhnev made relations with the East European allies his specialty. This specialization solved his problem of finding a grand strategy that would stand in world politics for the vision of inspirational accomplishment that he stood for at home. Pursuing his theme of emulating heroic feats of the past, Brezhnev claimed that the capitalist West continued to threaten the socialist countries. As his synecdoche for the capitalist threat, he initially selected NATO's proposal for a multilateral force (MLF), a nuclear-armed fleet manned by combined crews from participating NATO countries. By stressing the military threat from Germany, Brezhnev not only raised an issue of intense concern to many in the Soviet audience. He also justified a policy recommendation to shift

Soviet policy from subsidizing Eastern Europe's economic progress to guaranteeing its security. Brezhnev's argument for a cut in the subsidy echoed his contention in domestic politics that the standard institutions of socialist economy could continue to produce economic advance. As a reduction in the implicit subsidy to Eastern Europe would free resources, Brezhnev's proposal for a policy shift was likely to reinforce his appeal to those officials who welcomed his advocacy of a more extensive military buildup.

The Politburo reformists, allowing Brezhnev to dominate policy toward Eastern Europe in return for his tolerance of their leadership in other world regions, concentrated on protecting the decentralization of economic administration in progress or under consideration in all five of the loyal East European allies (i.e., other than Romania). The ultimate policy package combined their proposal to encourage reform in Eastern Europe with adoption of Brezhnev's proposals to reduce the subsidy and to make East European diplomatic initiatives toward West European governments conditional on NATO's abandonment of the MLF. Increasing demands on East European governments while reducing the payoffs to them for compliance, and approving economic reforms while taking away the resources needed for the reforms to succeed, this package displayed the counterproductive features characteristic of a foreign policy chosen by competitive politics.

Heroic Anticapitalism: Brezhnev's Grand Strategy

What grand strategy for world politics would replicate the symbolism of inspirational accomplishment that distinguished Brezhnev's domestic vision, recall the heroism of the past, and single out the Party cadre as the ideal Soviet official? Of the many strategies that might have been suitable for evocation of the heroic cadre, Brezhnev found most attractive a strategy based on the old association of the cadre with violent opposition to capitalism. Heroism was appropriate to a world in conflict. Brezhnev therefore depicted a socialist camp under siege and offered the unified resistance of communists as the solution. "Peace . . . ," he said in his first speech as Party leader, "depends increasingly on strengthening the cohesion of all anti-imperialist forces and primarily on the unity of the socialist countries and the world communist movement."[1]

1. October 20, 1964.

As his main symbol of the imperialist threat, Brezhnev initially picked the NATO proposal for the MLF, which he interpreted as a threat to give nuclear weapons to West Germany. His argument consisted of three claims. First, German leaders, "hypnotized" by the borders of 1937, were hoping to reverse the political results of World War II, even though this hope was futile and would result in a war that would destroy West Germany. Second, under modern conditions the West German leaders' only hope of giving this idea even slight plausibility lay in the acquisition of nuclear weapons. Third, NATO's presentation of its MLF plan as a substitute for a national German nuclear capability was in fact merely "camouflage" for the German leaders' long-term plan to gain full control over a national nuclear capability. The threat of West German nuclearization figured in ten of Brezhnev's fourteen speeches given on appropriate occasions and printed in *Pravda* during the period from 15 October 1964 to the Central Committee Plenum at the end of September 1965.[2]

Although Brezhnev's opposition to MLF looks like an instance of the standard prediction of international relations theories that a state will resist augmentation of an enemy alliance's military power, three circumstances reveal Brezhnev's knowing use of MLF as a synecdoche to communicate his grand strategy. First, MLF was only part of the nuclear threat facing the Soviet Union, and a minor part at that. Although very prominent in Brezhnev's speeches, the two hundred nuclear missiles proposed for the MLF would have added little to the threat already posed by the United States' thousand intercontinental ballistic missiles, six hundred strategic bombers, and Polaris submarine-launched ballistic missiles, in addition to French and British nuclear capability. Based on surface ships, these missiles would have been vulnerable to a nonnuclear Soviet preemptive attack, in contrast to the invulnerable U.S. retaliatory forces. MLF was a part of the threat that stood for the whole.[3]

Second, Brezhnev knowingly misrepresented NATO's deliberations over MLF. Most of his discussions of MLF occurred in exchanges of

2. Discussions of MLF: November 6, December 4, 1964; March 23, April 9, May 9, July 4, September 11, 15, 25 and 30, 1965. Omission of MLF: October 20 and November 21, 1964; July 11 and 28, 1965. Three speeches (on agriculture in March and to two Third World visitors) count as inappropriate occasions, as do eleven brief speeches at ceremonies for arriving or departing foreign leaders.

3. David N. Schwartz, *NATO's Nuclear Dilemmas* (Washington, D.C.: Brookings, 1983), 131.

public speeches with East European leaders. They described the intense controversy within NATO over whether to deploy MLF. In pointed contrast, Brezhnev said that the disagreements concerned merely details about the kind of forces and the number of fingers on the nuclear button. He said it was "clear" that NATO was preparing a new, dangerous concession to West German militarists.[4] Denials of dissension within NATO over MLF maintained the persuasiveness of Brezhnev's claims that the Soviet Union faced a monolithic enemy alliance, "headed by the United States of America" and comprising "world reaction" or "world imperialism," which was preparing to attack the socialist countries.[5]

Third, Brezhnev continued to demand resistance to the MLF even when he knew that its prospects for adoption were diminishing. Brezhnev launched his campaign to make MLF the main security issue two days before meetings in Washington at which President Johnson ordered the State and Defense departments to stop pushing for MLF in NATO councils.[6] Johnson's decision was publicized in U.S. press reports known to circulate among Politburo members. Even if Johnson still hoped to gain NATO's assent to the MLF, at the very least the December 1964 decision reduced the likelihood of its eventual adoption and, in retrospect, sounded its death knell. Yet, despite knowledge of MLF's dwindling prospects, Brezhnev intensified his campaign against it over the next eleven months. When NATO finally did abandon MLF in April 1965, Brezhnev's reaction combined a claim of credit for blocking the proposal with a not entirely reconcilable insistence that NATO's substitute for the MLF proposal (the Nuclear Planning Group, instituted as a forum for German participation in discussion of nuclear strategy) represented "camouflage" for continuing efforts to place nuclear weapons under German control.[7]

A description of NATO as a monolithic alliance bent on arming

---

4. December 4, 1964. See also April 9, September 25, 1965.

5. May 9, July 1, 4 and 11, September 11, 15, 25 and 30, 1965; January 15, March 30, 1966. Occasions when Brezhnev might have used this phrase or its variants but did not were July 21 and 28, August 28, October 5 and 24, 1965, and January 13, 14, and 16 and April 9, 1966.

6. Schwartz, *NATO's Nuclear Dilemmas*, 120–22.

7. Brezhnev's claims are to be found in his speeches in September 1965 to the East Europeans and on October 24, 1965, in Kiev, as well as in his speech to the XXIII Party Congress, March 30, 1966. The same line of analysis is found in "A Mine Dug under European Security," *Obozrevatel'*, July 20, 1965. On the NATO decision, see Schwartz, *NATO's Nuclear Dilemmas*, 120–22.

West Germany with nuclear weapons for renewal of aggression against Eastern Europe and the Soviet Union made plausible a policy recommendation that the socialist countries should match NATO's conduct. Accordingly, Brezhnev said the main goal of Soviet foreign policy should be to cohere the socialist countries. As "the main force today resisting imperialism," they had a "special role" in preventing war.[8] Brezhnev did not oppose the building of alliances with nonruling communist parties or with "anti-imperialist" Third World countries; but these activities, though "necessary," were not so "urgent" as his own program of "joint actions of the countries of socialism."[9] To improve coordination of the socialist countries, Brezhnev advocated creation of a standing commission of the Warsaw Treaty organization, perhaps similar to NATO's Atlantic Council. Brezhnev's little-known proposal encountered effective resistance from the East Europeans.[10]

For Brezhnev, the purpose of coordinating the Warsaw Treaty states' foreign policies was to prevent any of them from welcoming diplomatic overtures from NATO states. East European leaders proposed to cooperate with NATO governments or political parties that might join in reducing military confrontation. If NATO could persuasively be portrayed as monolithic, the East Europeans' strategy would seem infeasible. Brezhnev therefore denied the possibility of cooperation. For example, when Walter Ulbricht asserted that the "cleavage" between militarist and peaceful forces did not coincide with the East German state border but "proceeds across West Germany itself," Brezhnev located the "cleavage between the two German states."[11]

To counter the putative nuclearization of West Germany, Brezhnev advocated an acceleration of the program initiated in 1961 by General Andrei Grechko, at that time head of the Warsaw Treaty's unified command, to coordinate the national armies more closely by conducting joint maneuvers according to a common training outline that emphasized combat under nuclear conditions. The nuclear emphasis of Grechko's outline was a means of strengthening alliance cohesion, since it deprived the participating East European armies of the opportunity to train according to the alternative, "territorial de-

---

8. July 1, 1965; May 9, July 1, September 7, 1965; March 30, 1966.
9. May 9, 1965.
10. Robin Alison Remington, *The Warsaw Pact: Case Studies in Communist Conflict Resolution* (Cambridge: MIT Press, 1971), 83–86.
11. September 25, 1965. See also December 4, 1964; April 9, 1965.

fense" scheme developed in Romania and Yugoslavia (and under consideration elsewhere), which would have enhanced their ability to resist Soviet intervention.[12] Brezhnev was the only Politburo member to endorse Grechko's program of military cooperation.[13]

Brezhnev's stress on protecting socialist countries against the NATO security threat shifted the emphasis of Soviet policy away from Khrushchev's priority of ensuring economic progress. Brezhnev became the proponent of a cost-cutting strategy in Eastern Europe. The pattern of Soviet trade presented its East European allies with an implicit subsidy. The Soviets bought East European manufactures and sold fuels and ores, both at the world prices for equivalent Western goods, even though the Soviet raw materials could have been sold in the world market at full price while the East European manufactures sold only at a sharp discount.[14] Brezhnev couched his proposal to cut the subsidy in positive terms, as advocacy of increasing the share of manufactures in Soviet exports: "An increase in the volume of trade is not the only thing. What we trade is also very important. For the very structure of trade is a good indicator of socio-economic progress. In the trade of our countries mutual deliveries of machines and industrial equipment have an ever larger place."[15]

Brezhnev's proposal to trade manufactures for manufactures drew protests from the East European leaders whose economies were most dependent on Soviet deliveries of fuel and raw materials, particularly Czechoslovakia's Antonin Novotny, Poland's Wladyslaw Gomulka, and East Germany's Walter Ulbricht. Brezhnev discredited their appeals for an increase in the implicit subsidy by denying that their economies faced any long-term difficulties. Socialist institutions were a sufficient guarantee of rapid economic advance without external intervention, Brezhnev said. When Novotny raised the 1962 recession, Brezhnev countered by calling attention to the long-term trend, noting that Czechoslovakia's economic growth had out-

12. Christopher D. Jones, *Soviet Influence in Eastern Europe: Political Autonomy and the Warsaw Pact* (New York: Praeger, 1971), 106–63, 228–33.

13. September 15 and 30, 1965.

14. Michael Marrese and Jan Vanous, *Soviet Subsidization of Trade with Eastern Europe: A Soviet Perspective* (Berkeley: Institute of International Studies, 1983); Paul Marer, "The Political Economy of Soviet Relations with Eastern Europe," in Sarah Meiklejohn Terry, ed., *Soviet Policy in Eastern Europe* (New Haven: Yale University Press, 1984).

15. September 11, 1965. See also December 4, 1964; April 9, September 7, 11, 15, and 20, 1965.

paced that of selected capitalist countries by a factor of three or four. Any suggestion that socialism might encounter economic difficulties he dismissed as "the ill will of bourgeois propagandists."[16]

Brezhnev's effort to cut the implicit subsidy is also evident in his neglect of the topic of "socialist integration" of the economies of the Council for Economic Mutual Assistance (CEMA). The objectives of "cooperation and specialization" of industrial production included both intrabranch and interbranch components. The former involved exchanges of parts between industries with similar production profiles. The latter involved exchanges of fuels and raw materials from the richly endowed members (the Soviet Union, Romania, and Bulgaria) for manufactures from industrially more highly developed countries, particular Czechoslovakia and the German Democratic Republic.

Predictably, none of Brezhnev's speeches made any mention of either the international socialist division of labor or cooperation and specialization of industry until late September 1965, and even then he said that these processes must not be "artificially forced," and that it would be "impermissible and even incorrect" to give priority to the economic development of the whole socialist commonwealth over that of any of the individual countries.[17]

The expectation of issue specialization implies that Brezhnev's Politburo rivals should have generally refrained from objecting to his proposals on relations with East European countries, and they did. At the same time, these were Brezhnev's proposals, not the common property of the Politburo. Although his rivals said generally that socialist cohesion was desirable, and some echoed his positions on various single issues (particularly MLF), no other Politburo members repeated all of Brezhnev's arguments or devoted nearly so much space in their speeches to policy in Eastern Europe.

Brezhnev's proposals were ill designed to impress Soviet policy experts. The experts on NATO shared his access to U.S. press reports of Johnson's decision to abandon the MLF proposal, and they knew about the dissension among the Western allies. The experts on relations among socialist countries were fully cognizant of the East Europeans' dependence on Soviet fuel and raw materials, which had been the subject of extended public discussion in the preceding two years. The proposals were tailored to the inexpert.

16. December 4, 1964. See also April 9, September 7, 11, 15, and 20, 1965.
17. September 15, 1965.

The Construction of Opposition: Reform

The one divergence on East European policy between Brezhnev and his Politburo rivals—Kosygin, Podgorny, Mikoian, Shelepin, and after March 1965 Kirill Mazurov—concerned endorsement of the economic reforms in progress in five of the six European socialist allies. The main connection between domestic reform in the USSR and economic organization in Eastern Europe was the usefulness of East European experience for legitimating controversial reform proposals in the USSR. Opponents of economic reform objected on the ground that marketization amounted to a "capitalist restoration." If the objection to reform was creeping capitalism, the ability to point to the adoption of capitalist practices in the undeniably socialist countries of Eastern Europe offered the reform advocates a convincing counterargument. The reformers could not persuasively promise to protect reformist officials against Brezhnev at home if they allowed him to trample reform in Eastern Europe. Knowing this, when Brezhnev discussed economic reorganization in Eastern Europe, he confined himself to an expression of neutral skepticism: "Practical experience affirms the expediency of some forms and discards others."[18]

The pro-reform Politburo members described economic reform in Eastern Europe and in the Soviet Union as a single process of mutual learning. In a comment that typified the reformers' attitude, Podgorny said:

> We are devoting much attention to working out the most rational forms and methods of organizing and administering industrial and agricultural production, strengthening the connection of science and practice. . . . No one can doubt that active exchange of valuable experience accumulated in fraternal countries will help all of us deal with the complex tasks of economic and cultural construction even better.[19]

Support for reform resulted in one overt disagreement with Brezhnev's policy recommendations. CEMA's project of interbranch cooperation and specialization, which contravened Brezhnev's effort to increase the share of manufactures in Soviet exports, was initiated by reform economists. Despite Brezhnev's opposition, throughout 1964 and 1965 Kosygin openly and repeatedly "attach[ed] great sig-

18. April 9, 1965.
19. May 9, 1965. For others' comments, see March 2, May 7, July 1, September 28, October 2, 1965.

nificance" to coordination of plans and specialization of production within CMEA, as well as expansion of "broad economic ties among all socialist states," which would make it possible to reap more benefits from "the advantages inherent in the world system of socialism."[20] These statements placed limits on the reduction in the subsidy that Kosygin would accept.

Bargaining

As Sarah Meiklejohn Terry writes, "the most striking feature of Soviet behavior up to 1968 was the way it *fostered* the growth of reformism in the region."[21] In light of military intervention against reformers in Czechoslovakia three years later, it is remarkable that during 1965 economic reforms adopted or extended by every East European country except Romania obtained endorsement in consensus documents approved by the Soviet Politburo.[22] But the issue trade was the Politburo reformers' acquiescence in Brezhnev's proposal for a change in the mix of Soviet exports to Eastern Europe. Speeches during 1965 concerned the formulation of the plan for 1966. Brezhnev managed to reverse the 1963–1965 increase of the share of fuel and raw materials in relation to machinery in Soviet exports. In 1966 the value of fuel and raw material exports stayed constant, while the value of machinery exports increased by 86 million rubles. Deliveries of Soviet fuel and raw materials to every country had increased in relation to machinery and equipment from 1963 through 1965; Brezhnev succeeded in reversing this trend overall and in every country except Hungary.[23] This signal success bucked the trend: 1966 was the only year from 1960 to 1980 when the implicit subsidy declined. Brezhnev also gained a Politburo decision that his stand on the MLF should shape the final communiqué of the January 1965 Warsaw meeting of the Political Consultative

20. December 10, 1964. See also March 3, April 20, September 28, 1965.

21. Sarah M. Terry, "Theories of Socialist Development in Soviet–East European Relations," in Terry, *Soviet Policy in Eastern Europe*, 231. Wlodzimierz Brus mischaracterizes Soviet policy as failure to block economic reform in 1965–1966 rather than as encouragement of it, and attributes Soviet passivity to the East Europeans' willingness to decouple economic reform from political change: "Economic Reforms as an Issue in Soviet-East European Relations," in Karen Dawisha and Philip Hanson, eds., *Soviet–East European Dilemmas: Coercion, Competition, and Dissent* (London: Heinemann for the Royal Institute of International Affairs, 1981), 86–87. See also John C. Campbell, "Soviet Policy in Eastern Europe: An Overview," in Terry, *Soviet Policy in Eastern Europe*, 10.

22. E.g., "Liniia, proverennaia zhizn'iu," December 12, 1965.

23. Marrese and Vanous, *Soviet Subsidization*, app. C.

Commission of the Warsaw Treaty. The communiqué expressed the East Europeans' grudging concession that they should postpone any initiatives toward agreements with West European states so long as NATO was considering the MLF, as Brezhnev insisted.[24]

When foreign policy is a compromise among political competitors, events that diminish the persuasiveness of one rival's description of the world scene should force concessions by that rival in the bargaining. Brezhnev had made MLF the benchmark by which the urgency of his grand strategy should be judged. When NATO officially renounced MLF in July 1965, Brezhnev's image of NATO as a monolithically hostile alliance lost persuasiveness. Brezhnev was compelled to make concessions, which became manifest when he resumed making speeches after the August vacation.

During the September round of meetings with the East Europeans, Brezhnev made limited concessions on four issues that had occupied the agenda throughout 1965. First, he agreed to a Czechoslovak proposal that the Soviets increase future deliveries of fuels and ores in return for the Czechoslovaks' provision of investment capital to develop new deposits and refineries on Soviet territory. Second, Brezhnev now agreed that the experience of reform in Eastern Europe would be a valuable guide for Soviet decisions on economic reorganization. Third, Brezhnev's speeches began to incorporate statements favorable to Kosygin's and the East Europeans' proposals for multilateral economic integration.[25]

Fourth, Brezhnev altered his attitude toward negotiations between the Warsaw Treaty states and the European members of NATO. He shifted his response to a proposal by the Polish leader Gomulka to convene a conference of all European states on collective security. In an exchange of speeches in April, when Gomulka had said the conference proposal's "urgency is not open to doubt," Brezhnev had distinguished between demands on NATO which "we propose" and "Poland's initiative for . . . a conference of European states."[26] In September Brezhnev endorsed the strategic principles informing Gomulka's proposal, and by March 1966 he had agreed to include a specific reference to the conference in the list of Soviet foreign policy initiatives in his report to the XXIII Party Congress.[27]

Competitive politics produced a Soviet policy toward Eastern Eu-

---

24. January 22, 1965.
25. September 15, 25 and 30, 1965; January 16, March 30, 1966.
26. April 9, 1965.
27. September 25, 1965; March 30, 1966.

rope rife with misinformation and internal contradictions. Brezhnev's representation of all NATO countries by the U.S.-German proposal for MLF accomplished the purpose of portraying himself as a champion in a fight against capitalism at the expense of obscuring several NATO countries' real receptivity to negotiations. Brezhnev demanded East European leaders' submission to his veto of negotiations with NATO states at the same time as he reduced the implicit subsidy that was their reward for compliance with Soviet demands. His price for accepting Soviet reformists' endorsement of economic reorganization in Eastern Europe was a cutback in deliveries of fuels and raw materials which severely complicated the reformers' attempts to revive their economies. The 1966 cuts in Soviet deliveries to Czechoslovakia exacerbated the economic troubles that undermined Novotny and in 1967 brought to power the advocates of more sweeping reforms against whom Brezhnev would mount the intervention of 1968.[28]

Brezhnev's combination of emphasis on the security threat facing Eastern Europe with a cost-cutting strategy calls into question common explanations for the Soviets' willingness to provide the subsidy. Supposedly the Soviet Union subsidized East European regimes for security reasons, because they supplied either a defensive buffer zone or an offensive staging area against NATO.[29] If the subsidy was a payment for military security, one wonders why the Politburo member who was most concerned with the threat of war expressed least support for the subsidy. But if it represented a reward to ruling communist parties for adopting policies that would reflect favorably on the persuasiveness of Soviet leaders' domestic visions, Brezhnev's opposition to a subsidy that benefited reformists in Eastern Europe and Kosygin's support for it fall into place. After the reformists lost power to counterreformers in Czechoslovakia, Poland, and East Germany between 1968 and 1971, Brezhnev became an advocate of the subsidy and Kosygin tried to restrain it. As Brezhnev overpowered Kosygin, the subsidy increased rapidly during the 1970s.[30]

---

28. On the opposition to Novotny, see Galia Golan, *The Czechoslovak Reform Movement: Communism in Crisis, 1962–1968* (Cambridge: Cambridge University Press, 1971).

29. J. F. Brown, *Eastern Europe and Communist Rule* (Durham, N.C.: Duke University Press), 30–31; Marrese and Vanous, *Soviet Subsidization*, 68–86.

30. Michael Marrese and Jan Vanous, "The Content and Controversy of Soviet Trade Relations with Eastern Europe," in Josef C. Brada, Ed A. Hewett, and Thomas A. Wolf, eds., *Economic Adjustment and Reform in Eastern Europe and the Soviet Union: Essays in Honor of Franklyn D. Holzman* (Durham, N.C.: Duke University Press), 189.

Chapter 6

Suslov and International Communism, October 1964–April 1966

Suslov specialized in policy toward foreign communists. Recapitulating his domestic vision of socialism sustained by the Communist Party's special capacity to persuade, Suslov argued that those foreign communist parties that relied on persuasion instead of revolutionary violence could prevent war in the short run and win parliamentary majorities in the long run. Indoctrination of the mass public by communists would not only preserve socialism at home but protect and spread it abroad.

Suslov's apotheosis of foreign communists who favored a parliamentary strategy for the transition to socialism brought him into conflict with Brezhnev. Proposing to rebuild the grand alliance of states ruled by communists, Brezhnev recommended a reconciliation with Maoist China. One issue in the Sino-Soviet dispute was the Maoists' rejection of the nonviolent path to socialism. As a Sino-Soviet reconciliation would require negotiation of joint stands on the disputed issues, Brezhnev's proposal threatened to interfere with Suslov's attempts to recruit domestic support by preaching the merits of persuasion over revolutionary violence.

Suslov ultimately recaptured control of policy toward international communism by forming a coalition with Kosygin and Podgorny based on common antipathy to the Maoists, who were also polemicizing against the two Soviet leaders' proposals for economic reform and East-West cooperation. Logrolling between this coalition and Brezhnev produced a self-frustrating policy toward China, as the

Politburo approved Brezhnev's proposals for reconciliation on the condition that there be no concessions on any of the ideological or policy issues in dispute. Suslov's grand strategy also misrepresented world conditions by portraying the two strongest communist parties in Europe as typical of the rest of the parties in the industrial world, though he knew that even the two strong parties lacked the electoral strength to achieve his promise of parliamentary majorities.

The Broad Front: Suslov's Grand Strategy

Contrary to his reputation as a Stalinist, Suslov advocated an electoral strategy for the transition to socialism in advanced capitalist countries. A "bore" as a public speaker,[1] Suslov gave many fewer speeches than the other senior Politburo members. To communicate his grand strategy, he relied not only on his own speeches but also on those of his subordinate and associate for forty years, Boris Ponomarev. They both argued that peace depended on communists' "creation of a united workers' front and a broad popular front" composed of "forces struggling for peace, national independence, democracy, and socialism."[2]

These forces comprised three "detachments": "countries of the socialist commonwealth, peace-loving states of Asia, Africa, and Latin America occupying an anti-imperialist position and together with the socialist countries forming an expansive zone of peace," and "the working class and the broad popular masses of capitalist countries."[3] According to Suslov, "each [detachment] upholds both its own interests and the general interests [of world communism] in its world zone by means and methods particular to it."[4] This statement justified the pursuit of different strategies by communists in developing countries and communists in industrial countries. In the Third World, where industrial development was said to be retarded by capitalist states' policies of "colonialism and neocolonialism," the working class was correspondingly underdeveloped. Lacking a social base adequate for socialism, communist parties should devote their efforts to supporting local governments that would pursue policies of "resistance to the neocolonialist strategy of imperialism, di-

1. Zhores A. Medvedev, *Andropov* (Oxford: Basil Blackwell, 1983), 51.
2. October 5, 1965; June 5, July 18, 1965.
3. October 31, 1965; and see October 5, 1965; January 27, 1966.
4. January 27, 1966.

rected at tying the young nationalist states to the chariot of capitalism . . . and isolating them from the world system of socialism."[5] In countries that adopted the so-called noncapitalist path of development, "the greatest success in construction of the new society is achieved where the alliance and salutary collaboration of all revolutionary forces are ensured."[6] Whenever capitalist powers sought to block independence movements by force, communist parties should support "just wars of national liberation and uprisings of peoples against imperialist oppression."[7]

While Third World communists should back movements for national independence with violence if necessary, First World communists should try to win power by peaceful means. Suslov and Ponomarev advocated the Italian and French Communists' strategy of trying to win parliamentary elections by forming electoral coalitions with social democratic parties,[8] a goal referred to as "the unity of the working class." Criticizing a strategy of waiting for the "favorable moment" for revolution, Suslov praised "active and daily work to change the situation in the interests of democracy and socialism." Suslov noted that the Italian party had "enriched the workers' movement with new forms and methods of class and antimonopolist struggle" in the form of "the successes achieved by your party in recent years at parliamentary and municipal elections." He praised the late French leader Maurice Thorez for having "profoundly understood the necessity of the unity of the working class as the indispensable condition for success in the struggle against the oppressors." Suslov approvingly quoted Thorez's statement that "we communists and socialists cannot fail to find the path to agreement" and saluted this policy's "important results."[9]

During the process of developing parliamentary majorities for the

5. June 5, 1965. See Roger E. Kanet, "Soviet Attitudes toward Developing Nations since Stalin," in Kanet, ed., *The Soviet Union and the Developing Nations* (Baltimore: Johns Hopkins University Press, 1974), 35–36.

6. October 23, 1965. And see December 15, 1964; June 5, 1965; January 27, 1966. See also Jacques Levesque, *The USSR and the Cuban Revolution: Soviet Ideological and Strategical Perspectives, 1959–1977*, trans. Deanna Drendel Leboeuf (New York: Praeger, 1978), 55–57; Robert Legvold, *Soviet Policy in West Africa* (Cambridge: Harvard University Press, 1970), 187–235.

7. October 23, 1965.

8. Donald L. M. Blackmer, "Continuity and Change in Postwar Italian Communism," in Blackmer and Sidney Tarrow, eds., *Communism in Italy and France* (Princeton: Princeton University Press, 1975), 55–59; Ronald Tiersky, "Alliance Politics and Revolutionary Pretensions," in ibid., 442–45; Neill Nugent and David Lowe, *The Left in France* (New York: St. Martin's Press, 1982), 165–77.

9. April 28, 1965; January 27, 1966; and see Ponomarev, October 23, 1965.

left, the strategy of working-class unity would also maintain world peace. While agreeing with Brezhnev that the Soviet Union faced a monolithic imperialist alliance led by the United States, Suslov and Ponomarev disagreed with Brezhnev's comparison of the war danger in 1965 to the crisis that had faced the Soviet Union in the 1930s. One day before Brezhnev warned that the world situation had in some respects worsened since the 1930s, Ponomarev claimed that improvements in the world situation showed a "radical change" since the 1930s.[10] Denying any reason for "fear on our part of imperialism," Suslov said, "The conquests of world socialism are now reliably safeguarded." Because the danger of war had diminished, the purpose of the struggle against war had changed. Formerly necessary to protect the Soviet Union, the struggle for peace had now become a device that would mobilize broad popular support for communists, whose "struggle against the war danger is aimed at sparing the masses of people" the hardships of nuclear war.[11]

Portraying European voters as attracted to communist parties by the difference between capitalist governments' complicity in the Americans' plans of aggression and the communists' peace campaign, Suslov opposed Soviet diplomatic cooperation with capitalist governments. In public this stand needed delicate handling. As European publics identified local communists with the Soviet Union (and Suslov sought to encourage this identification), the Soviet Union must avow peaceful coexistence in order to symbolize peace. At the same time, to encourage the public to identify capitalists with war, the USSR must not be seen to negotiate agreements with capitalist governments. Suslov managed the tension by generally endorsing peaceful coexistence but never advocating any specific East-West agreements. Concurrently he and Ponomarev rejected the rationale for international cooperation by objecting to "profoundly mistaken and harmful" tendencies to overlook "the threat to peace from the imperialists."[12]

To communicate his strategy of preserving peace by relying on foreign communists' mobilization of European publics, Suslov used a synecdoche evidently directed at inexpert audiences, not at Soviet policy experts on European communism. France stood for the whole:

10. Ponomarev, October 23, 1965. See Suslov's speeches of June 5 and October 5, 1965. Cf. Brezhnev, October 24, 1965.
11. January 27, 1966.
12. October 23 and 31, 1965.

the French strategy of left unity "has played an important role in the mobilization and deployment of a broad movement for peace, embracing the most varied strata of society . . . , both in France itself and in the whole world."[13] Even in France and Italy the prospects for the electoral strategy were less optimistic than Suslov painted them, for until October 1966 French Socialists refused even to hold a public meeting with the Communists, and in Italy the Socialists preferred coalitions with the center.[14] Suslov extended the principles of unity of action among left parties throughout the capitalist world, even though outside France and Italy, most communist parties commanded much less electoral support and the much stronger socialists were usually unwilling to form electoral alliances. In the mid-1960s the communists controlled one-quarter of the parliamentary vote in Italy, one-fifth in France and Finland, and less in Iceland, Greece, and Luxembourg, but no other party commanded even 5 percent.[15] Soviet experts on European communism were well aware of the wide diversity of European parties and the atypicality of the French and Italian parties' relative strength.[16]

The Construction of Opposition: China

Relations with China belonged both to Suslov's specialty, the international communist movement, and to Brezhnev's specialty, relations among socialist states. The overlap caused policy toward the Sino-Soviet split to become a topic on which the four rivals differentiated their global strategies during 1965.

Suslov proposed to create the impression of worldwide communist approval for his grand strategy by conducting a new international conference of communist parties. The conference would display global communist opposition to Maoists' criticism of the electoral strategy, which in typically pithy language they dismissed

13. April 28, 1965.
14. Tiersky, "Alliance Politics," 443; Norman Kogan, "The Italian Communist Party: The Modern Prince at the Crossroads," in Rudolf L. Tokes, ed., *Eurocommunism and Détente* (New York: Council on Foreign Relations, 1978), 86–87.
15. R. Neal Tannahill, *The Communist Parties of Western Europe* (Westport Conn.: Greenwood, 1978), 249–64.
16. See Robert Legvold, "The Soviet Union and West European Communism," in Tokes, *Eurocommunism and Détente*, 314–84.

as "parliamentary cretinism."[17] At the same time, Suslov's proposal for the conference defended his grand strategy against a threat posed by European communists. The Italian "right Communist" Giorgio Amendola had just proposed to dissolve the Communist Party in favor of a unified party of the working class as a whole, not organized according to democratic centralism. Despite opposition from some Italian Communists, the futility of previous efforts to win with a multiparty electoral coalition led the leadership of the Italian party to approve Amendola's proposal.[18]

Since Suslov was offering the success of Italian communism as the benchmark for evaluation of his strategy, Amendola's proposal to dissolve the party threatened to undermine his persuasiveness to Soviet audiences. Suslov and Ponomarev found a common formula for rejecting claims to national autonomy by both the Maoists on the left and Amendola and other European communists on the right. Suslov and Ponomarev argued that communist parties must subordinate their policies "before all" to the interests of the international communist movement, called for an "unflagging struggle by the communist movement against manifestations of a nationalist character," and asserted that "nationalist egoism" in a communist party would inevitably lead to "the weakening of the party."[19]

The Italians explicitly recognized that Suslov's initiative for a new world conference would interfere with their domestic strategy. The late Italian Communist leader Palmiero Togliatti had opposed a world conference "because we feared (and we fear) that in this manner the Communist parties of the capitalist countries would be pushed . . . to enclose themselves in internal polemics of a purely ideological nature, far removed from reality," instead of devoting their efforts to the uniquely fruitful objective of leading the working class's political efforts.[20] Suslov knew Togliatti's views, for *Pravda* had published them. By proposing a world conference, he countered the recurrent threat posed by foreign parties' tendency to fragment or to dissolve into broader left movements.

17. Lilly Marcou, *L'Internationale après Staline* (Paris: Bernard Grasset, 1979), 157; quoted in Peter Jones and Sian Kevill, *China and the Soviet Union, 1949–1984* (New York: Facts on File, 1985), 33.
18. William E. Griffith, *Sino-Soviet Relations, 1964–1965* (Cambridge: MIT Press, 1967), 84, 132.
19. April 28, June 5, 1965; December 15, 1964; October 23, 1965. See also Willaim E. Griffith, "The Diplomacy of Eurocommunism," in Tokes, *Eurocommunism and Détente*, 401–9; Marcou, *L'Internationale après Staline*.
20. Quoted in Griffith, *Sino-Soviet Relations*, 377–78.

The proposal that bolstered the persuasiveness of Suslov's grand strategy represented an obstacle to Brezhnev's objective of reinforcing the grand alliance of communist-ruled states. Though Brezhnev devoted particular attention to Eastern Europe, he made it clear that he was proposing the "solidarity of all socialist countries"[21]—that is, including China—and favored taking advantage of "all opportunities . . . for friendly reconciliation of the existing divergences of opinion and for strengthening the combat unity of the world system of socialism." Disagreements among "sovereign socialist states" should not pose obstacles to cooperation against the common enemy "if we approach them correctly."[22] Brezhnev was motivated to seek Sino-Soviet reconciliation by his self-presentation as a heroic communist, which converged in many respects with Mao's. He shared Mao's doubts that nuclear war could be avoided, Mao's expectation that it would result in victory for socialism, and Mao's aversion to East-West cooperation.[23]

Moreover, differing with Suslov's view that communists in the Third World should restrict their goals to supporting national independence, Brezhnev said: "The more confidently these young states move in the direction of the socialist goals they have chosen, the more diverse, profound, and stable our ties with them become."[24] This position placed Brezhnev closer than any other Soviet leader to Mao's view that socialism rather than national independence should be the objective of Third World revolutions. Accordingly, Brezhnev differed with Ponomarev over Soviet ties with India, against which China nearly went to war again in late 1965. When Ponomarev placed India in the same rank with Algeria, Egypt, and Mali, the Soviet Union's closest Third World allies, Brezhnev relegated India to the category of bordering countries with which the Soviet Union sought "good neighbor" relations—that is, countries unlikely to move toward socialism, such as Turkey, Iran, and the Scandinavian states.[25]

In his efforts to promote reconciliation with China, Brezhnev criticized any conduct likely to impair Sino-Soviet relations. "All communists' sacred duty," Brezhnev said, "is to commit no actions capable of weakening the united front of the world revolutionary

21. March 23, 1965.
22. April 9, 1965.
23. May 9, 1965.
24. August 25, 1965. See also January 16, 1966.
25. November 6, 1964; September 11 and 30, 1965; January 16, March 30, 1966.

movement."[26] Brezhnev objected to polemics that might inflame discord, and he did so in language that applied as well to his colleagues on the Soviet Politburo as to the Chinese. In April 1965 he said, "Artificial puffing up of these disagreements can only weaken the forces of revolution, progress, and peace and bring joy to the imperialists."[27]

If Brezhnev opposed the raising of any issue likely to provoke discord, he should have resisted the proposal for a world conference. Maoist China was flatly refusing to attend a new conference, correctly perceiving Suslov's intent to use it as a forum for criticism of Maoist ideas. When he met the Chinese premier, Zhou Enlai, in November 1964, Brezhnev agreed to postpone the conference indefinitely; he then deleted the proposal from his speeches over the next sixteen months.[28] Now Brezhnev proposed additional bilateral meetings, which he praised as a "very necessary and useful practice."[29]

Though Kosygin and Podgorny shared Brezhnev's opposition to a new world communist conference, his pressure for reconciliation with China interfered not only with Suslov's measures to ensure the persuasiveness of his grand strategy but also with their efforts to accomplish economic reform and East-West cooperation. If the conference was intended to prevent the dissolution of European communist parties, and Suslov presented his strategy of relying on European communists as an alternative to Kosygin's and Podgorny's strategy of encouraging cooperation with European capitalist governments, then a conference would be as antithetical to the persuasiveness of their strategies as to Brezhnev's.

Kosygin accordingly proposed an alternative to the conference. During a swing through Asian communist capitals in February 1965, including two stopovers in Beijing, he called attention to the trip's suitability for restoring communist unity. On his return to Moscow, Kosygin said, "We consider the meetings and conversations that took place with the Chinese leaders useful. They facilitated clarification of opportunities for further development of our relations." Dur-

26. September 15, 1965.
27. April 9, 1965.
28. Griffith, *Sino-Soviet Relations*, 62–64; O. B. Borisov and B. T. Koloskov, *Sovetsko-kitaiskie otnosheniia, 1945–1970* (Moscow: Mysl', 1971), 330. "O. B. Borisov" was the pseudonym of Oleg Borisovich Rakhmanin, who was Ponomarev's deputy. For Brezhnev's last references to the conference until the XXIII Congress in March 1966, see October 20 and November 6, 1964.
29. September 30, 1965. See also January 16, March 30, 1966.

ing these meetings Kosygin proposed either a trilateral or a quadri-
lateral meeting (with North Vietnam, or also with North Korea in
attendance) to issue a joint declaration supporting the North Vietnamese in their conflict with the United States.[30]

At the same time, however, Kosygin and Podgorny differed with
Brezhnev by presenting their own criticisms of Maoist stands. Both
defended peaceful coexistence against Maoist charges that it required the sacrifice of Third World revolutions. "Experience shows
that peaceful coexistence and revolutionary struggle do not at all
contradict each other," Kosygin said. "On the contrary. The policy
of peaceful coexistence creates the most favorable opportunities for
the struggle of the toilers of capitalist countries for their rights and
interests, for the struggle of oppressed peoples against oppressors."[31]
Kosygin's defense of peaceful coexistence as promoting the class
struggle (rather than remaining "a form of class struggle") had been
the target of a specific complaint in the "Twenty-five Points" that the
Chinese Communist Party addressed to the Soviet party in June
1963, on which the Chinese were continuing to insist as the basis for
any reconciliation.[32]

Podgorny said that the view of peaceful coexistence as interfering
with world revolution was "a falsifier's interpretation."[33] Commenting on Chinese proposals that the two countries conclude a defensive alliance that would take effect only in case of U.S. aggression
while continuing to pursue independent foreign policies and revolutionary strategies, Podgorny drew attention to the unfavorable prospects for Brezhnev's proposed reconciliation with China by saying
that the Chinese proposal had "a very strange tone" with which
"one cannot agree." Kosygin and Brezhnev also rejected the Chinese
proposal for a limited alliance, but without Podgorny's pejoratives.[34]

30. February 27, 1965; M. S. Kapitsa, *Levee zdravogo smysla* (*O vneshnei politiki gruppy
Mao*) (Moscow: Politizdat, 1968), 80–81.

31. February 13, 1965.

32. See the sixteenth point, excerpted in Jones and Kevill, *China and the Soviet
Union*, 34–35. For Chinese insistence, see Borisov and Koloskov's account of the
meeting with Zhou in *Sovetsko-kitaiskie otnosheniia*, 330–32. For other statements by
Kosygin implicitly attacking Chinese positions, see February 12 and 13, May 8 and 15,
June 30, July 11, September 22, 1965.

33. April 1, 1966.

34. May 9, 1965; for the Chinese offer, see *Pravda's* text of a speech by Zhou, January 12, 1965, and W. R. Smyser, "The Independent Vietnamese: Vietnamese Communism between Russia and China, 1956–1969," Papers in International Studies, Southeast Asia Series no. 55 (Athens: Ohio University Center for International Studies,

Kosygin and Podgorny also objected to Maoist views on Soviet domestic issues, into which the Chinese had injected themselves. At the November 1964 meeting in Moscow Zhou demanded as "an indispensable condition of normalization of Soviet-Chinese relations" that the Soviet leadership renounce the decisions of the last three party congresses—that is, abjure the de-Stalinization begun at the XXth Party Congress in 1956 and extended in 1959 and 1961. Moreover, the Chinese greeted the fall of Khrushchev not only with accusations of "complicity with American imperialism" but also with warnings of an impending " 'restoration of capitalism' in the USSR."[35] Kosygin and Podgorny reacted to the Maoists' attacks on their reform projects by seizing the opportunity to tar their domestic opponents with Maoism. Chinese criticisms provided Kosygin and Podgorny with an occasion to issue general denunciations of opponents of the reform as "enemies" and "lackeys of the bourgeoisie."[36]

For all four leaders, the issue of Sino-Soviet relations stood as a synecdoche for the condition of the global conflict between socialism and capitalism. For Suslov, policy toward China symbolized the prospects for his strategy of relying on communist-led left electoral coalitions. For Brezhnev it symbolized the prospects for a solid alliance of communist-ruled states. For Kosygin and Podgorny it symbolized both the affirmation of their proposals for domestic reform and the prospects for cooperation with capitalist states.

Bargaining

As John Gittings wrote, although in their China policy the post-Khrushchev leaders displayed "much greater tactical circumspection than their predecessor," they remained "unprepared to yield on any substantive issue of policy."[37] Soviet policy combined adoption of Brezhnev's tactics for promoting a reconciliation (including both postponement of a world conference and a halt in explicit polemics against the Chinese) with adherence to Kosygin's, Podgorny's and Suslov's principles in foreign policy and revolutionary strategy.

1980), 88, quoting Aldo Natoli, an Italian Communist who claimed to have been shown the transcript of Mao's meeting with Kosygin in February 1965. For Kosygin and Brezhnev's statements on this issue, see May 8 and 9, 1965.

35. Borisov and Koloskov, *Sovetsko-kitaiskie otnosheniia*, 330–34.

36. September 28, 1965; April 1, 1966.

37. John Gittings, *Survey of the Sino-Soviet Dispute: A Commentary and Extracts from the Recent Polemics, 1963–1967* (London: Oxford University Press, 1968), 228.

Table 2. Soviet leaders' declared stands on Chinese demands, 1965

Chinese demand	For	Against
Postpone world conference of communist parties	Brezhnev Kosygin Podgorny	Suslov
Subordinate peaceful coexistence to Third World revolts	Brezhnev Suslov	Kosygin Podgorny
Subordinate national independence to socialism in Third World	Brezhnev	Suslov Kosygin Podgorny

Examination of the four Soviet leaders' declared positions on Chinese demands, summarized in Table 2, explains why Gittings's characterization of Soviet policy is apt. Brezhnev could obtain a temporary agreement to postpone the world conference of communist parties. Only Suslov opposed the postponement, and he lacked motivation for objecting too persistently. As the Soviet side admitted when Brezhnev, Suslov, and Ponomarev met the Austrian communist Franz Muhri as late as October 1965, opposition from a variety of foreign parties continued to preclude a conference in the near future.[38] Thus Brezhnev obtained approval to agree with Zhou in November 1964 to postpone the conference and to cancel the meeting of the Editorial Commission which had been scheduled for December. Suslov obtained an agreement that proposals for bilateral Sino-Soviet consultations would be portrayed publicly as a step toward an eventual international conference[39] and permission to convene representatives of parties willing to participate in the Editorial Commission under the guise of a "consultative meeting" held in Moscow in March 1965.[40] The consultative meeting provided Suslov with an opportunity to issue a communiqué reaffirming international communist support for continuing preparations for a new

38. Griffith, *Sino-Soviet Relations*, 136n.
39. E.g., "Edinstvo deistvii—povelitel'noe trebovanie antiimperialisticheskoi bor'by," June 20, 1965.
40. Gittings, *Survey*, 229, notes that the Soviet Party proposal to reschedule the Editorial Commission from December 15 to March 1 (when it became the consultative meeting instead) came in a letter sent to the Chinese on November 24, 1964, ten days after the meeting with Zhou that postponed the conference; but Borisov and Koloskov, *Sovetsko-kitaiskie otnosheniia*, 330–32, say the Soviet delegation proposed the rescheduling during the meeting with Zhou.

world conference, an agenda he had continued to pursue in bilateral talks with visiting foreign communists.[41]

Though Brezhnev could achieve a decision to postpone the conference, an agreement to subordinate peaceful coexistence to Third World revolution was impossible. Suslov agreed with him that revolutions in the Third World should take priority over cooperation with capitalist countries, but Podgorny and Kosygin would object. Any decision in favor of priority for Third World revolutions would immediately raise the question whether the goal of those revolutions should be advance toward socialism or national independence, and that issue would split Brezhnev from Suslov. Unless peaceful coexistence could be separated from Third World revolution, Brezhnev would find himself in isolation—and that separation was precisely what the Maoists found objectionable.

Consequently the Soviet leaders could agree on reconciliation with the Chinese only if they agreed to make no concessions on the disputed substantive issues of foreign policy and revolutionary strategy.[42] Table 2 also shows why they agreed to Brezhnev's proposal (expressed in his strictures against "artificially puffing up disagreements") for a halt in public polemics against the Chinese. Given that the opponents of his proposal for reconciliation disagreed among themselves over the substantive issues, either side would prefer Brezhnev's option of collective silence to a Politburo endorsement of the opposing view on that substantive issue.

The Soviets represented the policy of reconciliation without substantive concessions as a positive program called the "Joint Actions" policy. They offered this rationale for Joint Actions:

> Despite disagreements concerning the political line and many important problems of theory and tactics, it is altogether possible and necessary to achieve unity of actions in the struggle against imperialism, in the cause of full-scale support of the people's liberation movement, in the struggle for general peace and peaceful coexistence . . . in the struggle for the vital interests and historic goals of the working class.

41. Griffith, *Sino-Soviet Relations*, 87; November 15, December 17, 1964; January 28, 1965.
42. The best treatments of the Sino-Soviet disputes remain Donald S. Zagoria, *The Sino-Soviet Conflict, 1956–1961* (Princeton: Princeton University Press, 1962; New York: Atheneum, 1969), and Benjamin I. Schwartz, *Communism and China: Ideology in Flux* (Cambridge: Harvard University Press, 1968).

Joint actions in the struggle for these common goals are the surest ways
to overcome existing disagreements.[43]

This rationale invited the Chinese to cooperate toward Soviet objectives formulated in terms to which the Maoists were known to object.

The logroll that shaped Soviet policy toward the Sino-Soviet dispute during 1965 was tantamount to a demand that the Maoists sur-
render. It would have been reasonable only if the Chinese leaders
faced no alternative to accepting Soviet demands. If Yan Mei is right
when she argues that Mao was using the Sino-Soviet dispute to dramatize to domestic audiences his fears of the bureaucratization of
Chinese socialism,[44] even a conciliatory policy would probably not
have achieved a reconciliation. The actual Soviet policy quickly failed.

Because the Joint Actions policy was self-frustrating, from June
1965 Brezhnev's proposals for reconciliation with China rapidly lost
persuasiveness, and he was forced to make concessions in favor of
Suslov's proposal for a world conference. The first telling blow to
the policy came in a Chinese editorial of June 13, 1965, repeating the
accusation that the new Soviet leaders were professing revolution
while in fact they were colluding with the United States.[45] In response, *Pravda* accused the Chinese of impeding unity by publishing
"openly hostile" distortions of Soviet policy but also reaffirmed the
rationale for Joint Actions.[46]

The Chinese article in June touched off a sharp exchange among
the Soviet leaders during July. The Indonesian communist D. N.
Aidit, whose party was attempting to mediate the dispute, came to
Moscow for talks said to concern the international communist movement; he met a Soviet delegation led by Brezhnev, Suslov, and Ponomarev. The talks were held intermittently from July 7 to 31.[47] The
intensity of disagreement among the Soviet leaders over the line to
take in the talks with Aidit was evident. On the same day that
Brezhnev made his strongest plea against wasting "time and strength
on mutual attacks," Kosygin denounced Mao's view of war as iden-

43. March 10, 1965.
44. Yan Mei, "The Maturing of Soviet-Chinese Relations," in "Soviet Foreign Policy
in an Uncertain World," *Annals of the American Academy of Political and Social Science* 481
(September 1985): 73.
45. Griffith, *Sino-Soviet Relations*, 95–96; Jones and Kevill, *China and the Soviet Union*,
64.
46. "Edinstvo deistvii," June 20, 1965.
47. August 1, 1965; on Aidit's intermediary role, see Marcou, *L'Internationale après
Staline*, 149.

tical to Hitler's.[48] These disagreements culminated in early August when *Pravda* published a detailed defense of Soviet foreign policy against Chinese charges but again refrained from naming the Chinese as the target.[49]

China's publication of Lin Biao's "people's war" article of September 2, 1965, which denounced Soviet positions yet again, returned Brezhnev to the defensive. After further attempts to justify reconciliation in September, at the Central Committee Plenum he admitted for the first time that after "almost a year" of the Soviet "course to normalization" of relations with China, "unfortunately one must state that these efforts of the CPSU were not supported by the leaders of the Communist Party of China." Nevertheless, Brezhnev announced the leadership's decision that "we should persist in searching for ways to settle the disagreements . . . between our parties and countries."[50]

Although Brezhnev defended his policy, during October Suslov and Ponomarev demanded additional concessions. The first part of the compromise to give way was Brezhnev's postponement of the campaign for a new world conference. Suslov and Ponomarev both issued calls for the conference,[51] the first such appeals in any public speech by any Politburo member or Central Committee secretary since the previous December. In this instance there is good evidence that the demands for a conference were responses to the loss of persuasiveness suffered by Brezhnev's policy. Suslov and Ponomarev voiced their calls at two international communist meetings commemorating the thirtieth anniversary of the 1935 Seventh Congress of the Comintern. This congress, which had reversed as "sectarian" and "dogmatist" the previous ban on coalitions with social democrats, was regarded by the Chinese as a capitulation to "social fascism." As long as Brezhnev's proposal for reconciliation had retained persuasiveness, it had evidently precluded timely celebration of the anniversary of the Seventh Congress, which should have been commemorated during July or August—the months of its sessions thirty years earlier.[52]

A month later Brezhnev surrendered the ban on polemics as well. After another Chinese statement on November 11, 1965, rejected Joint Action with a typically pithy comment—"There are things that

---

48. July 11, 1965.
49. "Blagorodnye tseli sovetskoi vneshnei politiki," August 8, 1965.
50. September 30, 1965.
51. October 5 and 23, 1965.
52. Adam Ulam, *Stalin: The Man and His Era* (New York: Viking, 1973), 402.

divide us and nothing that unites us"—and called for "a clear line of demarcation both politically and organizationally" between "Marxist-Leninists" and the Soviet "revisionists," the Soviets finally published a detailed rebuttal naming the Chinese as the target.[53] They also ended one practice begun in November 1964 as part of the bilateral approach to restoring Sino-Soviet relations, ceasing to provide the Chinese with confidential foreign policy information.[54] Although Brezhnev again defended his initiative toward China during the next two months[55] while his Accounting Report to the XXIII Congress was being negotiated, and although the final text of the report defended the initiative too, the report incorporated two further concessions to Suslov: Brezhnev now joined in calling for a world conference, and he echoed Suslov's earlier warnings against "manifestations of nationalism, great-power chauvinism, and hegemonism" in international communism.[56]

Protection of issue specialties produced a maladaptive Soviet policy toward China during 1965. The policy discussion displayed a contest over the boundaries of issue specialization. China fell both within Brezhnev's specialty of relations among communist-ruled states and within Suslov's specialty of relations among communist parties. Because the Sino-Soviet dispute engaged substantive issues central to Kosygin's and Podgorny's grand strategies as well, Suslov was able to form a coalition that eventually frustrated Brezhnev's attempt to seize control of the issue. This coalition maintained issue specialization within the Politburo, but the logroll could effectively pursue neither Suslov's objective of concentrating world communism's attention on Togliatti's "internal polemics of a purely ideological nature" nor Brezhnev's objective of reconciliation with China.

At the same time Suslov's use of foreign communist parties to replicate the symbolism of his indoctrinational vision of socialism at home impaired their already slender prospects for winning parliamentary majorities. By denouncing "manifestations of a nationalist character," he insisted that they refrain from the one strategy by which communists might have built parliamentary majorities—abandonment of the Leninist organizational principles that enabled Suslov to use them as foreign symbols of his vision of Soviet communism.

53. Griffith, *Sino-Soviet Relations*, 456; November 28, 1965.
54. Borisov and Koloskov, *Sovetsko-kitaiskie otnosheniia*, 336.
55. January 13, 15 and 16, 1966.
56. March 30, 1966.

★ Chapter 7

*Kosygin and the
Capitalist World,
October 1964–April 1966*

Standing for economic efficiency at home, Kosygin stood in foreign affairs for reaping the gains from trade with capitalist economies. To recapitulate a domestic vision that embraced such capitalist symbols as markets, profits, and commodity exchange, he adopted a grand strategy of embracing capitalist governments. Arguing that trade and peace were mutually reinforcing, Kosygin made a principle of promoting cooperative security and economic arrangements potentially open for universal participation across the divide between socialism and capitalism. The United States' participation in these arrangements was central to Kosygin's strategy. As he said, "Peace can be assured only by active and joint actions of all peoples and of all governments."[1]

Kosygin's initiatives toward capitalist states drew intense opposition from his rivals after the United States escalated the fighting in Indochina in February 1965. Having made U.S. restraint in Vietnam the benchmark for evaluation of his grand strategy, over the course of 1965 Kosygin found himself compelled to accept not only a Soviet counterescalation in Southeast Asia but also restrictions on diplomatic and commercial initiatives to capitalist governments in general. Only with the failure of Brezhnev's initiative for reconciliation with China was Kosygin able to resume his East-West diplomacy, and then only to the exclusion of contacts with the United States.

1. May 13, 1965.

126

Policy toward the capitalist world displayed the self-frustrating consequences of symbolism and logrolling. Kosygin's futile demands that the Common Market and NATO remove their barriers to East-West trade stood for the much more complex task of integrating a command economy into a world capitalist market. During most of 1965 bargaining by convergent concessions over the linked issues of East-West talks and the response to escalation in Vietnam muted any internal contradictions in Soviet policy. But at the end of 1965, diplomatic initiatives pursuing negotiation of security arrangements in Europe became linked to further Soviet escalation in Vietnam and to continuation of the ban on negotiations with the United States. As the NATO allies and even some neutrals were unwilling to negotiate security issues without inclusion of the United States, this logroll proved self-defeating.

Negotiating Trade and Security: Kosygin's Grand Strategy

East-West trade symbolized the extension into world politics of Kosygin's self-presentation as the champion of economic efficiency at home. He linked foreign trade both to economic advance at home and to peace abroad. Describing a world in which trade and peace were reciprocally reinforcing, Kosygin characterized foreign states, presented by his rivals as threats to Soviet security, in terms that emphasized their potential responsiveness to cooperative overtures by the Soviet Union. This description of world conditions justified his policy recommendations for negotiations on economic and security cooperation with Western countries.

Foreign trade would promote realization of Kosygin's domestic vision: "Active international trade, exchange of goods and of scientific-technological experience, is an important factor in the acceleration of economic progress."[2] Among other benefits, technology exchange would "permit saving hundreds of millions of rubles on scientific-research work."[3]

Peace and trade would be mutually reinforcing. "The more vigorous and multifarious the trade-economic ties between states, the more trust in each other these states will have," Kosygin said; and a

2. March 2, 1965.
3. April 5, 1966.

peaceful foreign policy would "promote successful development of the USSR's foreign economic ties."[4]

In Kosygin's image of the world, capitalist countries were both motivated to expand trade and receptive to Soviet peace initiatives. Although repeatedly recognizing that Soviet industrial products "unfortunately cannot always withstand competition from the goods of the best foreign firms," he nevertheless boasted that "our industry is not backward and in a whole series of technological solutions is ahead."[5] To take advantage of foreign markets for advanced Soviet industrial products, the 1966–1970 economic plan "should provide for a substantial improvement of the commodity structure of exports and imports [by investments in] priority development of export of machinery, equipment, and other finished goods."[6]

To Kosygin the West was far less hostile than either Brezhnev or Suslov saw it. He avoided Brezhnev's and Suslov's claims that the Soviet Union faced a threat from a monolithic imperialist alliance led by the United States and West Germany; this image appeared in only one of the speeches he delivered on twenty-seven appropriate occasions. Even on this occasion he said that the imperialist alliance was directing its threat against former colonies, not against the socialist states.[7] Moreover, he consistently held out more promise of favorable changes in U.S. and West German policies than Brezhnev did. In 1964 Brezhnev took the position that if the governments of both countries responded to Soviet peace overtures, they would respond only grudgingly, under popular pressure. Kosygin, by contrast, portrayed the U.S. and West German governments as split over peace with the Soviet Union, with the peace advocates winning the contest in the United States.[8] After U.S. escalation in Indochina, Brezhnev began to deny the ability of popular opposition to restrain either German or U.S. policy makers.[9] Conceding that President Johnson had ignored the results of the 1964 elections in favor of "the policy of the extreme right reaction in the U.S.A., whose representative is Goldwater," Kosygin still drew attention to an "intensifying

4. May 15, 1965; April 5, 1966. See also December 10, 1964; March 2, September 14, 1965.
5. July 11, 1965, and see December 10, 1964, and April 5, 1966; March 3, 1965, and see May 20, 1965.
6. April 5, 1966. See also December 10, 1964.
7. June 30, 1965.
8. December 10 and 12, 1964.
9. May 9, 1965.

mood of concern and deep alarm in the United States itself" and raised the possibility that Johnson might reverse course.[10] He also saw the West German population as limiting its government's capacity for aggression.[11] The threat to peace, in Kosygin's view, lay not with hostile states but with hostile "forces" that threatened to take control of foreign governments against the will of their peoples.[12]

To combat the aggressive forces within foreign governments, Kosygin proposed alliances with foreign populations and with "realists" in foreign governments. "The Soviet Union expresses readiness to collaborate with all governments that stand or will stand for relaxation of international tension and stabilization of security of peoples."[13] To take advantage of the contribution of trade to securing peace, he proposed "to conclude long-term trade agreements" that "would place the trade relations of the Soviet Union with Western countries on a stable footing."[14] Kosygin repeated this offer during visits by leaders of Norway, Sweden, Denmark, and Great Britain.[15] To accompany his initiatives for trade, in December 1964 Kosygin proposed "talks with Western powers" that would "stubbornly and patiently seek settlement of disputed issues."[16] The objective of these talks, as he unfolded the proposal over the next sixteen months, was to negotiate "a reliable system of security in Europe."[17]

While presenting himself as the advocate of negotiations, Kosygin also posed as making demands on capitalist governments. In particular, Kosygin called on the capitalist states to abandon policies of "economic estrangement [*razobshchenie*] of states" and "creation of artificial barriers to international trade."[18] These statements were references to the European Economic Community's system of trade preferences and to restrictions on sales of technology to socialist countries. Kosygin presented the expansion of East-West trade as if it were merely a matter of political will. "If the West really wants to trade broadly with us on mutually advantageous terms, it would be possible to expand significantly both the scope of the Soviet market

10. March 2, 1965 (see also February 13 and June 30, 1966); April 20, May 15, 1965.

11. March 2, 1965.

12. April 5, 1966. See also November 26, December 10, 1964; April 8, 1965.

13. April 5, 1965. See also November 26, December 10, 1964; April 8, October 8, 1965.

14. December 10, 1964. See also April 5, 1966.

15. June 1 and 12, September 14, October 8, 1965; February 23, 1966.

16. December 10, 1964.

17. April 8, October 8, 1965; February 23, 1966.

18. March 2, 1965; April 5, 1966.

and Soviet deliveries of raw materials, equipment, and other goods in which Western countries are interested."[19]

Kosygin's demands for removal of trade barriers stood as a synecdoche for the much larger problems of integrating a command economy into the capitalist world market. Discrimination was a real obstacle to Soviet machinery exports, but only one. Irrational pricing made it difficult for planners to decide what to export. Inconvertibility of the ruble generated uncertainty among Western buyers about future prices of Soviet exports and raised the cost of negotiating deals. Pressures for rapid expansion of output diminished incentives for quality control, with the result that reliability of industrial equipment was low by world standards, manuals were lacking, and spare parts were in short supply. Specialized foreign trade organizations, not producers, managed exports, and they lacked marketing and service networks. Unable to make direct contact with potential Western buyers, Soviet producers found it hard to acquire information on the demand of potential buyers or on changes in their tastes.[20] Kosygin's references to the technological backwardness of Soviet industrial products make it clear that he understood some of the economic obstacles to rapid expansion of machinery exports to the West. His proposals for price reform and for incentives to spur innovation and improvement in quality of products promised changes in many of the institutional conditions that hampered export of industrial goods, and Kosygin said the economic reforms were designed to foster foreign trade. Still, he chose to focus his audiences' attention on the political barriers. This synecdoche rationalized his proposals for negotiation of security and commercial arrangements in tandem.

Like the grand strategies of Brezhnev and Suslov, Kosygin's proposals were appeals to the inexpert, not to the policy specialists in the Ministry of Foreign Trade, who knew the difficulties of penetrating highly competitive capitalist markets. Evidently recognizing the skepticism of the ministry's specialists concerning his proposals, Kosygin blamed them for the sluggishness of Soviet exports:

19. December 10, 1964.

20. Franklyn D. Holzman, *Foreign Trade under Central Planning* (Cambridge: Harvard University Press, 1974), 139–63; Paul Ericson, "Soviet Efforts to Increase Exports of Manufactured Products to the West," in *Soviet Economy in a New Perspective* (Washington: U.S. Government Printing Office, 1976), 709–26; Ed A. Hewett, "Foreign Economic Relations," in Abram Bergson and Herbert S. Levine, eds., *The Soviet Economy: Toward the Year 2000* (London: Allen & Unwin, 1983), 269–310.

Officials of foreign trade organizations are often isolated in their own sphere and take insufficiently into account that all their activity should be subordinated to the tasks of raising the efficiency of the economy as a whole. . . . Industry officials should study the conditions of sale of their production both in our country and abroad, and the Ministry of Foreign Trade is obligated to provide them the necessary information.[21]

Kosygin's rivals refrained from challenging his proposals on foreign trade, but silence did not signal consent. Nobody else discussed foreign trade in such detail. Opposition manifested itself in the difference between Kosygin's speech at the XXIII Party Congress in April 1966 and the draft directives for the five-year plan which his Politburo colleagues approved for later ratification at the Congress. He had more to say about East-West trade than about trade with socialist and nonaligned countries combined, but the directives devoted full paragraphs to socialist and nonaligned trade partners and only a single sentence to "further expansion" of East-West trade.[22]

The Construction of Opposition: Vietnam

When the United States began bombing North Vietnam in February 1965, Kosygin's rivals acquired an issue that they used to oppose his proposals for diplomatic and economic initiatives toward the main capitalist powers. Each of the four rivals turned Vietnam into a symbol of the urgency and feasibility of his grand strategy in world politics. The U.S. escalation also provided an opportunity for a fifth Politburo member, Shelepin, to begin defining a distinctive grand strategy of his own.

Disagreement over Vietnam began in December 1964 between Kosygin and Brezhnev. Kosygin argued that the Soviet Union must protect North Vietnam against a potential U.S. attack, but he warned that because of "the development of military technology and the presence in states' arsenals of weapons of mass destruction . . . , a new world war would signify the greatest disaster." Therefore, "we come out for talks with Western powers and are ready persistently and patiently to seek settlement of disputed issues." Favoring negotiations, Kosygin recommended that military aid for the defense of

21. April 5, 1966.
22. February 20, 1966.

North Vietnam should be conditional on U.S. action: it should be delivered "if the aggressors dare to raise their hand to them."[23]

Only six days earlier, Brezhnev agreed that the Soviet Union's most important goal was the elimination of the "threat of annihilation in the flames of atomic war." But to achieve this goal, he argued, the Soviet Union must "resist provocations by imperialists and any of their encroachments on the peaceful life of peoples of the socialist countries and on the freedom and independence of peoples of Asia, Africa, and Latin America, and support the just struggle of these peoples in every way." Consequently, he said, the Soviet Union "is ready to render necessary aid to" North Vietnam regardless of U.S. action, as a warning to the United States that a repetition of the August 1964 air and sea attacks on North Vietnam would be a "dangerous game."[24]

While Kosygin was visiting Hanoi in February 1965, U.S. bombers struck targets in the southern part of North Vietnam. This action, the continuing escalation of air attacks, and the introduction of U.S. combat units into the fighting in the South provided the occasion for the five Politburo members to differentiate their public stands on world affairs. Over the next year they disagreed over three linked issues: whether to negotiate, what military aid to supply, and what risks the Soviet Union faced in Indochina.

For Kosygin Vietnam provided a symbol of the urgency of his policy of negotiated resolution of international disputes, and he tried to restrain Soviet military aid in order to hold the door open for talks. Even after the initial attacks, when he returned to Moscow in February, he called for "finding a path to the settlement of the problems of Indochina around the negotiating table" after cessation of U.S. air raids.[25] Even after air raids resumed in March and U.S. combat troops began arriving in April, Kosygin continued to advocate negotiations, arguing that the United States might still decide to reverse course and seek a negotiated settlement.[26] He justified his calls for negotiations by warning of the risk of an uncontrolled escalatory spiral to nuclear war: because "in our time the U.S.A. has no mo-

23. December 10, 1964.

24. December 4, 1964. William Zimmerman has read Brezhnev's and Kosygin's statements as identical: "The Korean and Vietnam Wars," in Stephen S. Kaplan, ed., *Diplomacy of Power: Soviet Armed Forces as a Political Instrument* (Washington, D.C.: Brookings, 1981), 340.

25. February 27, 1965. See also February 9, 1965.

26. April 20, May 15, 1965.

nopoly on modern weapons," he warned in April 1965; "by expanding the scale of military actions against socialist Vietnam, the United States step by step approaches a very dangerous brink."[27] At the same time Kosygin was careful to define narrowly the purposes of Soviet military aid. While calling the guerrilla war in South Vietnam a "just and legitimate cause" that the "Soviet Union and all progressive forces have supported and will support," Kosygin said that Soviet aid would consist of "concrete measures" only for the defense of North Vietnam.[28]

For Podgorny the Vietnam conflict presented an opportunity to underscore both the feasibility and the urgency of a grand strategy of isolating aggressors by political containment. Like his domestic vision, Podgorny's stand on Vietnam split the difference separating Kosygin from Suslov and Brezhnev. Like Kosygin, Podgorny restricted Soviet military aid to the Democratic Republic of Vietnam (DRV) to "concrete measures for . . . strengthening its defense capability."[29] But like Suslov and Brezhnev, he rejected negotiations. Podgorny dismissed President Johnson's May 1965 bombing pause as an "effort to mislead world public opinion regarding the U.S.A.'s so-called 'love of peace.'"[30] In four speeches during May Kosygin expressed no skepticism about the sincerity of the U.S. signal.[31]

Podgorny argued that a global diplomatic coalition could form on the issue of the Vietnam conflict and could end the war. He stressed favorable information about international opposition to the war, saying that the United States' "aggressive actions in Vietnam evoke general condemnation."[32] Given the threat posed by U.S. actions in Vietnam to "the vital interests of all peoples," Podgorny said, "the task of all peoples of the world is . . . to halt American aggression in Vietnam."[33] Podgorny held out the prospect that even some U.S. allies in NATO had begun "a process of reevaluating foreign policy ideas" that might lead them to join the coalition against U.S. policy in Vietnam.[34] He conceded that U.S. militarists were considering use of nuclear weapons in Vietnam, but he downplayed the risks with

27. April 20, 1965. See also December 10, 1964; February 27, March 24, June 30, 1965.
28. February 11, 1965. See also February 7 and 27, April 20, 1965.
29. May 9, 1965. See also May 22, 1965.
30. May 22, 1965.
31. May 13, 14, 15 and 20, 1965.
32. May 22, 1965. See also April 1, 1966.
33. April 1, 1966; December 15, 1965.
34. April 1, 1966.

the assertion that his proposed coalition could succeed in "the struggle for prevention of imperialist aggression."[35]

For Suslov and his spokesman, Boris Ponomarev, Vietnam symbolized the problem that they proposed to solve by their grand strategy of strengthening the alliance among the socialist countries, independence movements in the Third World, and the "broad front" in the First World. "The naked aggression of the American imperialists against Vietnam is a challenge to the socialist countries, the national liberation movement, and the forces for democracy and peace."[36] Accordingly, their speeches, in contrast to Kosygin's and Podgorny's, treated protection of North Vietnam and the "liberation" of South Vietnam as equally important policy objectives. Their proposals for "aid to the DRV and to the patriotic forces of South Vietnam"[37] were justified by a lower estimate of the risks facing the Soviet Union in Indochina. Where Kosygin saw an escalatory spiral to nuclear confrontation, Suslov and Ponomarev saw toppling dominoes. One "can prevent the loosing of a new war," but "the danger of local wars is no less serious than in the past."[38] Suslov and Ponomarev classed U.S. conduct in Vietnam together with actions in the Dominican Republic, the Congo, Laos, and Cuba as "links in one chain—the chain by which international reaction wants to restrain the people's liberation movement."[39] By sending military supplies to the guerrillas in South Vietnam, Suslov and Ponomarev could hope to sustain the intensity of combat, which was useful for substantiating communists' assertions about the bellicosity of the United States. As Jacques Duclos wrote in *Pravda*, "We French Communists know how significant is the aid rendered to the people of Vietnam by the Soviet Union" for mobilizing "toilers imbued with the spirit of proletarian internationalism."[40]

For Brezhnev, Vietnam was a battle to be fought in which defeat promised terrible consequences, a familiar enemy could be identified, and the heroic past could be resurrected. In contrast to Ko-

35. May 9, July 25, 1965.
36. October 5, 1965.
37. June 5, 1965. See also December 15, 1964; January 1, April 17, May 24, October 5, 23 and 31, 1965; January 27, 1966.
38. October 5, 23 and 31, 1965.
39. June 5, 1965. See also October 5 and 23, 1965.
40. Jacques Duclos, "Partiia frantsuzskikh kommunistov—45 let," December 29, 1965.

sygin's and Podgorny's efforts to restrict military aid to specified "concrete measures," Brezhnev offered an unlimited commitment. "To strengthen the DRV armed forces, the Soviet Union is ready to render any aid that our Vietnamese friends need in order to resist the American imperialists' aggression. For us there has been and will be no stopping point here." Brezhnev exceeded even Suslov's description of the purposes of Soviet aid when he placed "expelling the interventionists" from the South ahead of defending the security of the DRV.[41] Brezhnev even raised the possibility of Soviet military intervention. He spoke of his sympathy with the "feelings of fraternal solidarity and socialist internationalism" that motivated "Soviet citizens who express readiness to take part in the struggle of the Vietnamese people for freedom and independence" in letters to the Politburo.[42]

Portraying Vietnam as a heroic fight, Brezhnev rejected negotiations. "We have declared more than once that the Soviet Union is not against good relations with the United States. . . . However, everyone should know that the Soviet Union will never tolerate encroachments . . . on the security of our friends and allies. We will never make these interests the subject of a deal with anyone at all."[43] Never speaking in favor of talks, he ridiculed Americans' claims that they favored a negotiated settlement.[44]

Brezhnev's images of U.S. purposes and of the risks facing the Soviet Union in Vietnam justified his recommendations for greater Soviet involvement and against negotiations. Brezhnev's descriptions of U.S. actions in Vietnam recurrently alluded to Nazi conduct in World War II.[45] (The defense minister, Rodion Malinovskii, spoke more bluntly: "The American aggressors have surpassed even Hitler.")[46] Brezhnev used a Munich analogy to describe the risks in Vietnam. Citing the experience of the origins of World War II, Brezhnev said of Vietnam: "If one does not extinguish these small fires in time, they can ignite and grow into the flame of general rocket-nuclear war. . . . That is why our country attaches such great signifi-

41. April 9, 1965. See also May 9, 1965.
42. March 23, 1965.
43. Ibid.
44. September 11, 1965; January 16, 1966.
45. See March 23, April 9, September 11, October 24, 1965.
46. May 8, 1965. See also April 3, 1966.

cance to . . . timely and resolute resistance to aggressors."[47] Whereas
Kosygin warned that nuclear war might result from an uncontrolled
escalatory spiral, Brezhnev warned that nuclear war would result
from the Soviets' failure to confront the aggressor in Vietnam.

In August 1965, after the United States announced the transfer of
another 50,000 ground troops to South Vietnam, Shelepin joined the
discussion with a proposal for a more far-reaching commitment to
North Vietnamese goals, a greater increase in the flow of military
aid, and a stronger rejection of negotiations. In place of the other
leaders' promises of "all necessary aid," Shelepin called for "necessary and ever-growing aid."[48] Leading a new delegation to Hanoi in
January 1966, Shelepin also twice called explicitly for the war in the
South to culminate in a "united" Vietnam.[49] This statement endorsed
the DRV's war goals instead of the Geneva conference's provision
for a neutral South Vietnam, the most that any other Politburo member had been ready to support.

Shelepin argued that the United States would never be willing to
negotiate, but nuclear confrontation presented no risks to the Soviet
Union. The Americans were attacking Vietnam, he said, for motives
innate to capitalism: "They want to ensure renewed growth of monopoly profits at the cost of war, at the cost of people's suffering."[50]
The United States was committing "bloody crimes against the Vietnamese people," because it had fallen heir to "the delusory plans for
the rout of communism and seizure of mastery over the world" once
harbored by "Hitler and his allies."[51] With these far-reaching motives
behind the U.S. intervention in Vietnam, a diplomatic settlement
was out of the question: "The U.S.A.'s actions in Vietnam do not
testify to the Americans' readiness to accept the DRV government's
four points, which correspond to the most important military and
political principles of the 1954 Geneva agreements, as the basis for a
settlement." At the same time, Shelepin denied any risk of nuclear
confrontation, because "the military power of the Soviet Union and
other socialist countries paralyzes imperialism."[52]

47. October 24, 1965. See also March 23, April 9, May 9, July 4 and 21, September
11 and 15, 1965; January 16, March 30, 1966.
48. August 18, 1965.
49. January 10 and 12, 1966.
50. January 10, 1966.
51. August 18, 1965.
52. January 10, 1966.

Bargaining

Soviet policy toward the West after Khrushchev has been described as combining two general features. First, according to William Zimmerman, "the USSR increased its support of North Vietnam as the United States increased its outlay for the war effort. . . . The Soviet contribution, however, was minuscule compared with American expenditure . . . [and] fell short of that sought or advocated by those . . . who demanded a direct confrontation with the United States and a willingness to take risks."[53] Second, as both Thomas Wolfe and Michael Sodaro have argued, during the initial period after Khrushchev's removal, "Soviet European policy remained relatively subdued."[54] Neither of these policies conformed to Kosygin's grand strategy of coupling East-West negotiations on military issues with increased economic exchanges. U.S. escalation in Vietnam explains why.

Because the Politburo linked the entire East-West relationship to events in Vietnam, Soviet policies in Europe and in Southeast Asia developed in tandem. Policy moved through three stages. In the first stage, Soviet policy pursued Kosygin's sweeping diplomatic initiatives, including negotiations over Vietnam. In the second, the escalation in Vietnam forced Kosygin to make concessions that resulted in decisions to increase Soviet military aid to Vietnam and abandon planned economic and diplomatic initiatives in Europe. In the third, the failure of Brezhnev's reconciliation with China and NATO's abandonment of MLF resulted in a new policy package that coupled further escalation of aid to Vietnam with pursuit of détente in Europe, to the exclusion of the United States.

The Politburo resolved the initial disagreement between Brezhnev and Kosygin over whether to supply defensive aid to North Vietnam or to seek a negotiated settlement as part of a broader East-West détente by a sequential exchange that approved both proposals. When he was preparing to lead a Soviet delegation to Hanoi in early February 1965, Kosygin reported, the Politburo had given him an "instruction" to promise resumption of military aid.[55] The fact that his delegation included two generals (G. K. Sidorovich, head of military aid in the foreign aid agency, and K. A. Vershinin, an expert on

53. Zimmerman, "Korean and Vietnam Wars," 353–54.
54. Thomas W. Wolfe, *Soviet Power and Europe, 1945–1970* (Baltimore: Johns Hopkins University Press, 1970), 280. See also Michael J. Sodaro, *Moscow, Germany, and the West from Khrushchev to Gorbachev* (Ithaca: Cornell University Press, 1990), 72.
55. February 27, 1965.

defense against tactical bombers) tends to confirm Kosygin's account.[56] Construction of launch sites for surface-to-air missiles (SAMs) beginning in late March and the delivery of SAMs and twenty-five fighter aircraft in May, as the first launch site neared completion, add substantiation to Kosygin's claim that he went to Hanoi with a promise of defensive aid.[57] A Soviet history would later date a new stage of military cooperation between the USSR and North Vietnam to the "end of 1964."[58] A Soviet-Vietnamese communiqué in April stated that the February agreement on military aid was "being carried out in the volume and order provided."[59] The Politburo reached its decision to provide aid before it could have known that U.S. aircraft would begin attacking North Vietnam on February 7, while Kosygin was in Hanoi.

Promising defensive aid, Kosygin also pursued a negotiated settlement to the Vietnam conflict. In Hanoi he carefully qualified Soviet support for North Vietnam's war goals, backing only a "neutral" South Vietnam even though this formulation had long been unacceptable to his hosts.[60] When Kosygin returned to Moscow, he took advantage of U.S. avoidance of further air raids from February 11 to March 2, 1965, to continue efforts to organize talks. While Kosygin spoke in favor of negotiations on February 15, Soviet representatives privately urged the British government to join in reconvening the Geneva conference, which had originally called for a neutral South Vietnam,[61] and private approaches were also made to France for mediation. Soviet diplomats in various capitals also pressed their U.S.

56. See Lyndon Baines Johnson, *The Vantage Point: Perspectives on the Presidency, 1963–1969* (New York: Holt, Rinehart & Winston, 1971), 123–24, where Sidorovich is misidentified as head of economic aid but Soviet policy is correctly described.

57. George C. Herring, ed., *The Secret Diplomacy of the Vietnam War: The Negotiating Volumes of the Pentagon Papers* (Austin: University of Texas Press, 1983), 53; CIA/OCI intelligence memorandum, 29 June 1965, SC no. 07354/G5L; "Special DCI Briefing for Senator Stennis," SC no. 04458/65, 9 April 1965; "The Situation in South Vietnam," OCI no. 0615/65; CIA special report, September 3, 1965, SC no. 00686/65B; CIA, "The Situation in South Vietnam," May 6–12, 1965, OCI no. 0619/65; CIA, "The Situation in South Vietnam," May 13–19, 1965, OCI no. 0620/65. All CIA documents referred to have been declassified (with deletions) and are stored in the Lyndon B. Johnson Library, Austin. See also Zimmerman, "Korean and Vietnam Wars," 346.

58. Mikhail Petrovich Isaev, *Sovetsko-v'etnamskie otnosheniia* (Moscow: Mysl', 1975), 180. I thank Judith Chase for this reference.

59. April 18, 1965.

60. February 9, 1965. See also CIA memorandum, "The Situation in South Vietnam," February 28, 1964.

61. William E. Simons, "Coercion in Vietnam?" *RAND Memorandum* RM-6016–PR (May 1969), 60–61; Wallace J. Thies, *When Governments Collide: Coercion and Diplomacy in the Vietnam Conflict, 1964–1968* (Berkeley: University of California Press, 1980), 80–82; Isaev, *Sovetsko-v'etnamskie otnosheniia*, 187.

counterparts to acknowledge the urgency of talks.[62] Possibly Kosygin's pursuit of negotiations delayed execution of the arms agreement with North Vietnam. Although the CIA estimated that delivery of SAMs by sea would take no more than a month, the missiles did not arrive for two months, and progress in constructing the launch sites was slow.[63]

Whatever the extent of Soviet interest in negotiations during February and early March, the steady escalation of U.S. air attacks and the arrival of U.S. ground combat troops in increasing numbers eroded the persuasiveness of Kosygin's pleas for negotiation and for restraint in Soviet military involvement. The effects of continuing U.S. escalation were manifest in verbal concessions by Kosygin, in an escalation of Soviet activity in Vietnam, in the cessation of diplomatic initiatives toward the major capitalist countries, and in East-West trade.

In June Kosygin ended both his effort to limit arms deliveries to the levels agreed in February and his pursuit of negotiations. He promised "an increase in aid and support to the Vietnamese people."[64] Kosygin's June concession presaged a new Soviet-Vietnamese aid agreement in mid-July, providing "supplemental aid above that already rendered according to agreements concluded previously."[65] After a promise in an April communiqué that Soviet "citizens" would be permitted to join the fighting if U.S. escalation continued, Soviet air defense personnel assigned as trainers to Vietnamese units received permission to begin operating the radars and SAMs in combat against U.S. bombers.[66] On July 24 the first SAM launch shot down a U.S. aircraft.[67]

At the same time, Kosygin ended his efforts to negotiate a peace settlement. After rejecting an appeal from the visiting Swedish prime minister for the Soviets' good offices in arranging negotiations, in late June Kosygin ·said, "American politicians speak of

62. CIA memoranda, "The Situation in Vietnam," February 24 and March 20, 1965; "Soviet References to Intervention in Vietnam," April 7, 1965.

63. CIA/OCI intelligence memorandum, June 29, 1965, SC no. 07354/G5L; memorandum: "Delivery of Surface-to-Air Missile Equipment to North Vietnam," February 10, 1965.

64. June 30, 1965.

65. July 13, 1965.

66. April 18, 1965; Maior A. Dokuchaev, "I my zashchishchali V'etnam," *Krasnaia Zvezda*, April 13, 1989. See Zimmerman, *Korean and Vietnam Wars*, 346–47; Daniel S. Papp, *Vietnam: The View from Moscow, Peking, Washington* (Jefferson, N.C.: McFarland, 1981), 68.

67. CIA memorandum, "Shootdown of US Aircraft on 24 July by Surface-to-Air Missile," July 26, 1965.

talks. But who believes in the sincerity of these declarations when the barbaric bombardment of DRV territory and punitive expeditions against patriots of South Vietnam continue?"[68] He also rejected other initiatives to persuade the Soviet Union to mediate.[69] In May Soviet Foreign Ministry officials had already refused even to transmit U.S. offers of negotiations to the DRV embassy in Moscow.[70]

While the July aid agreement, the authorization of combat activity by Soviet air defense experts, and the renunciation of talks moved the outcome of policy bargaining toward the preferences expressed by Suslov and Brezhnev, the policy remained a compromise. It was a bargain by convergent concessions. At one end of the policy dimension, Brezhnev and Suslov accepted the priority of Kosygin's and Podgorny's preference for protecting North Vietnam over their own preference for pursuing the "liberation" of the South. Deliveries were mainly air defense systems, and declaratory statements, even in private to other communist parties, emphasized the protection of the North.[71] North Vietnamese leaders, for whom the reunification of the country held overriding importance, were dissatisfied with the restraints on Soviet aid.[72]

The price Kosygin paid for limiting Soviet counterescalation in Vietnam was the abandonment of diplomatic and commercial initiatives toward Western countries. The original compromise linking aid for Vietnam to Kosygin's overtures toward the West had been complicated by Brezhnev's tactic of turning West Germany into a security threat as part of his campaign to tighten the East European alli-

68. June 12 and 30, 1965.
69. June 24, September 14, 1965. Neglecting this evidence, Victor C. Funnell characterizes the Soviets' "whole policy" from 1965 to 1967 as "clearly in favor of the termination of the war and a political settlement": "Vietnam and the Sino-Soviet Conflict, 1965–1976," *Studies in Comparative Communism* 11 (Spring/Summer 1978): 161. This assessment is apparently based on the perceptions of Vietnamese fighting in the South. It may be true that the Soviets urged the North Vietnamese to offer terms for negotiation and that their pressure led the Vietnamese to perceive the Soviets as seeking negotiation.
70. Herring, *Secret Diplomacy*, 60–62.
71. CIA, "A Review of the Situation in Vietnam," December 8, 1967; M. P. Isaev, *Istoriia sovetsko-v'etnamskikh otnoshenii: 1917–1985* (Moscow: Mezhdunarodnye Otnosheniia, 1986), 109 (I thank Judith Chase for this reference); "Secret Letter of the CPSU to Other Communist Parties Regarding the Split with the Chinese Communist Party," in *Yearbook of International Communist Affairs* (Stanford: Hoover Institution, 1968), 570.
72. CIA intelligence memorandum, "Hanoi's View of the War," December 14, 1965, SC no. 10526/65; Funnell, "Vietnam," 156–57; Thai Quang Trung, *Collective Leadership and Factionalism* (Singapore: Institute of Southeast Asian Studies, 1985), 34–35.

ance. West Germany could not be simultaneously a symbol of the nuclear threat, as Brezhnev wanted, and a partner eligible for talks and trade, as Kosygin preferred. The two leaders resolved this disagreement by excluding West Germany from the list of countries eligible for diplomatic and commercial initiatives.

Exclusion of West Germany from East-West rapprochement was visible in a change from Brezhnev's speech for the anniversary of the Revolution in November to Kosygin's Supreme Soviet speech in December. Evidently prepared before the ouster of Khrushchev three weeks earlier, Brezhnev's text included West Germany among the capitalist states with which the Soviet Union could improve relations.[73] Later in November, however, Kosygin singled out German nuclearization as his sole example of "the imperialists' intrigues . . . to place the peoples' security under threat."[74] Accordingly, after Brezhnev's speech on December 3 initiated his campaign to use the MLF threat as the justification for reconfiguring Soviet ties with Eastern Europe, on December 9 Kosygin omitted West Germany from his list of capitalist states eligible for closer relations.

The effect of U.S. escalation in Vietnam was to move the main Western powers off Kosygin's list of capitalist states eligible for diplomatic and commercial overtures and onto an ineligible list. Before escalation, Soviet policy had expressed Kosygin's plan to link security and trade issues. Kosygin had received the British trade minister in October 1964; in January 1965 the Soviet government announced that he would travel to Great Britain in the spring and Prime Minister Harold Wilson would reciprocate by visiting Moscow in the fall.[75] Soviet-American relations displayed a parallel linkage, with Kosygin receiving a delegation of ninety-two American business executives in November and *Izvestiia* calling for a Kosygin-Johnson summit on January 8.[76]

After escalation, the Soviet side canceled both initiatives. As an official history of Anglo-Soviet relations later commented, "The English government's support of the U.S.A.'s aggressive course was the reason the [Kosygin] trip . . . intended for 1965 was postponed

73. November 6, 1964.
74. November 26, 1964.
75. October 30, 1964; January 12, 1965.
76. November 20, 1965; Franz Schurmann, Peter Dale Scott, and Reginald Zelnick, *The Politics of Escalation in Vietnam* (Boston: Beacon, 1966), 53–56.

more than once."[77] Claiming credit at the September plenum, Brezhnev blamed British policy toward Vietnam for impeding Anglo-Soviet contacts, and he also said, "Naturally, events in Vietnam have placed a significant imprint on . . . our relations with the United States, [which] have become significantly complicated and show an obvious tendency toward a freeze."[78] Until the September plenum, among the OECD states only the heads of government of Finland, Sweden, Norway, and Turkey held meetings with Kosygin, and none was reported to have backed U.S. policy in Vietnam during the sessions.

The observations that Kosygin had linked trade and diplomacy and that escalation in Vietnam had damaged the persuasiveness of his image of world conditions should lead an observer relying on competitive politics theory to expect that Soviet trade with capitalist countries during 1965 should not conform to Kosygin's proposals for an increase in volume, an increase in Soviet imports, or an increase in the share of machinery in Soviet exports. The total volume of trade with OECD countries remained approximately constant only because Soviet exports increased sharply while imports fell. In constant dollars, it probably declined slightly. The estimated share of machinery in Soviet exports to the West declined from 23.5 percent to 21.8 percent.[79] Fluctuations in bilateral trade show no evident connection to changes in political ties with capitalist countries, despite Kosygin's effort to link diplomatic rapprochement with expansion of trade.[80]

By the end of 1965 Soviet policy began to show the effects of Brezhnev's admission at the September plenum that his efforts toward reconciliation with China were failing too. Brezhnev's loss of persuasiveness, coupled with Shelepin's August initiative for a new increase in aid to Vietnam, posed a problem for the Politburo: how could policy express both a shift away from Brezhnev's preferences and a move toward Shelepin's when both were at the same end of the Vietnam spectrum?

77. V. G. Trukhanovskii and N. K. Kapitonova, *Sovetsko-angliiskiie otnosheniia, 1945–1978* (Moscow: Mezhdunarodnye Otnosheniia, 1979), 161–62.

78. September 30, 1965.

79. John T. Farrell, "Soviet Payments Problems in Trade with the West," in *Soviet Economic Prospects for the Seventies* (Washington, D.C.: U.S. Government Printing Office, 1978), 697–702.

80. For statistics on East-West trade, see Bruce Parrott, ed., *Trade, Technology, and Soviet-American Relations* (Bloomington: Indiana University Press, 1985), 374–81.

The Politburo solved this problem by revising the linkage between Europe and Vietnam. Bargaining by convergent concessions gave way to sequential exchange. The conditioning of diplomatic overtures to the United States on an end to attacks on North Vietnam remained in force, but from the late fall of 1965 further increases in Soviet aid to Vietnam became linked to a revival of diplomatic and commercial openings to Western Europe, as a result of concessions by Brezhnev on European issues.

Soviet and Vietnamese representatives signed new aid agreements in December 1965 and January 1966.[81] Shelepin's initiative on Vietnam earned him a payoff in the form of an opportunity to go public by leading the first high-level delegation to Hanoi since Kosygin's visit eleven months earlier. A North Vietnamese official, previously critical of Soviet frugality, described his government's reaction to the Shelepin visit: "The Soviets are giving us substantially increased material and military aid. . . . Shelepin's trip was but the symbol of the increase of Russian aid to us."[82] The estimated value of Soviet military deliveries during 1966 exceeded the 1965 value by over 70 percent. The Soviet Union shipped 5.5 times as many SAMs, 50 percent more aircraft, twice as much artillery, 7 times as many radars, and 2.3 times as much ammunition by weight.[83] The estimated proportion of the North Vietnamese army's weapons supplied by the Soviet Union more than doubled from 1965 to 1966.[84] Shelepin's endorsement of the goal of "unity" of Vietnam became a repeated feature of Soviet comments.[85]

The separation of Soviet initiatives toward Western Europe from the ban on talks with the United States found expression in Foreign Minister Andrei Gromyko's annual foreign policy summation before the United Nations General Assembly. He drew a contrast between the Soviets' "readiness for expansion of contacts and areas of collaboration with France, England, Italy, and other capitalist countries"

81. December 24, 1965; January 15, 1966.
82. Quoted in Herring, *Secret Diplomacy*, 113.
83. CIA, "A Review of the Situation in Vietnam," December 8, 1967. Zimmerman, "Korean and Vietnam Wars," 345, provides the same estimates of the value of aid, though he attributes them to the International Institute for Strategic Studies in London.
84. Jon M. Van Dyke, *North Vietnam's Strategy for Survival* (Palo Alto: Pacific Books, 1972), 59–65, 222.
85. N. P. Firiubin et al., eds., *Sovetskii Soiuz—V'etnam, 30 let otnoshenii, 1950–1980: Dokumenty i materialy* (Moscow: Politizdat, 1982), 117, 124, 128, 130, 134. I thank Judith Chase for supplying these references.

and their desire for "good relations with the United States, too, but of course given the appropriate reciprocity and not at the expense of other countries [i.e., Vietnam]."[86]

The new policy became manifest in both commercial and diplomatic activity. Constant from 1964 to 1965, Soviet trade with OECD countries increased 10 percent from 1965 to 1966.[87] The increase in overall trade excluded the United States and West Germany; trade with these countries remained at low levels. In diplomacy, the August escalation in Vietnam had the opposite effect in Europe from the February escalation. The February escalation had canceled Kosygin's planned meeting with Prime Minister Wilson. The bargain reached at the September plenum authorized Gromyko to confer with the foreign ministers of four capitalist countries during the next seven months—France at the end of October, Great Britain at the end of November, Japan in January (when a new long-term trade agreement was signed), and Italy in April 1966.

Moreover, meetings with West European leaders now became authorized even when they expressed support for American policy in Vietnam. Immediately after the September plenum it was announced that agreement had been reached for a visit to Moscow by the Danish prime minister.[88] In Moscow he publicly promoted U.S. proposals for negotiations without a halt in bombing.[89] After the British foreign minister's visit in December, the long-postponed meeting with Wilson was scheduled for February 1966.[90] When Wilson arrived, a senior *Pravda* commentator wrote specifically that disagreements over Vietnam should not impede contacts with Great Britain.[91] During 1965–1967 Wilson would repeatedly act as a conduit for American peace feelers.[92] At each meeting with a European government the Soviet representatives echoed Kosygin's proposal for a comprehensive settlement of European security issues.[93] To justify the new policy in Europe, the opponents of East-West contacts began to exaggerate the Vietnam conflict's estrangement of American

86. September 26, 1965.
87. Parrott, *Trade*, 374–81.
88. October 4, 1965.
89. October 8, 1965.
90. December 23, 1965.
91. V. Nekrasov, "Vozmozhnosti sovetsko-angliiskogo dialoga," February 27, 1966.
92. Thies, *When Governments Collide*, 80–82, 159–65.
93. See the following communiqués: Kosygin-Krag, October 18, 1965; Gromyko-Couve, November 3, 1965; Gromyko-Stewart, December 4, 1965; Kosygin-Wilson, February 25, 1966; Gromyko-Fanfani, April 25, 1966.

allies. As Shelepin said in January 1966, "The war in Vietnam . . . further intensifies their political isolation in the international arena. . . . Even many U.S. allies in the aggressive military blocs of NATO, CENTO, and SEATO do not approve the American piracy against the Vietnamese people."[94]

Bargaining over East-West issues during 1965 displays the effects of logrolling on the adaptiveness of foreign policy. When Kosygin and Brezhnev used a logroll to resolve their initial disagreement over whether to pursue negotiations or provide defensive aid to North Vietnam, they approved a potentially self-frustrating policy. Possession of Soviet weapons was likely to make North Vietnam more intransigent in any talks with the United States, while Soviet pressure for entry into negotiations was likely to erase any gains (in the form of, say, North Vietnamese pressure on China to accept reconciliation) that might otherwise have been obtainable in return for the arms supplies.

These foreseeable effects remained unrealized when U.S. escalation compelled Kosygin to concede the negotiating half of the original logroll. When Vietnam and East-West issues then became bundled into a single dimension, the adaptiveness of Soviet policy improved. There was no self-contradiction in a policy of refusing to negotiate while supplying air defense for the protection of North Vietnam.

When the policy shifted in the fall of 1965 back to a logroll combining new increases in aid for Vietnam and the ban on talks with the United States with a broad diplomatic initiative in Western Europe, the maladaptiveness of logrolling reappeared. The West European allies might criticize U.S. conduct in Vietnam, but they were certainly unwilling to negotiate European security arrangements without the U.S. protector at the table. Soviet actions in Vietnam that could be interpreted as evidence of offensive intentions also intensified Western Europeans' worries about negotiating with the Soviets.

The consequences of symbolism also were noticeable. Each leader seized on Vietnam as a synecdoche for his grand strategy. Kosygin's willingness to allow Vietnam to stand as a synecdoche for U.S. peacefulness or hostility proved devastating to his program of East-West talks and trade. Only when the use of China as a synecdoche

94. January 10, 1966. For similar statements by other leaders, see November 6, 1965; January 16 and 27, March 30, April 1, 1966.

for the solidarity of communists proved equally damaging to Brezhnev's bargaining position did Kosygin recover the ability to pursue his grand strategy, and even then only to the exclusion of the element most vital to the success of the policy—negotiations with the United States.

⋆ Chapter 8

*Podgorny and
the Third World,
October 1964–April 1966*

Podgorny's grand strategy replicated the positional logic of his domestic vision. In domestic politics, Podgorny sought to build a reputation for advocating adoption of capitalist methods in economic management while concurrently upholding "the principle radically distinguishing the socialist order from the order of exploitation and gain."[1] Podgorny's stance in domestic politics positioned him between the reformer Kosygin, who espoused the takeover of capitalist techniques, and the antireformers Brezhnev and Suslov, who defended fidelity to socialist principles. Podgorny's grand strategy repeated this positioning. He built a reputation for advocacy of international cooperation while concurrently insisting on fighting "the great ideological combat of two social systems." Peace could be kept, Podgorny argued, by cooperation between the socialist countries and a "broad front of peoples,"[2] including a wide variety of Third World states and even some European capitalist governments, who had a common interest in preventing nuclear war. Cooperation among these states would achieve a quarantine of potentially aggressive capitalist states—in 1965, West Germany and the United States. At home and abroad Podgorny espoused the coupling of a pragmatic attitude toward capitalism with an emphasis on sustaining the ideological distinctiveness of socialism.

1. June 10, 1966.
2. July 25, 1965.

To cement cooperation with Third World countries, Podgorny proposed to continue Khrushchev's program of economic assistance to a broad variety of recipients, including both countries with capitalist institutions and countries on the so-called noncapitalist path of development. This proposal ran counter to the views of Soviet policy experts, who were expressing increasing skepticism about the effectiveness of aid to developing countries. The issue of economic aid turned controversial after U.S. escalation in Vietnam. Kosygin reacted to the frustration of his East-West program by intruding into what had evidently been intended to be Podgorny's preserve, proposing to limit economic aid to developing countries with capitalist institutions. A third figure participated in the aid dispute: Anastas Mikoian recommended a shift from aid to trade in Soviet economic relations with developing countries.

A separate controversy developed over security issues. Promoting his grand strategy of heroic anticapitalism, Brezhnev called for weapons aid both to governments that adopted socialist domestic policies and to movements engaged in armed struggle against colonialism. These proposals received backing from Suslov. Mikoian rejected armed struggle and called for a diplomatic program designed to assemble a narrow coalition of radical Third World states. Kosygin used the Third World as a venue for diplomacy designed to rebuild domestic audiences' confidence in the feasibility of his strategy of negotiating international conflicts.

The separation of economic and security issues produced a policy that shifted Soviet economic aid from governments on the noncapitalist path to governments on the capitalist path, while also enacting Brezhnev's increase in military aid and Mikoian's and Kosygin's diplomatic initiatives. The self-defeating tendency characteristic of logrolling was evident in a policy that denied economic aid to governments with which the Soviet Union was simultaneously pursuing closer military and diplomatic ties.

A Quarantine of Aggressor States: Podgorny's Grand Strategy

Less is known about Podgorny's grand strategy in the period immediately after Khrushchev's ouster than about the proposals of his rivals. He suffered discrimination in press coverage. *Pravda* published relatively full coverage of speeches by other leaders during foreign trips, but some of Podgorny's speeches were synopsized very briefly. At least once during 1965 the Politburo seems to have barred him from making any speeches at all.[3] Nevertheless, the few available speeches by Podgorny provide evidence of a grand strategy combining cooperative initiatives toward selected capitalist countries and a broad variety of Third World states with isolation of states portrayed as aggressors—in 1965, the United States and West Germany. This grand strategy replicated his domestic vision's coupling of an embrace of the capitalist concepts inherent in economic reform with an effort to insulate socialist collectivism from the corrosive effects of individualistic consumerism.

Podgorny described world conditions as favoring Soviet initiatives for cooperation with some West European countries. In contrast to Brezhnev's May 1965 description of a monolithic imperialist alliance eager to grant West Germany access to nuclear weapons, on the same day Podgorny claimed that only "some leading NATO countries" supported this plan.[4] Podgorny depicted the United States not as already leading an anti-Soviet alliance in NATO but, remarkably, as seeking to assemble such an alliance. President Johnson, he said, had urged "the unification of forces of the states of the so-called Atlantic civilization; in other words, the creation of a "holy alliance" of reaction against the socialist system and the national liberation movement."[5] But U.S. plans for "creation" of an aggressive alliance would fail, Podgorny said. "The peoples . . . have seen with their own eyes who is playing a dangerous game now. . . . Ever-broader strata of the public are drawn into the struggle for peace," and their efforts had occasioned a "reevaluation of foreign policy ideas even in countries that belong to military blocs." The resulting "moral-political isolation of aggressive imperialist circles" was causing "destabilization of aggressive alliances."[6]

In Podgorny's view, Third World governments were also threatened by the United States. "The U.S. ruling circles, cynically violating elementary norms of international law, more frequently resort to

3. Michel Tatu, *Power in the Kremlin: From Khrushchev to Kosygin*, trans. Helen Katel (New York: Viking, 1967), 522.

4. May 9, 1965.

5. May 22, 1965. Podgorny's commentary on Johnson's speech paraphrased a lengthy TASS analysis published the previous day (May 21, 1965). Though both the TASS analysis and Podgorny's speech had probably been approved by the whole Politburo, Podgorny's portrait of relations within the Atlantic Alliance was still highly unusual.

6. April 1, 1966.

direct interference in the internal affairs of sovereign states" and had "raised interference in affairs of other peoples almost to a norm of state activity."[7] In contrast to Kosygin, Podgorny never commented favorably on prospects for cooperation with the United States.

Podgorny's description of a security threat facing both Third World governments and U.S. allies in Europe justified a repeated policy recommendation in favor of "the unification of efforts of all anti-imperialist forces"[8]—a concept Podgorny defined far more broadly than Brezhnev or Suslov. In addition to the socialist countries and the international working class, in Podgorny's speeches these forces included "a broad front of peoples of Asia, Africa, and Latin America."[9] Podgorny fully recognized that Third World radicals were most likely to welcome Soviet overtures, describing "the aspiration of peoples of former colonial countries to socialism" as "one of the most important tendencies of contemporary social development." But unlike Brezhnev, he did not say that progress toward this aspiration should be a criterion for Soviet alliance, and unlike Suslov, he did not regard "major social transformations" in former colonial countries as a prerequisite to resistance to neocolonialism. Moreover, "an inseparable component" of Soviet policy should be "peaceful coexistence of states with a different social order," so that the USSR could "establish normal, businesslike relations with the majority of states of the world."[10] Proposing ties with the "majority" of foreign states, Podgorny remained careful to distance his strategy from Kosygin's proposals for cooperation with the United States: "The struggle for peace has nothing in common with appeasement of an aggressor."[11]

Podgorny used his first trip abroad to communicate his grand strategy. As secretary of the Central Committee responsible for personnel in January 1965, he had no official reason to lead a Supreme Soviet delegation to Turkey. But the trip did serve a competitive purpose. Turkey belonged to both categories of potential partners whose willingness to enter his "broad front of peoples" would prove controversial in Politburo speeches. Turkey was both a developing country with capitalist institutions and a member of NATO with grounds for disaffection in its conflict with Greece over the sover-

7. May 9, 1965 (see also May 22, 1965); July 25, 1965.
8. April 1, 1966. See also May 9 and 22, July 25, December 15, 1965.
9. July 25, 1965.
10. April 1, 1966.
11. May 9, 1965.

eignty of Cyprus. Podgorny's speeches during the trip expressed two salient precepts of his grand strategy: the use of economic ties to promote security cooperation and the effort to exploit conflicts among capitalist countries. To encourage Turkish leaders to accept rapprochement, he held out the prospect of increases in Soviet sales and purchases, and he paid more attention to Cyprus than would Kosygin, who failed to address the issue during a visit by the Turkish prime minister in August.[12] Occupying, in Podgorny's words, "the intersection of Europe, Asia, and Africa,"[13] Turkey served Podgorny as a synecdoche for the feasibility of a Moscow-centered coalition uniting states on all three continents.

The Construction of Opposition: Economic Aid

Once Brezhnev had specialized in relations among socialist countries, Kosygin in East-West issues, and Suslov in international communism, the Third World was the remaining issue specialty open to Podgorny. As his advocacy of attempting to isolate the United States from its European allies conflicted with Kosygin's proposals to negotiate concurrently with the West Europeans and the United States, a division of labor that allotted Europe to Kosygin and the Third World to Podgorny would have enabled each to pursue his grand strategy without overt conflict. Initially such a division of specialties appeared to be emerging. Kosygin's early speeches were inattentive to the Third World, and Podgorny's specific proposals focused on Third World issues.

If this specialization was intended, however, it broke down after Kosygin reacted to U.S. escalation in Vietnam by transferring his strategy of cooperation with capitalist countries to the Third World. Podgorny and Kosygin publicly disagreed over what Third World states should be eligible for economic aid, and both men found themselves at odds with Mikoian's proposals that aid should give way to trade. This pattern of opposition persisted until October 1965, when Brezhnev's admission of the failure of his proposal for reconciliation with China led him, like Kosygin after Vietnam, to

12. January 8, 1965. Cf. Podgorny's statements printed January 6 and 14 and February 7, 1965, with Kosygin's speeches for the visiting Turkish prime minister and with the communiqué, August 10, 11, 13, and 17, 1965.
13. July 25, 1965.

turn to the issue of aid for the Third World in a bid to restore the persuasiveness of his grand strategy.

Podgorny proposed to continue Khrushchev's program of offering economic aid to a broad variety of Third World recipients, whether they chose the capitalist or the noncapitalist path of development. A security alliance alone, he argued, was not enough to permit Third World states the freedom of action they needed if they were to cooperate with the Soviet Union.

> The USSR and other socialist countries not only have blocked the colonizers every time they tried to restore colonial regimes or to impose dependency on imperialism in new ways, but also have given and do give all forms of support to the peoples of weakly developed countries in their efforts toward creation of their own industry and development of their culture, which are the indispensable conditions for preservation of political independence.

While Podgorny recognized that radical regimes were more likely to cooperate with Soviet policy, his advocacy of economic aid did not discriminate among Third World countries by their domestic institutions. He proposed to aid Third World countries on both paths of development: "the great Indian people, the peoples of Algeria, the UAR [United Arab Republic], and other Arab countries, Indonesia and Burma, Ghana, Guinea, Mali, and many other young states of Asia and Africa."[14] This proposal placed Podgorny at cross-purposes with Soviet policy specialists, who had begun to call for evaluation of aid requests by criteria of economic effectiveness, not by the political criteria Podgorny cited.[15]

When Kosygin began to comment on economic aid in the spring of 1965, in contrast, he excluded states on the noncapitalist path (Algeria, the UAR, Indonesia, Burma, Ghana, Guinea, and Mali) from his list of eligible recipients. Kosygin signaled an end to his reticence on Third World issues on March 10, the week after U.S. air raids resumed in Vietnam, when the Soviet government announced that the Indian prime minister, Lal Bahadur Shastri, would visit in May. When Shastri arrived, Kosygin explicitly extended his earlier

---

14. May 22, 1965. See also July 25, December 15, 1965; April 1, 1966.
15. Roger E. Kanet, "Soviet Attitudes toward Developing Nations since Stalin," in Kanet, ed., *The Soviet Union and the Developing Nations* (Baltimore: Johns Hopkins University Press, 1974), 44–49; Elizabeth Valkenier, "Soviet Economic Relations with the Developing Nations," in ibid., 225–28.

commitment to aid Vietnam: "We consider it our internationalist duty to render moral and material aid not only to peoples struggling against colonialism but also to peoples attempting to . . . strengthen the economic independence of their states."[16]

Kosygin's promise of economic aid to India (to which he soon added Pakistan and Afghanistan)[17] contrasted with his reaction to public pleas for economic aid by visiting leaders of radical Third World governments—Milton Obote of Uganda, Sekou Touré of Guinea, Ne Win of Burma, and Houari Boumedienne of Algeria. On these occasions Kosygin said that local resources, social transformation, and independence would ensure economic development or that the Soviet Union would fulfill existing aid agreements.[18] Even at a ceremony honoring the first graduates of Lumumba University—a suitable occasion for a pledge of economic aid to radical states—Kosygin restricted the Soviet commitment to a promise to train technical cadres.[19]

Promises of economic aid to Third World states with capitalist institutions offered Kosygin an opportunity to rebuild Soviet audiences' confidence, eroded by U.S. escalation in Vietnam, in his grand strategy of cooperation with capitalist governments. As he said, "It is well known that our friendship [with India] can serve as an example of good-neighbor relations for many countries belonging to different social systems."[20]

Podgorny's proposal to extend aid to both types of Third World countries and Kosygin's proposal to restrict it to selected countries on the capitalist path opposed them both to Mikoian, the Politburo member who chaired the Presidium of the Supreme Soviet. Mikoian argued for a shift from aid to trade in economic ties with the developing world. Mikoian set forth no domestic vision and no grand strategy during 1965, but he did develop an elaborate position on policy toward the Third World. He expressed the economic component of his stand in a speech for the visiting president Gamal Abdel Nasser of the United Arab Republic: ". . . the economic difficulties of the formation period of young liberated states can be successfully resolved . . . when these states boldly conduct radical transforma-

16. May 14, 1965. For repetition of his commitment to economic aid, see May 15, 1965; January 13, April 5, 1966.
17. April 4 and 25, August 11, 1965; February 3, 1966.
18. July 23 and 30, September 22, December 18, 1965.
19. June 30, 1965.
20. January 13, 1966.

tions, mobilize their internal capabilities, and move toward mutually advantageous collaboration on equal terms with all countries, including the socialist states."[21] Coupled with Mikoian's failure to endorse economic aid when he spoke before Third World visitors,[22] his repeated references to "radical transformation" and "internal capabilities"[23] communicated an insistence that radical regimes rely on domestic political change for development, not on Soviet aid. Nasser expressed his dissatisfaction with Mikoian's position: "I will not hide from you that we feel that the specifically political aspect of our people's struggle sometimes arouses interest . . . at the expense of . . . expansion of the economic base."[24] All the other visiting leaders of radical Third World regimes also made public statements implying that they had privately objected to the Soviet leaders' unwillingness to extend additional aid.[25]

Mikoian's espousal of "mutually advantageous collaboration" continued to pursue the displacement of aid by trade, which he had proposed as early as 1961.[26] He proposed that trade should also dominate the economic relationship with developing countries on the capitalist path.[27] His formula "on equal terms" referred to an element of Soviet trade policy particularly objectionable to Third World radicals. They complained about a "fundamental contradiction" between Soviet claims that trade with socialist countries was nonexploitive and "the present attitude whereby the socialist country also pays the same price which the Western countries, because of their desire to exploit, have contrived to pay."[28] That is, Mikoian was understood to be proposing to replace aid with trade at world prices disadvantageous to the radicals.

Mikoian justified opposition to economic aid by raising fundamen-

21. September 1, 1965.
22. April 9, June 22 and 27, July 29, August 4, 6, 18, 19, 21 and 29, September 1 and 17, 1965.
23. July 29, August 18 and 19, 1965.
24. September 1, 1965.
25. Touré, July 29, 1965; Alphonse Massamba-Debat of Congo-Brazzaville, August 18 and 21, 1965; Ne Win, September 17, 1965; Modibo Keita, October 5, 1965; Boumedienne, December 18, 1965.
26. Elizabeth Valkenier, *The Soviet Union and the Third World: An Economic Bind* (New York: Praeger, 1983), 11–12.
27. April 9, June 22, 1965.
28. A Ghanaian newspaper editorial of July 1965, quoted in Robert Legvold, *Soviet Policy in West Africa* (Cambridge, Mass.: Harvard University Press, 1970), 251. See also Jacques Levesque, *The USSR and the Cuban Revolution*, trans. Deanna Drendel Leboeuf (New York: Praeger, 1978), 108–9.

tal objections to Podgorny's and Kosygin's proposals for cooperation with states developing on the capitalist path. Mikoian distinguished between two kinds of Third World states: those with "progressive" domestic institutions capable of following an independent foreign policy and "other governments, which are not so reactionary but are weak, [and] are acting on orders and contrary to their conscience."[29] In the "progressive" states, Mikoian said, "the revolution unblocks the people's creative forces, imbues them with faith in a better future, permits them to mobilize the country's internal resources more fully." In "countries where imperialists have managed to bring to power regimes congenial to them," on the other hand, "little has changed in economic life. . . . The people of these countries must still travel a long and difficult path to gain authentic independence."[30] Mikoian's claim that capitalist institutions subordinated Third World governments to imperialist control (a claim echoed by Brezhnev) drew an explicit rejection from Kosygin, who said that U.S. economic pressure on "young national states" would "not help the U.S. government, and the tactless methods it uses can only arouse people who are concerned for their dignity and the independence of their opinion even further against it."[31]

Until October 1965, Brezhnev remained aloof from the issue of economic aid. But he responded to the failure of his bid for reconciliation with China (which he finally admitted at the September plenum of the Central Committee) in a way that paralleled Kosygin's reaction to U.S. escalation in Vietnam. Just as Kosygin had responded to the resumption of bombing raids by inviting Shastri to Moscow in March, Brezhnev welcomed Modibo Keita of Mali—one of the countries with domestic institutions most closely patterned on the Soviet model—on October 4. *Pravda* announced Keita's impending arrival only two days in advance. The unusually short notice suggests that his trip was a response to the September plenum, and the announcement that Keita would come in his capacity as secretary general of the Soudanese Union Party (though he was also head of state and head of government) justified an exchange of speeches with Brezhnev rather than with Mikoian or Kosygin. Having arranged an appropriate forum, Brezhnev made his first statement in favor of economic aid: "In our day . . . the possibilities for successful

29. October 16, 1964.
30. September 1, 1965.
31. Brezhnev: March 30, 1966; Kosygin: May 15, 1965.

development of young states that have chosen the path of socialism are immeasurably more favorable than before. In their desire for progress these states rely on the aid and support of the world socialist system and of all anti-imperialist forces." In three further speeches, including his report to the XXIII Congress, Brezhnev explicitly justified not only military but also economic aid to radical, "socialist path" regimes such as Mali.[32]

The Construction of Opposition: Security

The extreme diversity of the Third World offered many opportunities for the Politburo rivals to find situations exemplifying the urgency of their various grand strategies. As the policy specialist Karen Brutents was to argue in early 1967, the situation in the Third World "is extremely unsettled and the class meaning and character of social processes . . . has still not crystallized."[33] For this reason, no single policy applied uniformly to all Third World countries would remain persuasive over time, and the Politburo contenders seized the chance to recommend a variety of policies.

Security problems, treated as separable from economic problems, provided the issue area for divergent policy recommendations. As an indicator of the urgency of heroic anticapitalism, Brezhnev pointed to the security threat facing Third World revolutionary movements that had not yet defeated colonial occupiers. Mikoian, who argued that transitions to socialism in the Third World should follow the peaceful path adopted in Europe, countered with a recommendation for a diplomatic coalition between the Soviet Union and Third World radical states. Kosygin and Suslov proposed aid in the form of arms to secure the independence of former colonies.

Diplomatic initiatives toward the Third World also figured in Kosygin's and Brezhnev's efforts to restore lost authority. When escalation in Vietnam threatened the persuasiveness of Kosygin's strategy of international cooperation, he turned to mediation of the Indo-Pakistani conflict to demonstrate the ability of negotiation to resolve disputes. When the failure of reconciliation with China undermined Brezhnev's persuasiveness, he too turned to a diplomatic move to-

32. October 24, 1965; January 16, March 30, 1966.
33. K. Brutents, "Natsional'no-osvoboditel'noe dvizhenie segodnia," February 1, 1967.

ward the Third World, with a proposal that the United Nations protect Third World states against outside intervention.

When Brezhnev discussed "support" for the Third World, he emphasized aid "for the national liberation movement of peoples still under the yoke of colonizers."[34] By 1965 anticolonial rebellions (outside South Vietnam, which was defined as an American colony in disguise) were confined to fighting on a tiny scale in the Portuguese colonies, the white-ruled states of southern Africa, six Latin American countries where the Soviet leaders agreed to consider domestic revolutionaries as attacking American colonialism, and a few other scattered locations. Thus, although completion of decolonization enjoyed substantial support in the former colonies, Brezhnev's advocacy of aid for anticolonial rebellions neglected almost all of the Third World, and outside Vietnam the potential recipients could not justify large demands on Soviet resources. Endorsement of aid to "the fearless fighters of the great army of freedom now pouring out its blood in stubborn struggle with the colonizers"[35] presented Brezhnev yet another opportunity to identify with the inspirational heroism of anticapitalist combat—an opportunity absent from the less glamorous, protracted task of economic development.

Both Suslov and Kosygin argued that military aid was necessary to block the efforts of capitalist countries to restore their influence over newly independent states,[36] though their reasons differed. For Kosygin, advocacy of military aid proved the sincerity of his declarations that he would enforce a norm of nonintervention on the United States as a condition for cooperation.[37] For Suslov, it emphasized his distinction between tactics appropriate to communists in Europe and those suited to the Third World. Though the electoral path was appropriate for Europe, arms aid was justified in the Third World to enable radical movements to seize power and defend it against the "fury in imperialist circles . . . , [which] dream of smothering the struggle . . . for national independence and socialism."[38]

Proposals for arms aid to Third World guerrillas encountered op-

34. September 11, 1965. See also October 20, November 6, 1964; April 9 and 23, May 9, July 28, September 4 and 30, 1965; January 16, March 30, 1966.

35. April 23, 1965.

36. For comments by Suslov and Ponomarev: December 15, 1964; June 5, October 23 and 31, 1965; January 27, 1966. Kosygin: October 20, December 10, 1964; February 9, 13, and 27, 1965.

37. December 10, 1964; May 8, July 18, 1965.

38. October 31, 1965. See also June 5, 1965; January 27, 1966.

position from Mikoian. Mikoian depicted the peaceful path to revolution as valid not only for Europe, with its large industrial proletariats,[39] but also for the Third World. He denounced advocates of arms shipments to violent rebels in the Third World as "either mindless or provocateurs."[40] He recommended that the Soviet Union foster security in the Third World by forming diplomatic coalitions with radical regimes, for the socialist countries must join with "all African countries that conduct a progressive policy."[41]

Mikoian made a specific proposal for consolidation of the diplomatic coalition between the Soviet Union and the Third World radicals: he called for Soviet participation in the abortive Second Afro-Asian Conference, known as the "second Bandung." His claim in September that geography, economy, history, and the record of aid to "Afro-Asian peoples" all qualified the Soviet Union to participate and his pledge to "devote all efforts to its successful work" were the only references to Soviet participation in the conference by a Politburo member during the year.[42] Ten days before the originally scheduled opening of the conference in June, Kosygin said the Soviet Union "attaches very great significance" to the conference, but he did not mention Soviet participation in it.[43]

Mikoian alone sought participation in the second Bandung conference because the proposal promoted his Third World strategy and interfered with those of Podgorny and Kosygin. Soviet participation was a divisive issue among Third World states, and when a coup overthrew the Algerian leader, Ben Bella, only days before the conference was scheduled to begin in Algiers, the question whether the conference should be canceled became equally divisive. Mikoian's proposal forced Third World interlocutors to identify themselves as either opponents of Soviet policy or potential members of his coalition of "countries that conduct a progressive policy."

In Kosygin's efforts to mediate Indo-Pakistani border clashes, he warned that conflicts between developing countries would benefit only the imperialists. "The Soviet people want these states to decide border and other questions in dispute among them by the peaceful

39. July 18, 1965.
40. October 17, December 1, 1964.
41. July 29, 1965.
42. September 1, 1965. See his statements on the Bandung principles of *panch sila*, April 6, 1965, and his statements on Afro-Asian solidarity, July 29, August 21, 1965.
43. June 19, 1965.

path."[44] Although Shastri rejected Kosygin's attempt to mediate in May,[45] after open warfare broke out in August, Kosygin renewed his mediation in early September with private letters to both Shastri and Pakistan's Mohammad Ayub Khan. Both sides eventually accepted his invitation to meet at Tashkent in January 1966.

Kosygin made Tashkent an explicit synecdoche for the viability of his strategy of negotiated settlement of international disputes, the persuasiveness of which had been challenged by the failure of his efforts to find a negotiated settlement in Vietnam. "Everyone to whom peace is dear followed this meeting with great attention and hope. They waited for news from Tashkent and hoped that the talks would be fruitful and that their results would strengthen the faith of all progressive people that even in difficult conditions paths for settlement of conflict can be found. And these expectations were justified."[46]

Brezhnev did not attempt to obstruct Kosygin's mediation between India and Pakistan, but he tried to turn the Tashkent initiative into an indicator of the urgent need for heroic anticapitalism. Instead of portraying Tashkent as an instance of achieving peace through talks, Brezhnev called it a blow against the West. Behind the Indo-Pakistani war, he said, "it is not difficult to see the hand of reactionary forces, and above all American imperialism." He denied Kosygin's claim that Tashkent proved the feasibility of achieving peace by negotiations among contending states. Only three days after Kosygin's statement, Brezhnev ruled out any policy except his proposed reliance on anti-imperialist solidarity. Commenting explicitly on the Tashkent meeting, Brezhnev said: "All this dictates again and again the necessity of strengthening the unity of communists throughout the world, the unity of all revolutionary liberation forces, the unity of all progressive forces in the world. There is no other path, comrades."[47] During September Brezhnev launched his own diplomatic initiative, announcing that the submission to the UN General Assembly of a draft resolution prohibiting interference in

44. May 15, 1965. See also April 4, May 14, 1965.
45. See his statement (May 15, 1965) accusing "certain countries" of coveting Indian territory and asserting that India's obligation to protect its territorial integrity must take precedence over all other goals.
46. January 13, 1966. See his rationalization for the conference itself, January 5, 1966.
47. January 16, 1966. See also September 11, 15, 25, and 30, 1965.

the internal affairs of foreign states was intended to protect small states' independence against imperialist powers' "blackmail."[48]

Bargaining

Soviet policy in the Third World displays a clear response to the twin variables of going public and bargaining. Most observers of change in Soviet policy toward the Third World after the ouster of Khrushchev discern a pattern of "retrenchment" or even "reversal" of his ambitious program of courting Third World allies.[49] "Soviet economic relations with the Third World began to shed their ad hoc and predominantly political character" in favor of a "pursuit of economic advantage" marked by "more stringent procedures" for evaluating aid projects and a "shift to more promising" Third World recipients.[50] At the same time there occurred a long-term "shift in overall commitments from economic to military assistance."[51] The changes in Soviet policy are regularly attributed to growing disenchantment with the "instability" of radical regimes, made evident during 1965 and early 1966 by the coups against Khrushchev's allies Ben Bella in Algeria, Sukarno in Indonesia, and Kwame Nkrumah in Ghana. The contingency of those changes on going public by Politburo members and bargaining has not been noticed.

Economic aid declined while military aid expanded because the public rhetoric of the Soviet leaders separated the two issues. The record of economic aid clearly displays the impact of bargaining. Figure 2 shows the positions taken by the three Soviet leaders who

48. September 25, 1965.

49. Carol R. Saivetz and Sylvia Woodby, *Soviet–Third World Relations* (Boulder, Colo.: Westview, 1985), 45; Valkenier, *Soviet Union and the Third World*, 11.

50. Valkenier, *Soviet Union and the Third World*, 13–22. See also Milton Kovner, "Soviet Aid to the Developing Countries: A Look at the Record," in J. W. Strong, ed., *The Soviet Union under Brezhnev and Kosygin: The Transition Years* (New York: Van Nostrand Reinhold, 1971), 61–64; Roger E. Kanet, "Soviet Policy toward the Developing World: The Role of Economic Assistance and Trade," in Robert H. Donaldson, ed., *The Soviet Union in the Third World: Successes and Failures* (Boulder, Colo.: Westview, 1981), 334–39; Neil MacFarlane, "The USSR and The Third World: Continuity and Change under Gorbachev," *Harriman Institute Forum* 1 (March 1988): 1, and "The Soviet Union and the National Liberation Movements," in Carol R. Saivetz, ed., *The Soviet Union in the Third World* (Boulder, Colo.: Westview, 1989), 37–38; Melvin A. Goodman, "The Role of Soviet Military and Economic Aid in the Third World under Gorbachev," also in Saivetz, 59.

51. Alvin Z. Rubinstein, *Moscow's Strategy in the Third World* (Princeton: Princeton University Press, 1988), 54.

		Aid countries on noncapitalist path?	
		Yes	No
Aid countries on capitalist path?	Yes	Podgorny	Kosygin
	No		Mikoian

Figure 2. Stands on economic aid to Third World, May–September 1965

discussed economic aid between May and September 1965. As long as economic aid is separated from other issues, a bargain by convergent concessions is available, and the bargain is located in the cell occupied by Kosygin. Mikoian concedes grants of economic aid to countries on the capitalist path and Podgorny concedes refusal of economic aid to countries on the noncapitalist path.

Soviet behavior displays the shift to be expected from this pattern of bargaining. As the Politburo began to reject radical Third World leaders' requests for further aid while seeking new recipients among countries on the capitalist path, new commitments of economic aid declined from $825 million in 1964 to $628 million in 1965.[52] This decline was a response to Kosygin's intervention in the aid issue with his March invitation to Shastri. In the first four months after Khrushchev's ouster, Politburo members outside the inner core justified continuation of his policy on economic aid, and minor new aid commitments were extended to Uganda, Kenya, Congo-Brazzaville, and Mali.[53] But in April the Lenin commemoration speech gave evidence of retrenchment: "Of course possibilities for rendering economic aid are not limitless, but the possibilities will grow together with successes in our country's development."[54] In May an Algerian delegation was unable to obtain more than an agreement to provide

52. Kovner, "Soviet Aid," 63. Leo Tansky, "Soviet Foreign Aid: Scope, Direction, and Trends," in *Soviet Economic Prospects for the Seventies* (Washington, DC.: U.S. Government Printing Office, 1973), 769, gives a figure of only $416 million but omits a $200 million aid commitment to Turkey, even though he mentions the commitment. See his table, 768, which gives a total of only $84 million for new commitments to the Middle East; this figure corresponds to Kovner's for Greece alone.

53. Ponomarev, December 15 and 22, 1964; Shelepin, December 25, 29 and 30, 1964; January 11, February 6, 1965; Polianskii, February 10, 1965; USSR Ministry of Foreign Affairs, *SSSR i strany Afriki, 1963–1970,* pt. 1 (Moscow: Politicheskoi Literatury, 1981), 162–68, 175–80, 187–91, 194–96.

54. April 23, 1965.

"technical assistance."[55] The assistance took the form of expert advisers for projects funded by the host country, a practice that was comparatively disadvantageous to the recipients, who had to pay for the experts' services in hard currency.[56]

Economic aid not only decreased but also shifted to countries on the capitalist path. During the rest of 1965 the radical regimes of Egypt, Ghana, Guinea, Mali, and Sudan were able to obtain moratoria on repayment of existing credits but not new aid commitments.[57] Senegal, Sierra Leone, Afghanistan, India, Pakistan, Argentina, Greece, and Turkey—all "capitalist path" countries—did obtain new commitments.[58] With the efficiency advocate Kosygin dominating the policy bargaining, it is not surprising that "economic rationality became the criterion" for aid grants.[59]

When Brezhnev entered the controversy with his proposal for aid to radical regimes, the policy gradually shifted. The shift was not immediate; even a public demand by Brezhnev during Keita's visit could not obtain a new commitment for Mali. The delay can be attributed to a bargaining problem apparent in Figure 3.

The former compromise by convergent concessions had now become unavailable, as refusal of aid to countries on the noncapitalist path would have disadvantaged Brezhnev. Had the situation depicted in Figure 3 remained intact, the leaders would have needed to

		Aid countries on noncapitalist path?	
		Yes	No
Aid countries on capitalist path?	Yes	Podgorny	Kosygin
	No	Brezhnev	Mikoian

Figure 3. Stands on economic aid to Third World, October 1965

55. *SSSR i strany Afriki,* 217–20.
56. Tansky, "Soviet Foreign Aid," 771.
57. Legvold, *Soviet Policy in West Africa,* 234; on Sudan, *SSSR i strany Afriki,* 240. On Egypt, see the communiqué, September 2, 1965; Yaacov Roi, *From Encroachment to Involvement: A Documentary Study of Soviet Policy in the Middle East* (New York: Wiley, 1974), 418n.
58. Kovner, "Soviet Aid," 63. Tansky, "Soviet Foreign Aid," 775–76, includes a trivial grant of $3 million to Indonesia, a "socialist path" country. The original source for their data is the U.S. government.
59. Valkenier, *Soviet Union and the Third World,* 14.

shift to a compromise by sequential issue trading—by taking turns in either granting or denying economic aid to their preferred countries. Instead, in December 1965 Mikoian retired from his office as head of state and ended his public activities (though he continued as a nominal member of the Politburo until April 1966).

With Mikoian's retirement, the compromise by convergent concessions shifted to Podgorny's position. Kosygin conceded his rejection of aid to countries on the noncapitalist path, while Brezhnev conceded his opposition to aid for countries on the capitalist path. Politburo members began to speak more favorably of aid. The junior secretary whose April speech had signaled the retrenchment now called "support to developing states" an "internationalist duty," and in January even Suslov for the first time legitimated "economic aid to help the strengthening of economic independence."[60] Despite Kosygin's public advocacy of restricting aid for the radical Algerian regime to fulfillment of existing commitments,[61] in February 1966 a Soviet economic delegation led by a deputy chairman of Gosplan arrived in Algiers to study "the condition of the Algerian economy and [make] recommendations concerning the further development of the country." The delegation's work culminated in an agreement on August 4, 1966, that the Soviet Union would subsidize the construction of a new metallurgical factory.[62]

Since the differences over security could not be resolved by convergent concessions, they were compromised by a logroll that approved all leaders' policy recommendations. In contrast to economic aid, arms deliveries to the Third World increased steadily each year from 1963 through 1966.[63] Aid to armed rebels in Angola, Portuguese Guinea, and Rhodesia was accelerated during 1965.[64] Moreover, despite Mikoian's reservations,[65] Brezhnev's and Suslov's public support for armed rebellions led to a compromise with Cuba over armed struggle in Latin America. This compromise found expression in the communiqué of a meeting held in Havana "at the end of 1964" and attended by delegates of Latin American communist parties, who

60. Petr Demichev, December 25, 1965; Suslov, January 27, 1966.
61. December 18, 1965.
62. A. A. Shvedov and A. B. Podtserob, *Sovetsko-Alzhirskie otnosheniia* (Moscow: Progress, 1986), 119.
63. Kovner, "Soviet Aid," 69.
64. Galia Golan, *The Soviet Union and National Liberation Movements in the Third World* (Boston: Unwin Hyman, 1988), 269–72.
65. October 16 and 17, December 1, 1964.

endorsed "active support" for six armed rebellions in Latin America in return for an agreement not to accept the legitimacy of any party set up by a Maoist faction.[66]

Mikoian's payoff for the rejection of his stand on violence in the Third World was approval of his initiative for Soviet participation in the Second Afro-Asian conference. This logroll displayed the typical self-defeating feature. During 1965 the Soviet Union increased deliveries of money and weapons, begun the previous year, to the political organization that controlled a few thousand guerrillas who sporadically raided Portuguese targets in Angola. The aid was channeled through Alphonse Massamba-Debat's regime in Congo-Brazzaville,[67] exposing it to the risk of retaliation from Zaire and from the Portuguese in neighboring Cabinda. The Politburo asked Massamba-Debat to accept this risk at the same time that it rejected his requests for new economic aid under its general policy of denying aid to radical regimes. He retaliated by refusing to cooperate with Mikoian's effort to obtain an invitation for the Soviets to attend the Second Afro-Asian conference. Guinea, Mali, and Afghanistan also refused to support Soviet attendance, and joined Pakistan in backing a Chinese proposal to postpone the conference indefinitely.[68]

The separation of economic aid from other issues produced another paradoxical effect, self-frustrating for Soviet policy but competitively advantageous for Kosygin. The shift in economic aid toward countries on the capitalist path rewarded countries that disagreed with the Soviet ban of negotiations on Vietnam while penalizing countries that endorsed Soviet policy. When India and Afghanistan obtained large new aid commitments, their leaders used the occasion of visits to Moscow to press publicly for negotiations on Vietnam.[69] Of course, that was the position Kosygin wanted Moscow audiences to hear, and unsurprisingly, he openly endorsed the right

66. January 19, 1965. See also Levesque, *USSR and the Cuban Revolution*, 102–4.

67. John A. Marcum, *The Angolan Revolution*, vol. 2, *Exile Politics and Guerrilla Warfare, 1962–1976* (Cambridge: MIT Press, 1978), 383–85; D. L. Wheeler and René Pelissier, *Angola* (New York: Praeger, 1971), 211, 215; Levesque, *USSR and the Cuban Revolution*, 187–90.

68. See the communiqués of meetings with these countries, August 1, 16 and 26, September 2, October 12, December 20, 1965; William E. Griffith, *Sino-Soviet Relations, 1964–1965* (Cambridge: MIT Press, 1967), 128.

69. May 15, 1965. See also his May 14 reference to peace in "Asia." Also see Yusuf's speech, April 25, 1965, in which he called (as Kosygin had done after his return from Hanoi) for implementation of the proposal of the Cairo conference of nonaligned states for a new international conference on Vietnam, and the speech by the Afghan king, Mohammed Zahir Shah, August 7, 1965.

of neutralist Third World states to take their own positions on international questions such as Vietnam.[70]

When Kosygin's irruption into Third World issues isolated Podgorny in the policy bargaining during much of 1965, Podgorny became vulnerable to decisions by his rivals to deny him access to opportunities to go public. The sudden improvement in his bargaining position after Brezhnev joined the controversy over economic aid may explain why he replaced Mikoian as chair of the Supreme Soviet Presidium in December 1965. Although often regarded as a maneuver by Brezhnev to remove Podgorny from the post of the Central Committee secretary responsible for appointments, Podgorny's shift to the Presidium did offer him the competitive advantage of many more opportunities to give public speeches. Though whether the move was a gain or loss for Podgorny cannot be resolved, a feature of his rhetoric deserves notice. By building a reputation for advocacy of housing and public services many months before his move to the Presidium, Podgorny positioned himself as the public advocate of the activities administered by the hierarchy of soviets that would come under his management after December 1965. His focus on Third World countries, with which the Soviet Union often maintained contact through the exchange of parliamentary delegations, repeated his domestic positioning in foreign policy. Perhaps he realized well in advance that Brezhnev would not long tolerate a rival in the vital post of personnel secretary. In any case, the impression is hard to avoid that Podgorny was campaigning for his new office.

70. August 7, 1965. See also February 3, 1966.

*   Chapter 9

Shelepin and Sectarianism,
May 1966–November 1967

Logrolls that result in self-frustrating policies and descriptions of world conditions that events discredit should erode constituents' allegiances, making them available for recruitment by new leaders with new visions. After the XXIII Party Congress in April 1966, a fifth Politburo member, Aleksandr Shelepin, innovated a vision and grand strategy evidently designed for appeal to officials disaffected by Brezhnev's concessions on European issues after the failure of rapprochement with China, by Kosygin's compromises on reform and Brezhnev's on Vietnam, and by the defeat of Mikoian's proposals to restrict economic aid. Shelepin devised an identity that merged Kosygin's consumerist reformism with Brezhnev's heroic anticapitalism, standing for an adamant rejection of cooperation with noncommunists. He denied that revolutionary democrats could lead social transformations in the Third World and opposed any form of negotiation with capitalist governments in the First World. In Leninist terms, Shelepin became a sectarian.

Shelepin's espousal of a new sectarian strategy enables a direct test of whether going public by Politburo members shaped foreign policy. If going public was useless or harmful to a Politburo member, neither the public stances of the four senior members nor the policy compromises need have changed in response to Shelepin's initiative. If, however, going public provided bargaining leverage, to block Shelepin's entry into the inner circle of the Politburo the four senior members would have needed to alter their public stands and the compromise policy in order to demonstrate to Soviet officials who might have been considering a transfer of allegiance that Shelepin's sectarianism could not control policy.

Sectarianism: Shelepin's Novel Grand Strategy

"Sectarian" in Leninist terms meant barring coalitions not only with capitalists but also with anyone who was not a communist. Shelepin's sectarian grand strategy combined continued espousal of his earlier proposal for increasing military aid to the North Vietnamese communists with a new affirmation of the futility of economic aid to noncommunist Third World countries, regardless of their adherence to the noncapitalist or the capitalist path. He also began to deny the feasibility of protecting the Soviet Union by negotiations with capitalist powers, going so far as to assert that Nazis were increasing their influence on U.S. policy. At home he continued to champion consumerism and economic reform but set himself apart from Kosygin by arguing that Party cadres, not the government bureaucracy, should take responsibility for reform of economic administration. He reconciled the seemingly opposed policies of consumerism at home and adventurism abroad by patriotic appeals to pride in Soviet achievements, arguing that progress at home had so far outstripped that of capitalist societies that resources could be directed both to consumerism and to an expansion of military power to protect the spread of communist revolution abroad. Thus he tried simultaneously to displace Kosygin as the advocate of reform and Brezhnev as the champion of the communist cadre. Shelepin's distinctive standard for evaluation of policy confirms the limits he placed on appropriate coalition partners: "The CPSU measures all its steps and actions against the internationalist tasks of the world army of communists."[1]

The forum for Shelepin's attack on economic aid for the Third World was his trip to Mongolia in June 1966. Like previous Politburo speakers to the Mongolian audiences, Shelepin turned Mongolia into a synecdoche for the Third World, saying that Mongolia's "experience and example serve many peoples of Asia and Africa as a convincing answer how to avoid the capitalist stage of development." But Shelepin's view of the Mongol experience differed radically from previous interpretations.

1. June 9, 1966. See also October 29, 1966.

Unlike either Kosygin or Brezhnev, Shelepin repeatedly attributed
Mongolia's economic development to three factors: (1) the leadership of a working-class party that (2) had adopted "the ideas of scientific communism" and (3) had prohibited any capitalist activity in
Mongolia. To draw attention to his emphasis on the importance of
leadership by a mass proletarian Marxist-Leninist party, Shelepin
used emphatic language and repetition. He attributed Mongolia's
ability to build socialism "above all" to the Mongolian party's choice
of "the immortal teaching of Marxism-Leninism" as its "guiding
light." He ascribed to Lenin the belief that "the main thing" about
Mongolia's prospects for successful development was that the Mon-
gols "consolidated these successes by the creation of a people's revolutionary party." Shelepin said, "We want to emphasize again and
again that the immortal ideas of V. I. Lenin . . . are the most reliable
and victorious weapon of the working class and of the national liberation movement." Explaining Mongolia's development, Shelepin
added: "The essence of all the changes that went on in your beauti-
ful and grim land is that . . . you did not allow capitalism and barred
its entrance into your country forever."

Shelepin omitted any mention of one-sided aid from the Soviet
Union as a factor in Mongol development. To underline the omission, he neither visited the site of an extraction and processing plant
being built by Soviet work teams at Darhan nor mentioned the project in his speech. Shelepin's pointed neglect of the Darhan project
broke with the established pattern: the leaders of both previous Politburo delegations to Mongolia, Brezhnev and Shelepin himself,
had made special side trips to Darhan, and Kosygin had devoted an
extended passage to it in a speech about Mongolia in April 1965.[2]

Shelepin's version of the lessons to be drawn from Mongolia's
successful development contrasted with the lessons drawn earlier by
Brezhnev and Kosygin. Both had said that aid from "more developed socialist states." was among the prerequisites for "a transition
to socialism bypassing capitalism." Neither had included adoption
of "scientific socialism."[3]

Shelepin differed not only about what lessons should be drawn
but also about who was capable of learning. Whereas Kosygin said
that the example of Mongolia's noncapitalist path "has become fixed

2. Shelepin's visit, February 3, 1965; Brezhnev's visit, January 14, 1966; Kosygin's
comments, April 20, 1965.
3. January 16, 1966; April 20, 1965.

in the consciousness of *many peoples*," Shelepin said its experience had become "the guide to action for . . . *many other worker and communist parties* of backward countries."

Shelepin cited the Mongolian experience to reject Suslov's distinction between communist tactics in developing and industrial countries. Suslov and Ponomarev took the position that the weakness of the proletariat in underdeveloped countries precluded the formation of a communist party strong enough to lead the transition to socialism. According to Shelepin, Lenin "thought that the party of Mongol herdsmen would become a mass one and would be the condition of the success of their struggle, that from the herder elements in your country a proletarian mass would gradually be created. So it happened."

In sum, Shelepin's discussion of the noncapitalist path implied that Soviet economic aid was either unnecessary or futile. Leadership of a country by a communist party, the Mongol example proved, ensured its industrialization, despite the contrary opinions of "good-for-nothing prophets" whom "history has severely and mercilessly whipped." A country not led by a communist party could not progress toward socialism. Soviet aid was superfluous for the first country and futile for the second. This attack on foreign aid was a novel stand for Shelepin. His newfound opposition represented a break not only with the views of Brezhnev and Kosygin but also with his own past position: in December 1964 and January 1965 he had defended economic aid to Egypt.

Shelepin's view evidently found a responsive audience among Soviet communists, but it drew sharp criticism from both schools of experts on the Third World—both those who shared Podgorny's optimism concerning the ability of revolutionary democrats to make the transition to socialism and pessimists who shared Suslov's views about the limits of their potential.[4]

A few days after the XXIII Congress, R. A. Ul'ianovskii, deputy head of Ponomarev's International Department and a Third World specialist, attacked as "the worst kind of doctrinairism" the view that because Third World radicals' views diverged in some ways from "scientific" socialism, "consequently it would not at all be in the interests and goals of the common struggle to support national

4. See David E. Albright, *Vanguard Parties and Revolutionary Change in the Third World: Soviet Perspectives and Their Implications* (Berkeley: Institute of International Studies, 1990), 34–37.

revolutionaries." Ul'ianovskii specifically rejected "the assertion that in all cases and countries, the tasks of the general-democratic stage of the revolution, of agrarian and anti-imperialist transformations, cannot be carried out without direct leadership by the working class, without the presence of power in its hands."[5]

The intended audience of Ul'ianovskii's article is indicative of the domestic appeal of the position Shelepin would adopt. The article appeared in *Pravda*'s column "In Aid of the Propagandist," an aperiodic series aimed at the teaching staffs of the Communist Party schools, in which some fourteen million communists and nonparty activists were studying in 1966[6]. Even after a series of further articles denouncing the ideas expounded by Shelepin,[7] *Pravda* claimed that "many readers" were still requesting clarification of "the basic differences between the Marxist-Leninist teaching on socialism and petty-bourgeois conceptions" and asking for an explanation of "the vitality of nonproletarian views of socialism."[8]

Shelepin's sectarianism also was evident in his comments on relations with capitalist countries. Concurring with the general perception that West Germany harbored aggressive intentions, Shelepin advocated a unilateral response. Shelepin's position contrasted with the policy undertaken by Brezhnev and Kosygin, who led the Soviet delegation to the Bucharest session of the Warsaw Pact Political Consultative Committee in July 1966, which approved a new diplomatic initiative intended to secure West European governments' adherence to a program of restrictions aimed at German militarism and centered on the proposed European security conference.

In late 1966 Shelepin would endorse "the constructive proposals to ensure European security set forth in the Bucharest declaration."[9] But although he once briefly listed the initiatives,[10] he never discussed their merits in detail and never spoke in favor of achieving

5. "Sotsializm i natsional'no-osvoboditel'naia bor'ba," April 15, 1966.
6. "Nastoichivo ovladevat' marksizmom-leninizmom," August 2, 1966.
7. V. Korionov, "Usiliia, obrechennye na porazhenie," June 19; V. Tiagunenko, "Korennaia zadacha natsional'no-osvoboditel'nykh revoliutsii," August 28; Iu. Arbatov, "Stroitel'stvo kommunizma v SSSR i mirovoi revoliutsionnyi protsess," September 7; G. Kim and P. Shastitko, "Proletarskii internatsionalizm i natsional'no-osvoboditel'nye revoliutsii," September 14; E. Bagramov, "Leninskoe uchenie po natsional'nomu voprosu i sovremennost'," October 17, 1966.
8. Timur Timofeev, "Nauchnyi sotsializm i melkoburzhuaznaia ideologiia," October 24, 1966.
9. December 10, 1966.
10. October 19, 1966.

them by the diplomatic means of convening an all-European conference. Instead, Shelepin developed his own view of the appropriate response to the West German threat. "The calculations of West Germany's ruling circles are doomed to collapse. The Soviet Union and other socialist countries have enough forces and means at their disposal to return the resurrected 'geopoliticians' of the resurrected 'reich' to reason if necessary."[11] In contrast to Brezhnev's and Kosygin's emphasis on the readiness of European governments to cooperate with the Bucharest program, Shelepin noted only that "some state figures of the West, if one is to judge by the facts, so far have not drawn the appropriate conclusions from the results of the Second World War." Fortunately, he said, these persons were not in a position to act on their illusions: "Peace in Europe does not depend on those who are displeased with the outcome of the Second World War, and no one will succeed in changing the borders of European states."[12]

While he dismissed the prospects and the urgency of negotiations on European security, Shelepin used the Nazis as a synecdoche to represent politics in the United States, where "the economy is increasingly being reorganized on a military basis. In the country the militarist hysteria grows, an unprecedented orgy of racism and nationalism reigns, the forces of extreme reaction grow and organize. The groups that openly espouse fascist goals in the United States now number nearly a thousand." Shelepin then quoted George Lincoln Rockwell on the American Nazi Party's adherence to Hitler's political program.[13] Various Politburo members compared U.S. conduct in Vietnam to Nazi activities in World War II and it was not unusual to warn of resurgent Nazism in Germany, but Shelepin's warning of growing Nazi political power in the United States was unique in the Politburo. Shelepin drew no conclusions from his description of U.S. politics, but the warning alone sufficed to deny the merits of any policy alternative to his own recommendation for "revolutionary vigilance" to be ready for an impending attack.[14]

In addition to sectarian stands on relations with the Third World and with the West, Shelepin retained both the militant stand on Vietnam and "national liberation" and the consumerist policy at

11. June 3, 1966.
12. December 10, 1966.
13. June 3, 1966.
14. June 3, December 10, 1966.

home that had distinguished his statements during 1965. Although he opposed economic aid, he still promised aid to "oppressed nations in their sacred struggle for freedom." Shelepin again compared the Americans in Vietnam to "Hitlerite bandits" and expressed commitment to the fighting in the South and the goal of prompt unification. He repeated his principle of "necessary and ever-growing aid."[15] On the issue of a negotiated settlement he became even more rejectionist than the normally recalcitrant Soviet leaders, who favored talks on terms defined by the North Vietnamese. He described the "way out" of Vietnam for the Americans as unilateral withdrawal without negotiations: "The United States should withdraw its troops from Vietnam and begin to live up to the Geneva accords."[16] He again called increased consumer satisfaction "the main issue," the item that "stands first on the agenda."[17]

How could one reconcile militancy and rejection of alliances abroad with economic reform and diversion of resources to consumer production at home? When Kosygin and Podgorny advocated reform and shifts of resources to consumer satisfaction, they tried to portray the capitalist powers as less threatening than in the 1930s and recommended East-West negotiations, yet Shelepin saw the Nazis on the verge of taking power in Washington. Shelepin's solution to this problem was to assert that his policy recommendations, which the four core Politburo members had portrayed as incompatible, could all be carried out simultaneously because the Soviet Union was now strong enough to ignore the West. "The main thing is that the correlation of forces in the world has shifted even further in favor of socialism. The international prestige of the Soviet Union, its economic and defense power, and its political and moral influence in the world have risen to unprecedented heights."[18]

Shelepin's assessment of the relative power of the socialist and capitalist worlds was anything but ritualistic. In June 1966 the senior Politburo members expressed a range of views on this issue. Furthest from Shelepin and most critical of his view was Kosygin, who said, "It would be incorrect . . . to belittle the capabilities and potential of the United States."[19] Podgorny and Brezhnev agreed with Shelepin that trends favored socialism; but Podgorny said that it

15. June 3 and 9, October 29, December 10, 1966.
16. June 3, 1966.
17. June 23, 1966. See also October 29, December 10, 1966.
18. June 3, 1966. See also January 3, 1967.
19. June 9, 1966.

would not do to "underestimate the struggle against imperialism, which . . . still possesses great economic resources and significant military potential," and Brezhnev, too, warned that "the enemy's forces are not negligible."[20] Closer to Shelepin was Suslov, who included "the further growth of the might and international influence of the world socialist system" among "the leading tendencies in the course of world events," but even he warned that "individual detachments of revolutionary fighters sometimes suffer defeat and temporarily retreat."[21] The diversity was not attributable to variation in audience, as each speaker delivered his assessment of the world balance to meetings of electors preceding the pro forma elections to the Supreme Soviet.

Shelepin developed another innovative position to reconcile his view that leadership by a Marxist-Leninist party was necessary for economic progress in underdeveloped countries with his support for economic reform, presented by Kosygin as limiting Party intervention. Whereas for Kosygin the instrument of reform was the Soviet manager, for Shelepin it was the Communist Party and the individual worker. "If every Party organization and member and every worker and every toiler take it upon themselves" to shoulder the task, "a decisive turn toward improvement in quality . . . can be [achieved]."[22] Shelepin was ascribing the main role to the new subordinates he had acquired in December 1965, when he relinquished his position as head of the Party-state inspectorate and took over supervision of the consumer-related departments of the Central Committee staff.

The Construction of Opposition: Reform, Vietnam, Aid, and Europe

If going public was futile or perilous for a Politburo member, Brezhnev and Kosygin had nothing to fear from Shelepin's sectarianism and no reason to alter either their public stands or their policies. If going public provided bargaining leverage earned by winning constituents' loyalty, Brezhnev and Kosygin had much to fear. The failure of the main recommendations in their grand strategies—

20. June 1, 10, and 11, 1966.
21. June 8, 1966.
22. June 3, 1966.

reconciliation with China and rapprochement with the United States, respectively—and their compromises on the issues of counterescalation in Vietnam and economic reform at home were precisely the kind of developments that competitive politics theorists expect to turn constituents away from a leader.

Shelepin's challenge and Brezhnev's and Kosygin's resistance make sense only if all three were uncertain about the loyalty of the two senior leaders' constituencies. Given mutual uncertainty, Brezhnev and Kosygin could try to reduce their constituents' incentive to defect by removing the causes of disaffection. If these causes were their compromises on reform and Vietnam, they could eliminate the incentive to defect by realigning their positions on reform and Vietnam to coincide more closely with the stand taken by Shelepin. In other words, Kosygin could move toward Brezhnev on Vietnam in order to bolster Brezhnev's appeal to his constituents, since Kosygin's own constituents were unlikely to be attracted to Shelepin's aggressive posture on this issue. Conversely, Brezhnev was unlikely to lose constituents to Shelepin on the issue of reform and could therefore reciprocate by moving closer to Kosygin's position to bolster his appeal.

While Shelepin's stands placed him in direct competition with Brezhnev and Kosygin on the issues of Vietnam and reform, his antipathy to economic aid and his rejection of East-West negotiations offered opportunities for Brezhnev and Kosygin to resist his challenge by demonstrating to constituents that Shelepin's policy recommendations could not survive bargaining over policy. To display Shelepin's ineffectiveness, Brezhnev and Kosygin should have moved policy on economic aid and East-West relations in the direction opposite Shelepin's recommendations.

To control policy, Brezhnev and Kosygin needed the acquiescence of the other two core leaders, Podgorny and Suslov. Despite their disagreements with Brezhnev and Kosygin, each should have preferred a coalition with them to a coalition with Shelepin. Podgorny preferred their stands to Shelepin's rejection of aid to noncommunist Third World states and of negotiations with capitalist governments, while Suslov opposed Shelepin's rejection of coalitions with noncommunists in both world regions.

In short, if going public won bargaining leverage by attracting constituents, Shelepin's challenge should have caused Brezhnev and Kosygin to reduce or eliminate their disagreements on reform and Vietnam and to shift their policies on aid to the Third World and East-West negotiation in the direction opposite to his recommendations. Podgorny and Suslov should have agreed to these policy changes rather than form a coalition with Shelepin.

Reform

Did Brezhnev move toward Kosygin's position on reform? Between April 1966 and September 1967, when Shelepin was finally dropped from the Central Committee Secretariat, Brezhnev repeatedly praised the reform. He affirmed that "the reform exerts a salutary effect on the economy" and that factories operating under the new rules "stand out from the rest by the superior results of the work."[23] Brezhnev even demanded loyal implementation of the industrial reorganization by his supporters in the Communist Party hierarchy. Saying that "Party organizations are called to help" Communists learn the new management techniques, Brezhnev added, "Communists working in the economy should understand that their efforts to turn the Party's economic policy into reality are one of the main indicators of their Party attitude toward the cause today."[24] Brezhnev's expression of support for reform remained nuanced in various ways, but his statements became much more positive.[25]

Suslov and Podgorny manifested little change in their respective positions on the issue. Suslov's first statement on the reform only noted the compromise combining centralization with increased initiative from below, and he spoke no words of praise for the reform until November 1966.[26] Podgorny, however, repeatedly "dwelt at length on the [reform] issues of further improvement in planning, strengthening and development of economic methods and stimuli in regulation of the economy, skillful management, economizing in everything."[27]

Brezhnev's reduction of the ideological distance between himself and Kosygin narrowed the bargaining range on the issues of institutional reorganization and resource allocation, and as a result policy in both areas shifted toward Kosygin's stated preferences.

The reform program envisioned gradual transfers, first of individual factories and later of whole "branches" of industry (consisting of factories producing similar products), to new rules of management

---

23. October 16, 1966. See also May 18, June 11, November 2, 1966; January 14, April 19, 1967.
24. November 2, 1966. See also June 11, November 30, 1966.
25. For his reservations, see May 20, November 30, 1966; January 14, 1967.
26. June 8, November 3, 1966.
27. June 1 and 10, 1966; March 4 and 10, 1967.

and new criteria for evaluation of performance, published in February 1966. As one would expect if bureaucrats disaffected by compromise were registering their attitudes by interfering with execution of policy, actual transfers of plants to the reform fell far behind the schedule announced in April 1966 by Kosygin, who expected to transfer enterprises employing a third of the industrial work force to the new system by early 1967. In fact, by November 1966, only 673 enterprises employing 10 percent of the industrial work force and producing 12 percent of industrial output had made the transition.[28] The slowdown was the result of a "moratorium" on transfers announced on August, ostensibly in response to "numerous difficulties, particularly with regard to supplies and marketing," experienced by the first enterprises to make the transition.[29] A sign of Brezhnev's intention not to make an issue of the reform at this time was his restraint from seizing upon these difficulties as an argument for delaying the reform.

The head of state planning announced a revised schedule in November 1966.[30] Apparently this new schedule was met. By the end of the first quarter of 1967, 2,500 enterprises producing a fifth of all output had made the transition; during the rest of the year the reform was carried out at another 4,500 enterprises producing another fifth of all industrial output. For 1968, the reformers envisaged transferring whole *glavki* ("main administrations" controlling factories with similar production profiles) to the new rules and extending the reform from its initial concentration in light and food industries to heavy industry.[31]

While the reform went forward during 1967, a decisive shift took place in resource allocation, favoring the consumer goods industries promoted by both Kosygin and Shelepin but formerly opposed by the other core leaders. The September 1967 plenary session of the Central Committee approved a revision of the 1966–1970 plan, for the first time elevating the rate of growth of the group B industries (those producing mainly processed foods and consumer goods) above the rate of growth of group A industries (producing producers' goods). This decision resulted in a transfer of resources from agriculture to

28. N. Baibakov, "Vnedrenie khoziaistvennoi reformy—vazhneishaia zadacha," November 4, 1966. Another source gives 8 percent of output: Ed A. Hewett, *Reforming the Soviet Economy: Equality versus Efficiency* (Washington, D.C.: Brookings, 1988), 236.
29. G. E. Schroeder, "Soviet Economic 'Reforms': A Study in Contradictions," *Soviet Studies* 20(1968): 5.
30. Baibakov, November 4, 1966.
31. Kirilenko, April 23, 1967; Schroeder, "Soviet Economic 'Reforms,'" 5.

the production of consumer goods. During the first three years of the plan, the amount invested in agriculture was almost 20 percent less than the amount originally authorized.

This decision is commonly attributed to the bumper crop of 1966, which diminished the urgency of food problems, and is represented as a defeat for Brezhnev (the leading advocate of agriculture's investment priority).[32] This interpretation, however, overlooks the evidence that Brezhnev's policy preferences had changed in response to Shelepin's challenge. Before the XXIII Congress Brezhnev had said that his agricultural investment program represented a long-term commitment and had specifically warned against relieving pressure in other sectors by diverting funds from agriculture.[33] Now he publicly advocated the expansion of funding for consumer goods, announcing in March 1967 that "more resources are allocated to the development of light industry," and promising further increases.[34]

Vietnam

Kosygin reciprocated by closing the ideological gap between himself and Brezhnev on Vietnam. As a result, the restraints on aid to Vietnam relaxed.

After May 1966, Kosygin virtually adopted Brezhnev's former position on policy toward Vietnam. He now said that American conduct in Vietnam "reminds us of the actions of the Hitlerites in occupied territories."[35] In July he even endorsed the principle of overt military intervention.[36] After July, like both Shelepin and Brezhnev, Kosygin promised "ever-increasing aid and support" to defeat "American aggression."[37] Kosygin continued to affirm that the war foreclosed any "improvement of Soviet-American relations."[38] Kosygin now saw no possibility of a negotiated settlement. He depicted American statements in favor of Vietnam talks as a deception intended to mitigate domestic opposition to the war.[39] In February

32. Werner G. Hahn, *The Politics of Soviet Agriculture, 1960–1970* (Baltimore: Johns Hopkins University Press, 1972), 190–97.
33. E.g., September 30, 1965.
34. March 11, 1967. See also June 11, 1966.
35. May 17, 1966.
36. July 15, 1966.
37. July 15, 1966. See also August 4, October 14, December 9 and 21, 1966; March 7, July 4, 1967. For Brezhnev's statements, see July 2, October 16, November 2 and 16, 1966; March 11, April 19, 21 and 25, May 13, 1967.
38. June 27, 1967. See also December 5, 1966.
39. May 17, 1966. See also August 4, 1966.

1967 Kosygin did support an informal feeler by the North Vietnam's foreign minister expressing willingness to begin talks after an unconditional halt to the bombing, but after the United States resumed bombing, Kosygin reverted to his earlier position.[40] When asked after the Glassboro summit whether he foresaw an end to the fighting in the near future, he answered tersely, "I would not say so."[41]

Podgorny and Suslov maintained their earlier positions on the war, except now that Kosygin had shifted toward Brezhnev's stand, Podgorny accepted a loosening of the restrictions on arms aid: "If it is required, our aid will be increased and intensified."[42]

Soviet policy on aid to Vietnam became regularized. Rather than respond to each American escalation with ad hoc aid agreements, the Soviets began to conduct what appeared to be annual aid negotiations at the end of the summer in 1966 and 1967.[43] Each of these negotiations produced an agreement to increase military and economic aid according to the "ever-increasing" principle. The dollar value of military deliveries rose 40 percent from 1966 to 1967.[44] In the first six months of 1967, the Soviets delivered 60 percent more SAMs than they had delivered in all of 1966, 77 percent as many artillery pieces, and 75 percent as much ammunition. With the completion of the North Vietnamese air defense network, only aircraft and radar deliveries declined.[45]

Third World Economic Aid

While Brezhnev and Kosygin changed their positions on reform and Vietnam to eliminate the incentive for their respective constitu-

40. February 11, March 7, June 20, 1967. Kosygin's public statements correspond to private behavior. In February, Kosygin privately encouraged Brezhnev to accept a U.S. concession, sent through Harald Wilson, to stop the bombing without demanding an end to Vietnamese infiltration from the north, but when the United States reneged, Kosygin reverted to describing the situation as "hopeless": George C. Herring, ed., *The Secret Diplomacy of the Vietnam War* (Austin: University of Texas Press, 1983), 398–401.

41. June 27, 1967. For Soviet unwillingness to pass along U.S. peace feelers, see Herring, *Secret Diplomacy*, 66–67, 506.

42. June 10, 1966. See also January 29, 1967. Podgorny used "necessary aid" in speeches on March 4, 7, and 10 and May 31, 1967, and "ever-increasing" aid only on June 2, 1967. For statements by Suslov, see June 8, November 3, 1966; January 6, 1967.

43. Aid agreements were reported on October 4, 1966, and September 24, 1967.

44. William Zimmerman, "The Korean and Vietnam Wars" in Stephen S. Kaplan, ed., *Diplomacy of Power* (Washington, D.C.: Brookings, 1981), 345.

45. CIA, "A Review of the Situation in Vietnam," December 8, 1967, Lyndon B. Johnson Library, Austin. Only statistics for the first half of 1967 are provided in this source.

ents to defect to Shelepin, on Third World economic aid they tried to show constituents that Shelepin could not gain approval of his policy recommendations. Their instrument was a new policy of increased engagement in the Third World.

Kosygin anticipated Shelepin's challenge by shifting to a new stand in favor of aid to developing countries on both the noncapitalist and capitalist paths of development. He first expressed this attitude in late April 1966, during a visit from the prime minister of a new, more radical Syrian government that had seized power in February 1966. Having opposed aid to countries on the noncapitalist path throughout 1965, he now said, "We accord great significance to development of Soviet-Syrian collaboration in both the political and the economic areas."[46] Kosygin now explicitly declared himself in favor of promoting industrial development in a variety of Third World countries, and even gave priority to "peoples who have chosen the path of noncapitalist development."[47]

Kosygin's shift also showed up in his descriptions of the USSR's relations with India. Through he continued to cite relations between the two countries as "an example of collaboration of states of different social orders," Kosygin now also described those ties "as an example of the collaboration and cohesion of forces of world socialism and the world national liberation movement."[48] Similarly, the Tashkent conference now became a synecdoche for more than "resolution of real disagreements between states. . . . Tashkent showed also that developing countries have no more reliable friends than the socialist countries."[49] The change in Kosygin's interpretation of the larger meaning of Soviet policy toward India directly addressed the issue raised by Shelepin's sectarianism: whether coalitions with noncommunist governments could further Soviet aims.

During 1966 Kosygin repeatedly rebutted Shelepin's arguments against coalitions with noncommunists in the Third World. Countering Shelepin's argument that the absence of an industrial working class condemned backward countries to political instability, Kosygin said, "History testifies that only active participation of workers at all levels of the population in determining their country's fate forms the basis of the success and stability of the regime as a whole."[50] Soviet

46. April 20, 1966.
47. May 12, August 4, 1966. See also April 20, May 13, 18, and 19, June 9, July 29, August 4, December 24 and 27, 1966.
48. July 15 and 16, 1966.
49. July 15, 1966.
50. April 21, 1966.

economic aid, moreover, far from being futile, promised to create the social conditions that Shelepin claimed ensured political stability: "The Soviet Union favors economic aid and economic collaboration of a kind that . . . helps other countries to create their own national industry, and this in turn ensures employment of workers."[51]

Countering Shelepin's insistence that development could be achieved only by the exclusion of foreign capital, Kosygin represented Soviet economic aid as a means of offsetting imperialist influence. "The lever that [imperialist powers] most often use [to prevent development] is so-called economic aid. . . . Therefore it is important that economic collaboration not be converted into political pressure." Responding to Shelepin's denial of the possibility of industrialization by regimes not led by communist parties, Kosygin said that the Soviet people "know well that Indians are talented people who have become accustomed to working hard and productively. We believe in their strength and their potential to find a solution to any task."[52]

Brezhnev backed Kosygin by repeatedly calling for "solidarity with liberated countries, assisting the consolidation of their national independence and social progress."[53] These statements represented a change in Brezhnev, as they made no distinction between countries on the socialist and capitalist paths.

Suslov and Podgorny, too, backed Kosygin. In June 1966 Suslov identified himself with aid to noncapitalist countries by meeting a secretary of Mali's Soudanese Unity Party and promising "measures . . . to strengthen the economic independence of the Republic of Mali."[54] His associate Ponomarev advocated economic aid and criticized Shelepin's sectarian position by asserting that unless the "experience" of Third World radical parties was taken into account, "the development of the theory of Marxism-Leninism in contemporary conditions is impossible."[55] Podgorny tried to define the category of states eligible for economic aid even more broadly than Kosygin, adding "young independent states of Africa," which did not figure in Kosygin's policy.[56]

---

51. December 27, 1966. See also May 13, June 9, July 15, August 4, 1966.
52. July 15, 1966. See also August 4, December 5, 1966; July 20, September 26, 1967.
53. November 16, 1966. See also June 11, November 2, 1966; April 25, July 6, November 4, 1967.
54. June 14, 1966. See also Ponomarev's meeting with the Syrians, February 12, 1967.
55. June 3, 1966; November 1 and 16, 1967. See also April 13, 1967.
56. June 1 and 10, September 20 and 23, 1966; June 2, October 3, 1967. Less clear

Policy on economic aid shifted sharply against Shelepin's recommendations. During 1966 and 1967 significant new aid commitments were extended to Syria, Egypt, Mali, India, Iraq, Algeria, Morocco, Turkey, Ethiopia, Afghanistan, Pakistan, and Iran. The series of new aid commitments raised the total for 1966 to $1.24 billion, or double the 1965 amount.[57] At the same time, the new aid policy fell far short of Podgorny's preferences. Visitors from Zambia, Upper Volta, Cambodia, and Somalia obtained only symbolic commitments or none at all; significantly, the Zambian delegation was promised only a continuing supply of arms for the Zimbabwean rebellion.[58]

Adoption of this policy enabled Brezhnev and Kosygin to secure a continuing flow of information contrary to Shelepin's description of the world situation. Documents signed with foreign delegations during 1966 repeatedly affirmed that economic aid would produce trade benefits for the Soviet Union, registered progress toward industrialization along both socialist and capitalist paths, and demonstrated the support of developing countries for many Soviet foreign policy goals. New aid commitments dropped sharply in 1967, but by that time a substantial public record had been built discrediting Shelepin's position.

East-West Issues

Brezhnev and Kosygin rejected Shelepin's unilateralist approach to security in Europe. Their instrument was the "Bucharest program," a policy of diplomatic engagement in Europe adopted by the members of the Warsaw Treaty Organization in July 1966.

The Bucharest program consisted of seven proposals in four categories. First was expansion of East-West economic and technological

---

are Podgorny's statements of October 27, 1966, and February 28 and July 6 and 7, 1967, when he "sincerely" or "warmly" wished Morocco, Ethiopia, and Cameroun "success . . . in the development of their independent national economy and culture." Such expressions of sympathy for economic development often signified a tactful refusal of aid, but the meetings produced initial Soviet commitments to both Morocco and Ethiopia, though apparently not to Cameroun.

57. Milton Kovner, "Soviet Aid to the Developing Countries: A Look at the Record," in J. W. Strong, ed., *The Soviet Union Under Brezhnev and Kosygin* (New York: Van Nostrand Reinhold, 1971), 63; Leo Tansky, "Soviet Foreign Aid: Scope, Direction and Trends," in *Soviet Economic Prospects for the Seventies* (Washington, D.C.: Government Printing Office, 1973), 768, 775; April 26, May 19, June 3 and 14, July 17, August 4 and 5, September 29, October 29, December 27, 1966; March 3, June 4, October 5, 1967.

58. August 27, September 29, 1966; February 18, June 7, 1967.

collaboration. Second was a pair of military proposals: (*a*) simultaneous abolition of NATO and of the Warsaw Treaty Organization, or of their military organizations as a first step, and (*b*) partial measures such as troop reductions. Third was a set of three proposals aimed at the so-called threat posed by West Germany: (*a*) prevention of any access by West Germany to nuclear weapons, (*b*) acceptance of the principle that peace depended on the stability of postwar borders in Europe, and (*c*) negotiation of a German peace treaty. Fourth was a proposal to negotiate all of these substantive points at a conference of all European states. Bilateral contacts among East and West European governments were encouraged to pave the way for the conference at some future date. "As for participants in such discussions, the Warsaw Treaty states make no exclusions. Whether or not to participate in the discussion and resolution of European problems is a matter for each state to decide."[59]

The Bucharest program was a logroll among the four core Politburo members: each promoted those elements of the program that fitted his grand strategy. Although Brezhnev now reversed his former opposition to negotiations between the Warsaw Pact and NATO countries, he continued to pose as the heroic anticapitalist, concerned with security above everything else. Adopting a stand in favor of "assurance of European security" by "joint efforts of all European states," he justified this shift by claiming to perceive a change in the world situation, in the form of "new forces, new countries, new longings, new people . . . in Europe" prepared to cooperate with Soviet peace initiatives.[60] Of the seven points in the Bucharest program, however, Brezhnev endorsed only the three aimed at building a European coalition against West Germany. He demanded three actions by West Germany as conditions for peace in Europe: recognition of the permanence of European borders, recognition of the sovereignty of the GDR, and renunciation of nuclear weapons.[61] After accepting inclusion of the European conference in the Central Committee's report to the XXIII Congress, Brezhnev waited more than a year to endorse the conference again.[62] Brezhnev also disagreed with the principle of "no exclusions" from the conference.

59. "Deklaratsiia ob ukreplenii mira i bezopasnosti v Evrope," July 9, 1966.
60. June 1 and 11, October 16, 1966. See also November 16, 1966; March 11, April 19, 21, 25, November 4, 1967.
61. June 1, 1966. See also October 16, 1966; January 14, March 11, April 19 and 25, July 6, 1967.
62. April 27, 1967.

He said that "the issue of military threat will be taken off the agenda" in Europe "if constant interference in European affairs by foreign forces whose goals have nothing in common with the vital interests of European peoples is eliminated." The "foreign forces," of course, were groups influential in the United States.[63]

With a grand strategy of encouraging rather than limiting East-West cooperation, Kosygin took a noticeably more positive stand toward the Bucharest program.[64] He explicitly endorsed the "all-European conference" almost a month before the Bucharest declaration.[65] He remained the Politburo member most favorable to inclusion of the United States in negotiations, although his stand was nuanced. Kosygin avowed that "assurance of European security depends, in our opinion, above all on the European states themselves,"[66] but he carefully avoided Brezhnev's language asserting that European security required elimination of the interference of "external" or "transoceanic" forces. He left open the issue of U.S. participation in the conference: "It seems to me that this is a question that the European countries themselves should decide."[67]

Kosygin also differed from Brezhnev in endorsing all seven Bucharest proposals, which he repeatedly called "broad and in our opinion realistic."[68] Besides endorsing the three points that Brezhnev favored, Kosygin saw "a realistic prospect of relaxing military tension in Europe by abolishing military alliances or, as a first step, abolishing their military organizations and also by eliminating foreign military bases on the European continent."[69]

Kosygin's espousal of the economic point of the Bucharest program led to a renewal of his continuing disagreement with Brezhnev over the relative priority of security and economic goals. Kosygin's proposals for expansion of East-West trade had from the start incorporated active hostility to the Common Market. Kosygin rejected the possibility of negotiation of trade arrangements between the Com-

63. June 1, 1966. See also October 16, November 2, 1966; March 11, April 25, May 13, 1967.

64. June 18, 1966. See also July 15, August 4, December 21, 1966; March 17, 16, and 21, July 4 and 9, 1967.

65. June 18, 1966. See also July 15, August 4, December 21, 1966; March 16, 17, 21, July 4 and 9, 1967.

66. June 14, 1966. See also June 18, July 1, 1966.

67. December 5, 1966. See also December 3, 1966.

68. July 15, 1966. See also August 4, October 14, 1966; February 7, 1967.

69. October 14, 1966 (see also June 18, August 4, December 5, 1966; February 7 and 9, September 21, 1967); August 4, 1966 (see also February 7, 1967).

mon Market and CMEA; he said, "Closed markets bring no advantage to Europe. Therefore we must have markets that give all European states an opportunity to collaborate on completely equal terms."[70] Brezhnev argued, by contrast, that economic integration of European capitalist states could further Soviet security goals: "It is altogether obvious that such plans are depended upon to strengthen European capitalism. . . . But something else is obvious too. At the same time these plans disrupt the united front of world capital, opening new opportunities . . . to broaden the struggle for peace and security in Europe and throughout the world."[71]

Finally, Kosygin differed from Brezhnev on the desirability of bilateral East-West contacts. "The Soviet Union's efforts to strengthen European security open additional opportunities also for development of bilateral relations between the Soviet Union and Western states," Kosygin said.[72] He endorsed a broader range of bilateral contacts than Brezhnev. Brezhnev tended to approve contacts with France, Italy, "and others"; Kosygin spoke for developing ties with England, Japan, and Canada as well as the small states of Europe.[73] And Kosygin even held out hope of West Germany's cooperation with the Bucharest program.[74]

Once again, Kosygin framed his discussion to muster opinion against Shelepin's sectarian unilateralism. Kosygin defended negotiations as keeping Soviet enemies off balance: "Active political and diplomatic struggle . . . complicates the imperialists' implementation of their plans."[75] Although he joined Shelepin in exaggerating the threat of a resurgence of Nazism in West Germany, Kosygin rejected the unilateralist response. Kosygin called the National Democratic Party's entry into the Bavarian and Hessian state parliaments "one more signal that should alarm even the most complacent."[76] But whereas Shelepin wanted the Soviet Union to respond by "revolutionary vigilance," Kosygin said, "The Soviet Union will struggle together with other states that hold dear the cause of European security and peace against a revival of fascism in West Germany."[77]

70. December 5, 1966; February 11, 1967. See also March 21, 1967.
71. April 25, 1967.
72. August 4, 1966.
73. Cf. Kosgyin, August 4, 1966, with Brezhnev, January 14, 1967. Brezhnev's March 11, 1967, election speech mentions a broader range of "state visits" but subordinates the bilateral ties to the preparation of the multilateral contacts.
74. August 4, 1966.
75. October 14, 1966.
76. December 3, 1966.
77. December 3, 1966; February 11, 1967. See also March 7, 1967.

Podgorny welcomed the Bucharest proposals as "a concrete program of peaceful settlement of urgent European problems and creation of a stable system of security in Europe,"[78] but he never explicitly endorsed the "all-European conference." Instead he favored the provision calling for bilateral diplomacy with West European states. Podgorny continued to depict opportunities for dividing the NATO allies. In a series of European capitalist countries, he said, "sentiment is turning increasingly in favor of collaboration free from discrimination and confinement within a bloc."[79] While avoiding endorsement of the conference, however, Podgorny loyally conformed to the compromise policy by privately pressing his West European counterparts to accept the conference proposal.[80]

When Podgorny paid official visits to Austria and Italy, the program of bilateral contacts authorized at Bucharest gave him an opportunity to unveil a distinctive program for East-West trade that recapitulated his earlier effort to make economic contacts serve security interests in the Third World. In contrast to Kosygin's assertion that trade and peace were mutually reinforcing, Podgorny repeatedly said that "mutually advantageous economic, scientific-technical, and trade ties between states foster . . . peace."[81] He dissociated East-West trade from Kosygin's objective of accelerating Soviet economic growth, instead holding out the Soviet market as a lure to persuade West Europeans to reorient their security policies away from the United States. Rather than ask the capitalists to absorb Soviet machinery, Podgorny offered them markets for their own industrial products, to be paid for by Soviet raw materials and fuels.[82] Trade with the USSR, he argued, would sustain employment without requiring the sacrifice of political independence allegedly incumbent on states that participated in trade regimes sponsored by the United States or by West Germany.[83]

Suslov and Ponomarev were restrained in their approval of the Bucharest program because of its effects on the European communist parties, which were the principal instruments of their grand strategy. The divisiveness of the Bucharest program was the reason given for summoning European communist parties to a conference

78. June 10, 1966. See also March 4 and 10, May 31, June 2, 1967.
79. March 4, 1967.
80. See communiqués of meetings in which he participated: July 1, November 22, 1966; January 31, July 9, 1967.
81. January 26, 1967. See also January 25, 28, and 29, 1967.
82. January 28 and 29, 1967.
83. November 18, 1966. See also November 17 and 19, 1966; January 28, 1967.

at Karlovy Vary in April 1967.[84] West European communists felt at least three concerns. First, they feared that if they became identified with the Bucharest program, West Europeans would feel confirmed in their suspicions that the communist parties were merely tools of Soviet diplomacy. "During preparations for the present conference, individual parties expressed fears that we might narrow the prospects of mobilization of the masses . . . if we discussed issues of peace and security . . . at a conference of communist parties."[85] A second concern was that diplomatic contacts with the Soviet Union would increase public approval of West European governments and consequently diminish the popular appeal of communist parties' electoral platforms.[86] "Our fraternal parties in the countries of the 'Common Market'" also worried that if the Common Market were disbanded, as Kosygin insisted it must be, industrial workers in the member states would suffer.[87]

With Ponomarev saying that Soviet policy toward capitalist states should be evaluated by its "approval within the fraternal Marxist-Leninist parties," Suslov and Ponomarev approved the security goals agreed upon at Bucharest (they were shared by the European communists) but did not favor multilateral negotiations and only tepidly acknowledged bilateral ties between the Soviet Union and West European governments as "of course a positive fact."[88]

One observer has characterized the change in Soviet European policy in June 1966 as a shift from a "relatively subdued" phase to a "new policy line" aimed at "a European settlement that would . . . exclude the United States from any substantial influence in European affairs."[89] This change has customarily been attributed to the Soviet's recognition of the strains within the Atlantic Alliance caused by the Vietnam conflict and evinced by Charles de Gaulle's dramatic expulsion of NATO headquarters from France. But this explanation is insufficient.

84. See Brezhnev's speech at Karlovy Vary, April 25, 1967.
85. Janos Kadar, April 29, 1967. See also the statements by the Italian Luigi Longo and by Ulbricht.
86. April 25, 1967.
87. Speech of John Hollan, April 28, 1967. See also the speech by Luigi Longo, April 29, 1967.
88. June 3, 1966. See also June 8, October 3, 1966.
89. Thomas W. Wolfe, *Soviet Power and Europe, 1945–1970* (Baltimore: Johns Hopkins Press, 1970), 280–81. For an elaborate list of all the foreign policy considerations supposed to have influenced the Soviets' adoption of the Bucharest program, see Lawrence L. Whetten, *Germany's Ostpolitik: Relations between the Federal Republic and the Warsaw Pact Countries* (London: Oxford University Press for the Royal Institute of International Affairs, 1971), 69–71.

Favorable international circumstances did count in the Politburo's policy choices. Had de Gaulle been unwilling to visit Moscow, had Harold Wilson not compensated for his rejection by the Common Market with overtures to the East, had the Italian government not tried to draw the sting from left criticism by its diplomacy toward the socialist countries, the Politburo would presumably have pursued some other policy. But as indicated by the disagreement over reliance on unilateral mobilization to guarantee Soviet security or on an attempt to exploit disunion among the capitalist governments, the effect of these favorable foreign circumstances was to enhance the persuasiveness of the policy favored by the coalition of senior leaders over Shelepin's recommendation that these international circumstances be ignored.

Whether this coalition would even have formed in the absence of the need to counteract Shelepin's sectarianism is doubtful. The Bucharest proposal for a European conference has been generally and accurately described as a Soviet attempt to compete with the United States for hegemony in Europe.[90] Until Shelepin's challenge, three of the four leaders who backed the Bucharest program had preferred grand strategies other than competition with the United States for the loyalty of Europe. Kosygin had advocated incorporation of the United States in a general program of East-West cooperation, Brezhnev had opposed cooperation with both Europe and the United States, and Suslov had favored diplomatic proposals that would force the West European governments into the arms of the United States in order to make communist parties appear more convincing representatives of European interests. Meanwhile, the one leader who earlier had favored competing with the United States for the cooperation of West European governments, Podgorny, did not advocate the European conference. It was a policy no one wanted.

90. Gerhard Wettig, *Europäische Sicherheit: Das Europaeische Staatensystem* (Cologne: Bertelsmann Universitätsverlag, 1972), 36–38; John Erickson, "The Soviet Union and European Détente," in Kenneth Dyson, ed., *European Détente: Case Studies of the Politics of East-West Relations* (New York: St. Martin's Press, 1986), 175–77; Kenneth Dyson, "The Conference on Security and Cooperation in Europe: Europe before and after the Helsinki Final Act," in ibid., 87; Robert Legvold, "France and Soviet Policy," in Herbert Ellison, ed., *Soviet Policy toward Western Europe* (Seattle: University of Washington Press, 1983), 80–83; Robert H. Donaldson, "An Analysis of the Warsaw Pact Conference Proposals," in Louis J. Mensonides and James A. Kuhlmann, eds., *The Future of Inter-bloc Relations in Europe* (New York: Praeger, 1974), 68; Mojmir Povolny, "The Soviet Union and the European Security Conference," *Orbis* 18(1974): 202–4.

The Course and Consequences of Shelepin's Decline

The core leaders' demonstration of Shelepin's inability to control foreign policy paved the way for his demotion from the Secretariat at the Central Committee meeting in September 1967. Before he could be removed, the advocates of sectarianism squared off against the coalition in favor of engagement in the Third World and Europe at two sessions of the Central Committee in December 1966 and June 1967. The striking feature of these clashes was the central role of foreign policy rather than domestic issues in determining the outcome of Shelepin's bid for leadership. Symbolism and logrolling shaped the policies that maintained the coalition responsible for Shelepin's defeat.

At its December meeting the Central Committee, having heard Brezhnev deliver an unpublished review of foreign policy activity during 1966, approved a resolution that achieved unanimous acceptance only by an agreement to paper over all controversial issues. The published text expressed "approv[al of] the position of the Politburo and Soviet government on the Vietnam issue" and confirmed the abandonment of attempts at reconciliation with China. The text did not address policy toward the Third World; it mentioned European security only as "an important task" to be undertaken according to the "principles" established at Warsaw in January 1965 and at Bucharest; as the Warsaw meeting had given priority to the unilateral policy and the Bucharest session to the negotiating strategy, this passage simply agreed with both contending points of view.[91]

Conforming to the agreement reached at the December session to defer resolution of the dispute, the Politburo members agreed to refrain from going public. Although its members reached out to constituencies beyond the Central Committee membership, they confined themselves to unpublished speeches at gatherings of territorial organizations of the Party. The December 1966 plenum was the only one during the first three post-Khrushchev years to be followed by the dispatch of all full Politburo members across the country to discuss what had happened.

The June 1967 session heard the sectarians confront the adherents of engagement again. Symbols that displaced objective conditions in policy making produced policy failures that opened the door to the

91. "O mezhdunarodnoi politike SSSR i bor'be KPSS za splochennost' kommunisticheskogo dvizheniia," December 14, 1966.

sectarians' attack on the policy of engagement, while the gains from logrolling held together the coalition that successfully resisted the new challenge.

Both the Bucharest program in Europe and the new aid policy in the Third World substituted synecdoches for objective circumstances facing the Politburo. France and de Gaulle stood for the readiness of capitalist Europe to break its ties with the United States. As Kosygin said, "a strong and independent France that decides for itself alone what is useful to it and what, on the contrary, is against its national interests" is "a most important factor of international and above all European security."[92] In actuality, however, as de Gaulle told the Politburo in public, he sought to mediate an accommodation between the Soviet Union and the United States while remaining firmly on the Western side, not to draw Europe into separate negotiations with the Soviets.[93] As long as the Soviets' proposed European conference excluded the United States, it was a nonstarter. That was one reason for Brezhnev and Suslov to agree to the Bucharest proposal.

Throughout the Khrushchev and early Brezhnev years, the Aswan High Dam in Egypt stood as a symbol of Soviet ties to the Arab world. In December 1964, even Shelepin had called it "the living and eternal symbol of Soviet-Arab friendship."[94] When the coalition of senior leaders launched their initiative to increase economic aid in April 1966, they tried to repeat the symbolism of Aswan by promising to build the Syrians a dam on the Euphrates.[95] Although the new dam symbolized the continuity with past actions in the Third World that the anti-Shelepin coalition was trying to communicate, attention to the symbolism of the dam displaced awareness of objective conditions in the Third World.

The promise of economic aid to the new Syrian regime was an integral part of an attempt to demonstrate the ability of noncapitalist Third World countries to promote Soviet security by assembling an alliance of four "progressive" Arab states: Syria, Egypt, Iraq, and Algeria. From its inception the Soviet plan for an alliance was hampered by conflicts among the four participants, and the promise to build a dam on the Euphrates only exacerbated the tensions be-

92. December 3, 1966.
93. June 21, 1966.
94. December 29, 1964; for other instances, see December 25, 1964; January 11, August 25, 1965; May 13 and 18, 1966; October 27, 1967; January 19, 1971.
95. April 26, 1966.

tween Syria and Iraq. A dam would both diminish the flow of irrigation water to Iraq and place the upstream Syrians in a position to
control the flow.[96] Consequently, when the Iraqi prime minister arrived in Moscow in July, he displayed no public interest in Kosygin's proposal for an alliance of Arab progressives, despite Kosygin's offer to assist hydraulic projects in Iraq.[97] Kosygin recognized
the tensions among the Arabs, reportedly responding in frustration
to Iraqi complaints about the Syrians: "It would be better if you
spent less time hitting each other over the head and more time hitting Israel on the head."[98]

With the channel of economic aid dammed, the coalition against
Shelepin turned to Kosygin's idea of using Israel to open a new
channel to an alliance of Arab progressives. In May 1967, the Soviet
ambassador approached Nasser with a false intelligence report that
the Israeli army was mobilizing on the Syrian frontier. The deception induced Nasser to stage a military demonstration in Sinai.[99]
When this move brought Israeli and Egyptian forces into direct confrontation, the Soviet leaders reportedly urged Nasser to confine
himself to "political" forms of struggle. Nasser accordingly ordered
the troops to withdraw, deploying them in vulnerable road convoys
just at the moment when the Israeli government decided on a preemptive attack.[100] "To summarize," writes Jon Glassman, "in the
weeks before the Six-Day War Soviet diplomacy had played a dangerous game that had backfired."[101]

Within days after the defeat of the Soviets' Arab allies, at a plenary session of the Central Committee the first secretary of the Moscow committee, N. G. Egorychev, renewed the sectarians' criticism
of the coalition policy. In a speech not published at the time,

96. John Waterbury, "Dynamics of Basin-wide Cooperation in the Utilization of
the Euphrates," typescript (January 1990), 16–17.

97. July 29, 1966; for the agreement on water projects, see the communiqué, August 4, 1966.

98. Mohamed Heikal, *The Sphinx and the Commissar: The Rise and Fall of Soviet Influence in the Middle East* (New York: Harper & Row, 1978), 166.

99. William B. Quandt, "Lyndon Johnson and the June 1967 War: What Color Was
the Light?" and Richard B. Parker, "The June 1967 War: Some Mysteries Explored,"
Middle East Journal 46 (1992).

100. Dan Schueftan, "Nasser's 1967 Policy Reconsidered," *Jerusalem Quarterly*, no. 3
(Spring 1977), 137.

101. The Arabs' allegations against the Soviets and the background to the war are
carefully examined in Jon D. Glassman, *Arms for the Arabs: The Soviet Union and War in
the Middle East* (Baltimore: Johns Hopkins University Press, 1975), 39–43. The quota-
tion is on p. 43.

Egorychev accused the coalition of having exaggerated the extent of progressive social transformation in Egypt. He called Nasser's threats against Israel "careless and irresponsible" and asked for a "more demanding" Soviet policy toward the Arabs. Rehearsing Shelepin's arguments, he linked excess confidence in noncommunist Third World movements with inadequate attention to Soviet defenses. His speech was understood as a personal attack on Brezhnev, and during the interval between sessions, Brezhnev persuaded Central Committee members already scheduled to speak to rebut Egorychev, who the next day tendered his resignation as Moscow first secretary. When asked why he surrendered so easily, Egorychev later told an interviewer: "The Moscow committee must not sow dissension in the unity of the Party. And I understood that the whole Party had placed its confidence in Brezhnev."[102] Recognizing the futility of further resistance, Shelepin then accepted demotion to head of the trade union council.[103]

Why did a disastrous Middle East policy produce a political victory for the coalition of the senior leaders? One reason is that the sectarians failed to go public with their attack, trying to exploit their opportunity in private bargaining inside the Central Committee without generating outside leverage. The failure to go public was not necessarily a mistake. When Egorychev said there were "people who held about the same views as I did," he referred to a constituency that Shelepin had been trying to mobilize for more than a year. Shelepin had failed to convince the core leaders that he had enough loyal supporters so that the senior leaders must concede him a place in the bargaining over policy. When Brezhnev's mobilization of the rebuttal during the Central Committee session showed that the senior leaders continued to disbelieve that even the failure of their Mideast policy would alter the distribution of adherents, Shelepin conceded defeat. The shared uncertainty that had justified his challenge had been resolved.

102. "Poslan Poslom," *Ogonek*, February, 4–11, 1989. Rumors of the contents of this speech misled previous analysts, who argued that Egorychev called for more energetic measures on behalf of the Arabs (Harry Gelman, *The Brezhnev Politburo and the Decline of Détente* [Ithaca: Cornell University Press, 1984], 97; Malcolm Mackintosh, "The Soviet Military: Influence on Foreign Policy," *Problems of Communism* 22 [September–October 1973]: 6–7) or that Soviet military aid had been a waste of resources (Wolfe, *Soviet Power and Europe*, 339n.).

103. July 12, 1967. When, a "few days" earlier, Brezhnev and Suslov proposed the transfer, Shelepin says, "I answered that I had never chosen my work and had never refused any": "Istoriia—Surovyi uchitel'," *Trud*, March 19, 1991.

The coalition itself remained solid because the logroll continued to give each of its members opportunities to promote his grand strategy in public. The Soviet reaction to the Mideast crisis allowed Brezhnev, Kosygin, and Podgorny to engage in a division of labor that enabled each to claim credit for the effectiveness of his grand strategy. Brezhnev was authorized to convene an assembly of the Warsaw Treaty leaderships, which the Central Committee characterized as having "confirmed again that joint actions of socialist states are a powerful factor in the struggle against the aggressive intrigues of international imperialism."[104] Kosygin received authorization to go to New York for the special session of the U.N. General Assembly and even to conduct, at long last, an informal summit with President Johnson at Glassboro. Podgorny handled the negotiations with the nonaligned nations, conducting three summits with the Arab leaders plus two meetings with Tito.[105] These meetings produced documents giving Podgorny credit for strengthening "friendship and collaboration" between Arab countries and the Soviet Union.[106]

Soviet crisis management remained the logroll among the three leaders. The forum was a special session of the U.N. General Assembly lasting more than a month. Initially Soviet policy called on the General Assembly to adopt a three-point resolution condemning Israel as the aggressor in the Six-Day War, demanding withdrawal of all troops to the positions held at the onset of fighting, and requiring Israel to pay immediate, full compensation for all losses suffered by the Arab states.[107] When the proposal failed to command much support beyond the socialist countries and the Arabs, Kosygin and Gromyko obtained authorization to make a concession to nonaligned states that tried to broker the disagreement between the U.S.-Israeli coalition and the Warsaw Treaty and Arab states. Despite Brezhnev's public insistence that all three demands be pressed,[108] Kosygin spoke no more about Israeli aggression and compensation and concentrated on withdrawal of troops as the first priority.

Brezhnev evidently swapped the concessions to Kosygin in return

104. June 9, 1967; "O politike Sovetskogo Soiuza v sviazi s aggressiei Izrailia na Blizhnem Vostoke," June 22, 1967.

105. June 22, 25, and 26, July 4 and 5, 1967.

106. June 25, July 5, 1967. An exception was the Syrian notice (July 4, 1967), which said only that issues of strengthening friendship and collaboration had been examined.

107. Kosygin, June 20, 1967; "O politike Sovetskogo Soiuza v sviazi s aggressiei Izrailia na Blizhnem Vostoke," June 22, 1967.

108. Cf. Brezhnev, July 6, 1967, with Gromyko, July 5, 23, 1967, and Kosygin, July 9 and 20, 1967.

for Kosygin's acceptance of Soviet rejection of a West European proposal for a ban on further arms shipments to the belligerents. The rejection manifested Brezhnev's principle that the Soviet Union should provide military aid to armed struggles against "colonialism in the Third World." Podgorny also received concessions when Kosygin publicly attributed Soviet policy at the U.N. to "conversations and meetings with representatives of almost all Arab countries" and rejected President Johnson's proposal at Glassboro to link "the whole complex of issues" in Arab-Israeli relations.[109] Together with support by Kosygin and Gromyko for the resolution of the nonaligned states, these positions instantiated Podgorny's global strategy: the Soviet Union should give preference to coalitions with the nonaligned countries over cooperation with the United States.

If Soviet foreign policy during 1966–1967 was shaped by concerted efforts of the senior leaders to block Shelepin's bid for membership in the Politburo's inner circle, Shelepin's expulsion from the Secretariat in September 1967 should have brought Brezhnev's coalition with Kosygin to an end. In fact, Brezhnev and Kosygin resumed their public contest.

Brezhnev, who had spoken favorably of economic reform while the threat from Shelepin loomed, now denounced "reformists and revisionists."[110] Kosygin resumed his attempts to seize the peace issue. A relatively brief summary of a speech in Kishinev at the beginning of October repeated six times that peace must take priority over all other goals. Drawing the connection between peace abroad and economic progress at home, Kosygin now once again sought "an end to the United States' war in Vietnam" rather than victory, as well as "stable relaxation of tension in Europe."[111] During the next six months, Brezhnev and Kosygin faced off in what George Breslauer has called "a multi-issue polemic."[112]

The breakdown of their coalition presaged reversals on all the foreign policy issues affected by Shelepin's challenge: West Europe, the Third World, even Vietnam. During 1968 the Soviets stopped pressing for an all-European conference on security and cooperation. This loss of interest has been attributed to Soviet preoccupation with the

---

109. June 27, 1966.
110. November 4, 1967.
111. October 3, 1967.
112. George W. Breslauer, *Khrushchev and Brezhnev as Leaders* (London: Allen & Unwin, 1982), 176–78.

Prague Spring,[113] but it was predictable if the conference proposal had been a policy that no one wanted and each had agreed to only because sectarianism could not be countered without an offer of some compromise alternative. At the same time, the Soviet Union sharply reduced new commitments of economic aid to the Third World. The estimated value of Soviet military aid to Vietnam in 1968 dropped to 40 percent of the 1967 total.[114]

113. Raymond L. Garthoff, *Détente and Confrontation* (Washington, D.C.: Brookings, 1983), 112–13; Robin Alison Remington, *The Warsaw Pact* (Cambridge: MIT Press, 1971), 114–15; A. James McAdams, *East Germany and Détente* (Cambridge: Cambridge University Press, 1985), 95–96.

114. Zimmerman, "Korean and Vietnam Wars," 345.

★ Chapter 10

Brezhnev Turns to Détente,
1970–1972

During 1970–1972 both the domestic visions and the grand strategies of the four members of the Politburo's inner circle underwent realignment. While Suslov, Podgorny, and Kosygin continued to pursue their various designs of reliance on foreign communists, isolation of the United States, and global cooperation based on the mutually reinforcing effects of security agreements and economic exchange, Brezhnev radically altered his former stands. Even as he tried to preserve his established reputation for heroic anticapitalism, Brezhnev turned into the leading proponent of East-West détente by selectively incorporating variants of policy recommendations formerly identified with Kosygin. At the same time Brezhnev's new policy recommendations displayed a second significant trait: he was careful to position them at a median more acceptable to Suslov and Podgorny than Kosygin's earlier proposals on the same issues.

By the end of 1969, new international and domestic conditions lent persuasiveness to proposals for a new foreign policy of East-West détente. In the United States Richard Nixon had taken office with a strategy of negotiating the withdrawal of ground forces from Vietnam through Moscow and Beijing while offering economic inducements for Soviet and Chinese cooperation. In West Germany Willy Brandt had taken office with a strategy of negotiating in Moscow to work out compromises that would permit expansion of contacts with Eastern Europe and particularly the GDR. Exchanges of gunfire along the Sino-Soviet frontier had dramatized the impossibility of looking east for a grand alliance. The reinvigoration of NATO had made proposals to split Western Europe from the United States seem less promising. Yearly deployments of two hundred ICBMs, authorized in 1965, had secured strategic parity with the United States. An economic slowdown, intensified by bureaucratic obstruction sponsored by Politburo critics of the reform adopted in 1965, put pressure on the leadership to seek credits and technology abroad.

Though these new conditions favored a shift to détente, circumstances seem insufficient to explain it. If domestic and international circumstances alone motivated Brezhnev's change, why did the other three leaders, facing the identical circumstances, not change with him? Though conditions external to the political collectivity seem insufficient to explain a change in only one contender's grand strategy at a time, such a shift is predicted by competitive politics theory. A leader encounters an opportunity to change the grand strategy when events diminish the persuasiveness of rivals' strategies to their constituencies. All competitors' grand strategies lose persuasiveness over time, but not necessarily at the same rate. A competitor who achieves ascendancy in the contest may recognize a unique opportunity to expand his or her constituency. Because constituents react to a lead in the contest independently of their evaluation of the contenders' relative appeal, disaffected constituents of rivals become available for recruitment by an ascendant leader who selectively incorporates variants of the rivals' policy recommendations. While preserving the reputation established earlier by continuing to advocate policies with which he or she has already become identified, the ascendant leader chooses new policy recommendations that fall at a midpoint between the grand strategies of rivals. The rivals do not change their own strategies for fear of alienating their constituents further by seeming to be inconsistent. The combination of constituency expansion and strategic position should enable the ascendant leader to dominate bargaining over policy.

Brezhnev's move into the median with new policy recommendations produced a new foreign policy of détente. The Politburo abandoned the ban, imposed within four months of the ouster of Khrushchev, on publicly admitted bilateral negotiations with the United States and West Germany. This ban had not prohibited unpublicized contacts, which were frequent, nor had it barred public participation with the United States in multilateral negotiations, such as the crisis management of the 1967 Arab-Israeli war that culminated in a Johnson-Kosygin summit or the U.N.-sponsored talks that produced the Non-Proliferation Treaty of 1968. In response to Brezhnev's change of strategy, the Politburo lifted its earlier ban, turning to eager pursuit of negotiations on a wide range of security and economic issues with both the United States and West Germany.

New Elements in Brezhnev's Grand Strategy

In both domestic and foreign policy Brezhnev broke dramatically with the images of the situation and the policy recommendations he had offered during the first eighteen months after the removal of Khrushchev. In domestic policy Brezhnev combined his standing opposition to economic reform with a new espousal of a variant of Kosygin's consumerism.[1] In foreign policy, while continuing to present himself as the leader most supportive of military programs and most able to sustain the socialist alliance, Brezhnev abandoned his former rejection of East-West cooperation in favor of advocating diplomatic initiatives toward the United States, West Germany, and other capitalist states.

Reiterating his commitments to the alliance with other socialist states and to coalitions with "anti-imperialist" states and movements fighting for "liberation," in April 1970 Brezhnev recommended "development of mutually advantageous collaboration" with capitalist countries and resolution of international conflicts by negotiation. He changed his description of world conditions. In contrast to the pessimism of his earlier warnings about growing preparations for a new war, Brezhnev now said, "We have every reason to look optimistically on the development of the international situation." Optimism did not, however, justify a policy of pressure on the capitalist world. "Of course, all this does not mean that one may forget or minimize the danger that imperialism presents. Imperialism will not collapse of itself, automatically. No, it is still strong." Like Kosygin's earlier assessment of the continuing strength of capitalism, this statement justified a policy of negotiations.[2]

Negotiations had become possible, Brezhnev said, because "a new

1. George W. Breslauer, *Khrushchev and Brezhnev as Leaders* (London: Allen & Unwin, 1982), 179–99.
2. April 15 and 22, 1970.

political situation has developed" in the capitalist countries. In contrast to his earlier view that capitalist governments would negotiate only under popular pressure, if at all, he now began to say that "even in the ruling circles of a series of capitalist countries warnings can increasingly be heard that it is better to take care, better not to expand hotbeds of dangerous tension, but to think of more realistic paths of foreign policy."[3] Like Kosygin earlier, he began to affirm the capability of "reasonable" capitalist elites and their publics to control the "influential circles that try to hinder plans for peace and collaboration."[4]

Describing new circumstances, Brezhnev now emulated Kosygin's earlier calls for international cooperation on security issues. He now spoke in favor of "the replacement of military blocs and groupings by systems of collective security."[5] This had been the element of the Bucharest program to which Brezhnev had objected most strongly in 1966. In 1965 he had used realist logic to criticize Kosygin's view that international collaboration could prevent war. In 1971 he adopted a variant of Kosygin's former proposal.

Brezhnev combined these new elements in his grand strategy with statements that preserved his established reputation for heroic anticapitalism. He continued to call the alliance of socialist countries "the decisive barrier" to war, and he continued to insist that "we will render all necessary aid to those who fight for their freedom and independence."[6] Moreover, while incorporating variants of Kosygin's proposals for international cooperation, Brezhnev maintained differentiation by his proposals on two issues: the objectives of arms control and the priority of security over economics in East-West negotiations.

Occupying the Median on Arms Control

Whereas Brezhnev had once insisted that the war in Vietnam precluded bilateral economic or diplomatic cooperation with the United

3. April 22, May 8, 1970. See also June 13, August 29, 1970; May 27, June 12 and 17, December 9, 1971; June 6, November 2 and 14, December 1 and 22, 1972.
4. December 22, 1972; May 15, 1971. See also November 25, 1970; March 31, December 9, 1971; March 19, 1972.
5. June 12, 1971. See also June 13, 1970; October 30, 1971; June 28, December 22, 1972.
6. April 22, June 13, 1970. See also April 16 and 22, August 29, November 30, 1970; March 31, May 15, 1971; June 6 and 28, November 14, December 1, 15, and 22, 1972.

States, he now became the principal advocate of strategic arms limitation talks (SALT). In April 1970 he said, "We consider that even in the conditions the prevail today, when the world is divided into states with different social and political structures, when socialism and capitalism are locked in political and ideological struggle in the international arena, practical steps in the direction of disarmament can and should be taken."[7]

Brezhnev's newfound enthusiasm for "practical steps" on arms control incorporated a position formerly found in Kosygin's statements but not in his own or those of Podgorny or Suslov, who had limited their endorsements of arms control to the abstract principle of disarmament. At the same time Brezhnev distinguished his arms-control recommendations from Kosygin's.

In 1967 Kosygin had advocated negotiating restraints on offensive weapons but allowing continued development of strategic defenses, specifically antiballistic missiles (ABMs). Compromising with Johnson at Glassboro, Kosygin had then proposed that the negotiations should couple defensive and offensive limits.[8] The negotiations now endorsed by Brezhnev reversed Kosygin's 1967 priorities. In the initial rounds of negotiations during 1970, the Soviet delegation willingly accepted U.S. proposals for an agreement on ABMs while rejecting proposals for limits on offensive arms and proposing to defer those limits to a later stage of the talks.[9] Moreover, the agreement to begin talks on *limiting* future deployments of strategic arms preserved existing Soviet forces against Kosygin's May 1970 assertion that the talks should also encompass "reducing strategic arms."[10]

When an exchange of letters between Kosygin and Nixon in January 1971 resolved the U.S.-Soviet disagreement over coupling offensive and defensive limitations, Brezhnev found a new proposal to maintain the difference between his proposals and Kosygin's. Commenting in early January 1971 (before the exchange of letters with Nixon), Kosygin had said that the USSR "would welcome a reasonable agreement" without any "unilateral advantages."[11] Kosygin's statement could be interpreted as a call for a symmetrical arms-con-

7. April 15, 1970. See also March 31, June 12, 1971; March 19, 1972.
8. February 11, June 27, 1967.
9. Raymond L. Garthoff, *Détente and Confrontation* (Washington, D.C.: Brookings, 1983), 133–51; Chalmers M. Roberts, "The Road to Moscow," in Mason Willrich and John B. Rhinelander, eds., *SALT* (New York: Free Press, 1974), 28.
10. May 5, 1970.
11. January 3, 1971.

trol agreement. Two months later Brezhnev added a condition: equal security. "Talks on disarmament, especially when very delicate military technical matters are to be discussed, can be productive only if the security interests of both sides are taken into account equally and no one seeks unilateral advantages."[12] In March 1972 he repeated that "the key to their success is recognition by both sides of the principle of equal security."[13]

Soviet negotiators would interpret Brezhnev's principle of "equal security" as entitling their side to a variety of unilateral concessions to compensate the Soviet Union for supposed strategic advantages enjoyed by the United States, such as easier access to the open seas, the British and French nuclear deterrents, and Europe-based U.S. tactical aircraft technically capable of carrying nuclear bombs to Soviet territory. According to a Soviet commentator, the principle of equal security "makes it possible to fix the essential parity of the balance of strategic arsenals . . . while permitting certain possible inequalities in certain individual systems of strategic weapons."[14] The ultimate agreement compensated the Soviet Union with allowances for extra submarine-launched ballistic missiles and about three hundred "heavy" land-based missiles, unmatched by any U.S. equivalent.[15]

Brezhnev's "equal security" made his arms-control proposals more acceptable to Podgorny and Suslov than the alternative recommended by Kosygin: prohibition of unilateral advantages. When Podgorny and Suslov, neither of whom ever endorsed strategic arms limitations during 1970 or 1971, finally expressed approval of the ABM Treaty and of the interim agreement on offensive weapons at the Presidium's ratification ceremony in September 1972, both drew attention to the agreements' combination of "equal security" and "no unilateral advantages." Suslov even called these principles "the chief point" in the two agreements. He then asserted, "The Soviet

12. March 31, 1971.
13. March 19, 1972.
14. G. A. Trofimenko, "Voprosy ukrepleniia mira i bezopasnosti v sovetsko-amerikanskikh otnosheniiakh," *SShA: Ekonomika, Politika, Ideologiia,* 1974, no. 9 (September), quoted in Kenneth A. Myers and Dimitri Simes, "Soviet Decision-Making, Strategic Policy, and SALT," ACDA-PAB-243, Final Report (December 1974), 97; and their discussion, pp. 97–100. For an example of a Soviet demand for compensation for putative American advantages, see Garthoff, *Détente and Confrontation,* 162–63.
15. Garthoff, *Détente and Confrontation,* 157–58, 162.

Union will never concede any kind of infringement of the principle of equal security" in future arms control talks.[16]

Preserving a Reputation in Arms Control

While commitment to the principle of equal security positioned Brezhnev's recommendations between Podgorny and Suslov's opposition to arms control and Kosygin's proposals, expressions of commitment to arms programs helped to preserve his reputation for special attentiveness to defense needs. Brezhnev recognized that his incorporation of variants of Kosygin's recommendations for East-West cooperation would alienate supporters of the military in its hostile stance toward the West. A change in his attitude toward the desirability of identifying himself with military symbolism is evident in his choice of audiences. In 1965, 1966, and 1967 he had spoken at the Kremlin receptions for graduates of military command and staff colleges. From 1970 to 1972 Brezhnev avoided these speeches entirely, leaving Defense Minister Andrei Grechko to make brief remarks.

Brezhnev also displayed dwindling concern for the military leadership's preferences by rejecting Grechko's arguments against a strategic arms treaty. In contrast to such diplomatic agreements as the treaty with West Germany and the European security conference, which Grechko endorsed,[17] strategic arms control would directly affect military programs. In February 1971, when Kissinger and Dobrynin were privately negotiating the "equal security" deal, the defense minister went public in an apparent effort to mobilize opposition to an arms-control treaty. He cited historical precedent to cast doubt on the likelihood that the negotiations would succeed. When Lenin had offered peaceful coexistence, "this deeply humane initiative, corresponding to the vital interests of all peoples, was rebuffed by international imperialism." He also expressed suspicion of U.S. intentions. "The imperialists refuse to recognize," he wrote, that the Soviet armed forces could defeat any attack. Substantiating his suspicions of U.S. intentions by listing U.S. deployments of strategic offensive forces, Grechko evidently considered accurate information insufficient to prove his point. At a time when U.S. tactical air forces,

16. September 30, 1972. See also August 24, 1972.
17. May 9, 1970. See also February 23, September 2, November 8, 1970; February 23, April 3, May 9, November 8, 1971; February 23, May 9, November 8, 1972.

including all services and reserves, numbered 6,251 aircraft, Grechko alleged that the Pentagon possessed "25,000 other aircraft."[18] This exaggeration stood for expansion of offensive capabilities "aimed at the Soviet Union and other socialist countries" which remained the United States' top strategic priority. "Imperialism," Grechko concluded, "has always aimed and always will aim at smashing socialism and at changing the correlation of forces in its favor."[19]

In June, Brezhnev explicitly rejected those views:

> People may say: But the Soviet state advanced such proposals more than once in the past, too, but they were not accepted by the other side. Does this not testify to the unreality of disarmament plans and of limitation of the arms race in a world where capitalism still exists and where imperialists continue to exert no small influence on the international situation?

In an argument typical of leaders wrestling with the problem of expanding their constituencies with new appeals while preserving the reputations that appealed to their original constituencies, Brezhnev claimed that the success of his original proposals had changed world conditions in a direction that justified his new proposals. "Only a few years ago," he said, the U.S. imperialists had "seriously hoped" that an arms race would enable them both to dominate the international arena and to impede Soviet economic progress. "Now the failure of our enemies' plans has become completely apparent. Now everyone sees that socialism is powerful enough to ensure both reliable defense and development of the economy." Furthermore, "even the richest capitalist country, the United States of America, is increasingly feeling the negative economic and political effects of an unrestrained arms race." Because the excessive costs of defense were a concern to the public and "even to a portion of the ruling circles of Western states," arms limitation "becomes a more realistic cause than before."[20]

While rejecting criticism of his arms-control diplomacy, Brezhnev also proffered both symbolic and material benefits to officials concerned about military strength. Though he avoided occasions for

18. House Committee on the Armed Services, *Hearings on Military Posture and H.R. 3818 and H.R. 8687*, 92nd Cong., 1st sess., HASC no. 92-9 (Washington, D.C.: U.S. Government Printing Office, 1971), 2575.
19. February 23, 1971.
20. June 12, 1971.

public speeches that would dramatize the inconsistency between his contemporary posture and his earlier appeals to military audiences, Brezhnev kept his fences mended with supporters of the military by private speeches. In March 1970 he gave an unpublished "big speech" to the assembled high command at a ceremony marking completion of major military maneuvers.[21] Immediately after meeting Kissinger to agree on the agenda for the May 1972 summit, which would finalize the arms-control agreements, Brezhnev addressed another unpublished speech to a two-day conference attended by Grechko and by the senior command and political officers of the armed forces.[22]

In public speeches Brezhnev promised to protect military programs. In May 1970 he called further strengthening of the armed forces "our sacred duty."[23] He explicitly denied that SALT need interfere with this duty. In June 1971, calling attention to the fact that Washington had "reached several very major decisions on augmenting its strategic forces" even while the talks were in progress, Brezhnev rejected U.S. demands that the Soviet Union halt its own "programs already adopted."[24] During the May 1972 summit, Brezhnev followed through on his promise to protect ongoing strategic programs by rejecting U.S. treaty language that would have interfered with deployment of the SS-19 missile, instead proposing ambiguous wording that ultimately legalized the deployment.[25]

Although Brezhnev's pledge to protect ongoing strategic programs from SALT was less desirable from Grechko's standpoint than Brezhnev's earlier justification of military programs with hostile descriptions of U.S. intentions, Brezhnev's pledge encouraged Grechko to soften his public opposition to arms control. Now Brezhnev held that "further development of the defense industry and concrete programs for its activity will depend to a great extent on the international situation."[26] Grechko preferred to have the "constant strengthening of the Armed Forces" depicted as "an objective necessity . . . deriving from the established regularities of social development and the specificities of class struggle between capitalism and socialism."[27]

21. March 15, 1970.
22. April 26, 1972.
23. May 27, 1970. See also June 13, October 3, 1970.
24. June 17, 1971. See also April 15, 1970.
25. See Harry Gelman, *The Brezhnev Politburo and the Decline of Détente* (Ithaca: Cornell University Press, 1984), 134; Garthoff, *Détente and Confrontation*, 169–74.
26. March 31, 1971.
27. April 3, 1971. See also February 23, 1972.

Even so, with Brezhnev promising to protect arms programs, Grechko's 1972 article for Armed Forces Day omitted the objections to SALT that he had voiced in February 1971. Without revising his interpretation of the United States' warlike intentions, Grechko shifted his focus from the nuclear threat of U.S. missiles and bombers to the conventional threat posed by NATO's land and air forces in Europe. He also confirmed agreement on continuing military programs, now saying that the continuing obligation to strengthen the armed forces was "undisputed."[28]

Occupying the Median on East-West Issues

Negotiations on strategic arms control formed a component of a general program of diplomatic initiatives toward the capitalist world. Brezhnev's espousal of this program represented a sharp break with his 1965–1967 effort to minimize East-West contacts. Brezhnev now actively pursued closer ties with the United States and West Germany, linked contacts with France into the German-American initiative, and revived the proposal for a European security conference—but from June 1970 he no longer excluded U.S. and Canadian participation. This program incorporated major features of Kosygin's earlier foreign policy posture, but, as in the case of arms control, Brezhnev adopted a variant designed to be more acceptable to Suslov and Podgorny. Another parallel to his strategy in arms control was a provision for retaining the appeal he had originally used to motivate supporters—in this case, his self-presentation as the leader capable of ensuring the cohesion of the socialist commonwealth.

Brezhnev's East-West program contained both bilateral and multilateral initiatives. Having sought to wall off the socialist countries from the West during 1965–1967, he now switched to advocating bilateral contacts with West Germany, the United States, and France as well as other capitalist countries. This stance included advocacy of concessions on disputed issues. Though he had claimed throughout 1965–1967 that U.S. intervention in Vietnam precluded bilateral agreements with the United States, and though the fighting still continued, he now said, "We proceed from the viewpoint that improvement of relations between the USSR and the U.S.A. is possible."[29] In October and November 1970 he called Franco-Soviet collaboration "a

---

28. February 23, 1972.
29. March 31, 1971. See also June 13, 1970; June 12, 1971; March 19, 1972.

significant achievement."[30] In November he endorsed "some invigoration of contacts with England" and noted opportunities for developing ties with Italy and other European countries.[31]

Having formerly described West Germany as the main source of the threat of war, Brezhnev argued from May 1970 on that the FRG "can make a substantial contribution" to peace in Europe.[32] Referring a month later to "certain hopeful prospects" in negotiations with West Germany, he proposed to continue talks with its representatives, with the result that the two countries signed the Moscow Treaty on Renunciation of Force in August 1970. In the same speech Brezhnev justified the key Soviet concession that later made possible the conclusion of the treaty.[33] He noted that the "cardinal issue" was "inviolability of frontiers" in Europe. "Inviolability" was the West Germans' term, denoting a commitment not to attempt forcible revision of boundaries but refusing the earlier Soviet demand, once sponsored by Brezhnev, for agreement on "immutability" of borders, understood as also prohibiting peaceful revisions.[34] After the signing, Brezhnev again praised the treaty's "clear and unambiguous recognition of the inviolability of the existing frontiers in Europe, including the Oder-Neisse line [Poland's western frontier] and the borders of the GDR."[35] Later Brezhnev defended the treaty against criticism that it contained excessive concessions. "It must be said that the opinions encountered in some places as to which side 'won more' and which 'less' are in our view completely unfounded. All won equally."[36]

Brezhnev was no less eager to identify himself with the multilateral approach to East-West diplomacy. In contrast to his resistance in 1965 to the Polish proposal for a European security conference, during 1970 he repeatedly said that the conference was "becoming ever more topical" and called attention to the favorable response from the West European countries. In contrast to 1966–1967, when Brezhnev had depicted the conference as a means of ending U.S. interference in Europe, after April 1970 he ceased to accompany his

30. November 20, 1970. See also October 3, 1970.
31. November 30, 1970.
32. May 8, 1970.
33. June 13, 1970.
34. N. Edwina Moreton, *East Germany and the Warsaw Alliance* (Boulder, Colo: Westview, 1978), 150–52.
35. August 29, 1970.
36. October 3, 1970. See also June 17, 1971; December 22, 1972.

discussions of the conference with attacks on outside governments that allegedly opposed peace in Europe.[37]

While altering his grand strategy to incorporate variants of policy recommendations formerly identified with Kosygin, Brezhnev also designed his East-West program to be more acceptable than Kosygin's to such rivals as Podgorny and Suslov. The feature of Brezhnev's program tailored for this purpose was his proposal to schedule achievement of security goals before pursuit of economic goals. Podgorny had argued for subordinating economic contacts to security interests, and Suslov had argued that the main purpose of East-West collaboration should be prevention of nuclear war because of this program's appeal for European publics. Kosygin, by contrast, had argued that security negotiations and trade expansion were mutually reinforcing and should proceed in tandem.

Brezhnev's placing of security issues ahead of economic collaboration was evident in his discussion of the German treaty, the European conference, and bilateral relations during 1970. The main subject of discussion in the talks with the West Germans, he said, was a guarantee that German territory would never again become a source of war. Depicting the treaty as a means of blocking revanchist forces, Brezhnev named his goal of "inviolability of borders" as the main objective for a European security conference.[38] Brezhnev raised the issue of "development of mutually advantageous economic relations and cultural ties" only after the German treaty was signed.[39] While commenting favorably (during his speech to the XXIVth Party Congress in March 1971) on the "significant scale" of trade with a variety of capitalist countries, Brezhnev still noted that unresolved security issues (territorial disputes and foreign bases) were delaying the development of trade with Japan.[40] It was only during Brezhnev's trip to France in October 1971, when he had already secured the Politburo's assent to his program on arms control and European security, that he began to emphasize "read[iness] . . . for such measures as would ensure the carrying out of large projects and the growth of Soviet-French trade for ten or even twenty years ahead."[41]

Podgorny and Suslov made explicit their approval for the prece-

37. November 30, 1970. See also April 4 and 15, May 8, June 13, November 25, 1970.
38. May 8, June 13, 1970.
39. November 30, 1970.
40. March 31, 1971.
41. October 28, 1971. See also October 29, 1971.

dence of security over economics in Brezhnev's program. During the Moscow summit in May 1972, Podgorny even disagreed with Brezhnev in front of Nixon to underline the precedence of security issues. When Nixon tried to convince the Soviet leaders that they could not obtain an expansion of U.S.-Soviet trade without first accepting a SALT agreement, Brezhnev and Kosygin insisted that trade was important in its own right. Podgorny then entered an even stronger objection that "SALT was more important than commercial ties because it dealt with national security." When Brezhnev accepted this correction but added that trade was still important, Podgorny repeated that the security issue must be given priority.[42] In November 1970 Suslov said that initiatives in Europe that others justified as encouraging East-West trade drew their significance from the particular importance of preventing nuclear war. Later Suslov said of the German treaty, "Obviously if the treaty does not go into force, then the FRG, having lost political confidence, would also lose its significance for the Soviet Union as a serious partner in economic relations."[43]

Given the other three senior leaders' demands that security take precedence over economics, Kosygin had little choice but to go along. In accordance with the general expectation that occupancy of the median enables an ascendant leader to secure compliance because of his or her ability to join the other coalition, Kosygin publicly agreed to give priority to security goals. In July 1970 he told a Romanian audience that despite the Soviets' desire for wider East-West economic cooperation in Europe, "in matters of war and peace we cannot be indifferent to the course taken by this or that country."[44] It was Romania's leaders that the Soviets were vainly trying to prevent from breaking ranks with the Warsaw Pact nations for independent deals with the West; but Kosygin's acquiescence in the security-before-economics strategy was evident also in his reticence about economic issues in other speeches. Kosygin waited until his speech to the XXIVth Party Congress in April 1971 to press his foreign economic goals.

When Brezhnev began to emulate Kosygin's arguments for economic cooperation with the West, he found a new proposal to differentiate his stand from Kosygin's. As in 1965, Kosygin remained

42. Henry Kissinger, *The White House Years* (Boston: Little, Brown, 1979), 1213.
43. November 7, 1970; April 18, 1972.
44. July 8, 1970.

"against exclusionary economic groupings of the 'Common Market' type."[45] Kosygin encouraged bilateral trade by "the member countries of CMEA . . . with industrially developed capitalist countries. We stand for expansion of such ties."[46] With Kosygin promoting an erosion of the barriers between socialist and capitalist economies in Europe, Brezhnev positioned himself in favor of forms of cooperation that would preserve those barriers. Brezhnev said that the belief that "in general our policy in Europe is directed at undermining . . . the 'Common Market'" was an "absurd invention." Instead he linked Soviet acceptance of the Common Market to West European recognition of CMEA. Then in December 1972 Brezhnev raised the issue of developing "bases for some form of business ties between the international trade-economic organizations existing in Europe— between CMEA and the Common Market."[47]

In comparison with Kosygin's proposal to allow the East Europeans to make their own deals with the capitalists, Brezhnev's proposal to organize East-West trade via institutions that preserved Soviet dominance in Eastern Europe was closer to Podgorny's insistence on maintaining the subordination of economic to security goals and to Suslov's insistence on preserving the special character of ties among socialist states. With Brezhnev in the median, Kosygin was forced to make a concession from his earlier rejection of the EEC. He now asked the Common Market only "not to create additional difficulties,"[48] whereas earlier he had claimed that the Common Market *was* a difficulty impeding the growth of East-West trade.

Preserving a Reputation in East-West Issues

While transforming his approach on East-West issues, Brezhnev sought to retain his original appeal as the defender of the socialist alliance. If he was to pursue a strategy of seeking collaboration with capitalist countries on security issues, Brezhnev could not revert to his 1965 strategy of encouraging cohesion of the socialist alliance by exaggerating the security threat from West Germany and the United

45. April 7, 1971. See also October 25, 1971; October 25, 1972.
46. November 25, 1971.
47. March 19, December 22, 1972. See also Angela Stent, *From Embargo to Ostpolitik: The Political Economy of West German–Soviet Relations, 1955–1980* (Cambridge: Cambridge University Press, 1981), 244–46.
48. October 25, 1972.

States. Instead he now emphasized the change in the character of the threat posed by capitalism and the success of his policies in both meeting the threat and achieving East-West cooperation on security issues.

Brezhnev continued to pose as the epitome of the heroic communist—the bearer of a historical charisma capable of transforming society and therefore of responsibility for doing so. "We communists are answerable for the fate of our country," he said in Poland in December 1971.[49] Brezhnev used his choice of audiences as a synecdoche to associate himself with the inspirational past. He spoke at Red Csepel, the factory complex that had been the fortress of the 1919 Hungarian revolution, and at Auto-Praha, the Prague factory from which ninety-nine workers had ostensibly sent a letter to *Pravda* in July 1968 appealing for Soviet aid against counterrevolution.[50] Brezhnev justified East-West collaboration on security by using these occasions to claim that the imperialists had shifted from wagering mainly on military power in their campaign against socialism to attempting to dismember socialism from within. The imperialists were trying not only "direct aggression" in Vietnam but also "invigoration of nationalist prejudices and encouragement of any deviation from the international solidarity of socialist countries. Sometimes promises of economic advantages are heard, addressed to one or another socialist country."[51]

Linking the heroic struggle against counterrevolution inside the socialist countries to the maintenance of peace in Europe, Brezhnev also gave his program for socialist cohesion the credit for progress on European security. Brezhnev variously attributed the 1970 Moscow Treaty with the FRG, the willingness of the NATO countries to attend a European conference, and the putative worldwide popular appeal of Soviet foreign policy to the socialist countries' "development and conduct of a foreign policy line unified in its fundamentals and close coordination of practical actions."[52] As Edwina Moreton has argued, the coordination of foreign policies was a "public facade"

49. December 9, 1971. See also December 1, 1972.
50. May 28, 1971; December 1, 1972.
51. December 1, 1972. For other comments on this theme, see April 4 and 22, May 8, 1970; March 31, May 27 and 28, September 23 and 24, December 9, 1971; June 28, December 22, 1972.
52. May 27, 1971; August 29, 1970; December 9, 1971; March 19, 1972. See also April 22, June 13, November 25 and 30, 1970; March 31, April 22, May 15 and 28, June 17, September 23, 1971; June 6 and 28, December 1 and 22, 1972.

behind which each East European state pursued "autonomously defined foreign policy interests based on nationally determined priorities" that variously converged or diverged from the policy of the Soviet Union or of the other allies.[53] For Brezhnev's political purposes at home, however, this public facade supplied visible evidence for the argument, which any leader engaged in constituency expansion must adopt, that new goals not only can be achieved at no cost to original goals but are even a natural extension of success in achieving the original goals. Accordingly, throughout 1970–1972 Brezhnev would repeat: "Today, comrades, the task of strengthening the consolidation and development of all-round collaboration of socialist countries becomes especially topical and important."[54]

Continuity in the Rivals' Grand Strategies

Had the other three members of the Politburo's inner circle changed their grand strategies at the same time Brezhnev did, there would be no reason to attribute his shift to competitive politics. Observed changes in the world situation would suffice to explain an observation that all four leaders altered their strategic preferences in a uniform fashion. But in fact during 1970–1972 Suslov, Podgorny, and Kosygin responded to new domestic and international circumstances by reiterating their established preferences concerning the strategic principles that should guide Soviet foreign policy.

Suslov and his spokesman, Ponomarev, reacted to the new circumstances by reaffirming the validity of their strategy of relying on foreign communist parties to mobilize European publics against a new world war under the slogan of the "unity of the working class." Their main forum for advocating this grand strategy was a series of six "theoretical conferences" on Marxism-Leninism.[55] Ponomarev repeated that "ideological and political support for those detachments

53. N. Edwina Moreton, "Foreign Policy Perspectives in Eastern Europe," in Karen Dawisha and Philip Hanson, eds., *Soviet–East European Dilemmas: Coercion, Competition and Dissent* (London: Heinemann for the Royal Institute of International Affairs, 1981), 173. See also Lawrence L. Whetten, *Germany's Ostpolitik* (London: Oxford University Press for the Royal Institute of International Affairs, 1971), 79–80; Michael J. Sodaro, *Moscow, Germany, and the West from Khrushchev to Gorbachev* (Ithaca: Cornell University Press, 1990), 183–88, 207–10.

54. April 22, 1970. See also November 25 and 30, 1970; March 31, May 15 and 27, June 17, September 23, December 9, 1971; June 6 and 28, December 22, 1972.

55. January 21, February 25, November 18, 1970; March 18, September 30, 1971; June 14, 1972.

that are in the vanguard of international class struggles" constituted "the most profound principle of the policy of communist and workers' parties."[56] Suslov stressed the favorable prospects not for East-West diplomacy but for revolution in the capitalist countries. In November 1970, for example, Suslov quoted Lenin: " 'The annihilation of capitalism and its vestiges and the introduction of the foundations of the communist order constitute the content of the new epoch of world history begun now.' "[57] A year later he said, "All the vital changes of the age—social, economic, scientific-technical—do not weaken but rather intensify the world-historical role of the working class as the gravedigger of capitalism."[58]

Suslov and Ponomarev's emphasis on the potential for revolution in the capitalist world seemed specifically intended to challenge the descriptions of the world conditions that justified Brezhnev's proposals for East-West cooperation. Because of the accumulation of "flammable material" in contemporary capitalist society, Ponomarev said, "any acute political crisis—internal or international—can lead to the appearance of a revolutionary situation."[59] If the creation of a revolutionary situation was desirable, why should the Soviet Union reduce the likelihood of international crises by cooperation with capitalist governments beyond the minimum necessary to avoid nuclear war? Brezhnev objected so sharply to their description of the prospects for revolution in capitalist countries that his report to the XXIVth Party Congress deleted the separate heading on this topic in the report to the previous Congress.[60]

In 1965–1967, their grand strategy of relying on European communists to prevent war had encouraged Suslov and Ponomarev to object to agreements between the Soviet Union and capitalist governments in Europe. Now on successive days in October 1970, Foreign Minister Gromyko and Ponomarev would disagree overtly about Brezhnev's claim that capitalist governments had become ready to welcome Soviet initiatives for détente. Gromyko said: "Elements of a realistic position have become more palpable and apparent, although in different degrees in different states, and not in all. It is understood that such manifestations of realism and responsibility

56. November 18, 1970.
57. November 7, 1970.
58. September 30, 1971.
59. September 30, 1971.
60. See Franklyn Griffiths, "Ideological Development and Foreign Policy," in Seweryn Bialer, ed., *The Domestic Context of Soviet Foreign Policy* (Boulder, Colo.: Westview, 1981), 22–23, 35–36.

are welcomed by all who in fact are aiming at peace."[61] The next day Ponomarev described the small European states indiscriminately as precluded from adopting a peaceful foreign policy by their membership in "the aggressive North Atlantic bloc."[62]

The preliminaries to negotiation of the German treaty repeated this pattern. Before the treaty was concluded, when Brezhnev claimed that "realistic" leaders in West Germany predominated over "revanchists" and "militarists" and Kosygin called the revanchists' plans "dangerous but unachievable," Ponomarev drew attention only to "the fact that forces of revanchism and reaction continue to act in the FRG."[63] Suslov ignored the entire subject.[64]

The contest to define the Soviet relationship with West Germany only intensified with the signing of the German treaty in August 1970. In Moscow, Brandt told Brezhnev that the Bundestag would ratify the treaty only if the Soviet Union made concessions on the status of Berlin.[65] Both opponents and advocates of the treaty then alerted Soviet audiences to their disagreements over whether the treaty was worth further concessions.

Suslov's differences with Brezhnev were evident in their first public comments on the treaty. In speeches of similar length, Suslov devoted two paragraphs to the German treaty and Brezhnev devoted six. Both leaders used the treaty as a synecdoche for both "relations between our two countries" and "the whole international situation in Europe," but Brezhnev twice linked these two situations while Suslov separated them. Brezhnev said the treaty advanced a whole series of Soviet foreign policy objectives, while Suslov minimized its accomplishments by saying it merited approval "precisely because" it "legally secur[ed] the inviolability of borders in Europe." Brezhnev called the treaty "a very important event that will have great positive significance when it goes into force," while Suslov said that the treaty's significance had to be acknowledged, but it "will play its role fully only when it goes into force." Brezhnev took a sanguine view of the prospects for ratification, noting the "realistic approach" of the Brandt government and expressing "hope" for "successful completion and . . . further development" of the treaty process, while Suslov said ratification faced a "sharp struggle" in

61. October 23, 1970.
62. October 24, 1970.
63. June 11, 1970; June 3, 1970.
64. June 10, 1970.
65. A. James McAdams, *East Germany and Détente* (Cambridge: Cambridge University Press, 1985), 105–6; Sodaro, *Moscow, Germany, and the West*, 185.

West Germany, where "influential reactionary forces . . . short-sightedly fired up from outside" were opposing the treaty. In the historical long run, Suslov said, these forces were helpless, but meanwhile "it would be unforgivable to overlook the energetic activity in Europe of forces of aggressive militarism and revanche" supported by the United States. Suslov did not mention the German treaty again until April 1972, while Brezhnev discussed it in all three of his foreign policy speeches in the fall of 1970 alone and endorsed the negotiations on Berlin necessary to achieve ratification.[66]

Podgorny continued to advocate exploitation of divisions within NATO as part of a grand strategy of isolating the United States in world politics. In contrast to Suslov, Podgorny endorsed both the German treaty and the proposal for a European security conference. But Podgorny's opposition to bilateral talks with the United States caused him to refrain until May 1972 from any endorsement of arms control except in multilateral forums. Podgorny joined Suslov in especially resisting linkage between the Soviet proposal for a European security conference and NATO proposals for talks on reducing conventional forces in Europe, for a Berlin agreement, and for progress on SALT.

Podgorny manifested his aversion to the U.S.-Soviet component of Brezhnev's East-West program by avoiding any statement in favor of either bilateral arms talks or U.S.-Soviet trade until September 1972. In June 1970, after Brezhnev and Kosygin had specifically endorsed SALT, Podgorny said only: "We are ready for agreed actions on questions of peace and international security and for an end to the arms race with those countries that want this." As an example of desirable "agreed actions," Podgorny cited the Nonproliferation Treaty, which had been negotiated in a multilateral forum.[67] His next reference to nuclear arms control came in September 1971, when he argued that disarmament should be achieved by a world disarmament conference.[68] In April 1972 he said that the Biological Weapons Convention "can serve as a good example for the solution of other urgent problems of disarmament also," noting specifically that "many other states made a weighty contribution . . . especially by taking part in the talks."[69]

While delaying endorsement of the U.S. component of Brezhnev's

66. November 7, August 29, 1970. For Brezhnev's other comments, see October 3, November 25 and 30, 1970. See also Kosygin, August 13, 1970.
67. June 12, 1970.
68. September 15, 1971.
69. April 11, 1972.

214 Public Politics in an Authoritarian State

program, Podgorny spoke favorably of both the bilateral and the multilateral initiatives toward Western Europe. Describing the extension of the Soviet treaty with Finland as "a very important link" in Soviet efforts to improve the European situation, he continued, "As is known, the recent signing of the Soviet-French protocol and the Soviet-French declaration, and also the conclusion of a treaty between the USSR and the FRG, serves these same goals."[70] In contrast to Suslov, Podgorny said as early as September 1970 that the German treaty "is undoubtedly an important contribution to the cause of strengthening peace."[71] During the spring 1970 exchanges over the relative strength of "revanchist" and "realistic" forces in West German politics, Podgorny had evidently sought the middle ground; while he said, "Even now there are certain forces obsessed with the revanchist and militarist itch," he also held out the possibility that the "revanchists" could not control West German policy. Podgorny said Soviet policy should "express the hope that understanding of the need for a more sober and realistic approach to evaluation of the situation in Europe, of the interest of European security, and of the future development of the FRG will triumph."[72]

Podgorny also repeatedly stressed "the important and topical problem [of] preparation and summoning of an all-European conference."[73] Advocacy of the conference was a departure from his position during 1966–1967, when he preferred bilateral initiatives toward West European governments. Now Podgorny occupied Brezhnev's 1966–1967 position on this issue; he linked the conference to the goal of excluding U.S. influence from Europe. "Efforts to solve Europe's problems," Podgorny said, should be made "above all within a European framework" by "European states."[74] He was joined by Suslov, who called for a "meeting of all states of our continent."[75] As Brezhnev had done in 1966–1967, Podgorny blamed the United States for impeding Soviet initiatives: "There are also forces outside Europe which delay a settlement of vitally important problems."[76] Unlike Brezhnev and Kosygin, during 1970–1972 Podgorny

70. November 4, 1970.
71. September 24, 1970.
72. March 27, June 12, 1970.
73. October 7, 1970. See also March 27, June 12, September 24, October 1 and 14, 1970; June 3, 11, and 15, December 9, 1971; April 13, June 1, July 7, 1972.
74. October 7, 1970.
75. November 7, 1970.
76. June 11, 1971.

never endorsed participation by the non-European NATO countries, Canada and the United States, in the European security conference.[77]

Because Podgorny continued to advocate an East-West policy that competed with the United States for West European cooperation rather than linking Soviet policies toward all the capitalist governments, he evidently resisted concessions to NATO's demand for a linkage between the Soviet proposal for a European conference and the West's proposals for a Berlin agreement, for negotiations on reducing conventional forces in Europe, and for progress on SALT. Unlike Brezhnev and Kosygin, on several occasions Podgorny blamed NATO for blocking progress toward a European conference.[78] Kosygin, in contrast, never identified NATO as the obstacle to progress, and in December 1971 Brezhnev even raised the possibility that a NATO summit in Brussels might decide in favor of the European conference.[79]

In contrast to Brezhnev's optimism concerning the international situation, until the beginning of 1972 Podgorny repeatedly described it as "complex and contradictory" or "complex and tense."[80] Thus he seems to have been the target of Brezhnev's statement: "One cannot agree with those who try to use the complexity of the European situation to stop the summoning of a conference."[81] Kosygin also spoke against "any kind of preliminary conditions" for a conference, and Brezhnev objected to turning the conference "into an object of political horsetrading."[82] But in contrast to Podgorny, during the spring of 1971 both Kosygin and Brezhnev explicitly endorsed a concession to NATO's demand for commencement of talks on mutual reduction of conventional forces.[83] In return NATO would agree to the European conference.

With Brezhnev espousing variants of many policy recommendations formerly identified with Kosygin, the latter found himself frequently cooperating with his earlier antagonist on East-West issues. However, Kosygin continued to differ with Brezhnev in arguing that

77. For Brezhnev's and Kosygin's endorsements, see May 19, October 26, 1971; March 19, October 25, 1972.
78. October 4, 1970; June 11, 1971; June 1, 1972.
79. December 9, 1971.
80. March 30, June 12, October 29, 1970; June 11, November 17, 1971.
81. April 4, 1970.
82. January 3, May 27, 1971. See also June 10, 1971.
83. March 31, April 22, May 15 and 19, June 12, 1971.

East-West cooperation should take priority over superpower competition in the Third World, reiterating his 1965 claims that "peaceful coexistence" would foster development and social progress in developing countries.[84] He repeated his earlier assertions of the need to include "all states" in cooperation for peace,[85] and he still expected that cooperation on security and economic exchange would prove mutually reinforcing. In September 1971 he said:

> Many factors determine . . . the interconnection and interdependence of events in world politics and in the world economy. On the one hand, this is a consequence of the scientific-technical revolution, which has immeasurably intensified the process of internationalization in world economic life. But no less important is the strengthening, growing solidarity and cohesion of all forces in the world that want to see the policy of peaceful coexistence turned into a generally recognized norm of international relations.[86]

84. October 7, 1971.
85. October 20, 1971.
86. September 29, 1971. See also May 19, October 7, 20, 25, and 27, November 25, December 4, 6, and 7, 1971; March 15, October 25, 1972.

* Chapter 11

Bargaining for Détente,
May 1971 and May 1972

Brezhnev's occupancy of the median between Kosygin, who advocated U.S.-Soviet agreements, and Podgorny and Suslov, who opposed even negotiating with the United States, enabled the Politburo to enter East-West talks and even to sign such treaties as the August 1970 agreement with West Germany. But to maintain a median position, Brezhnev had to take a stance more acceptable to Podgorny and Suslov than Kosygin's. If Brezhnev proposed to conclude U.S.-Soviet agreements, the difference between his position and Kosygin's would narrow, and he would vacate the median. Thus in his median position Brezhnev could begin negotiations but not conclude them, a circumstance sure in the long run to undermine the persuasiveness of his descriptions of the Western powers as "reasonable" and "realistic" negotiating partners.

The opponents of U.S.-Soviet talks recognized that they could block conclusion of agreements if they could prevent Brezhnev from linking the various issues in dispute between East and West. In particular, both Suslov and Podgorny objected to NATO's demand for a package deal: ratification of the German treaty and approval of a European conference in exchange for Soviet agreement to U.S. initiatives for talks on reducing conventional forces in Europe, for progress on offensive weapons in SALT, and for a Berlin agreement. Because the West Europeans remained unwilling to settle issues without the U.S. guarantor at the table, Brezhnev could complete neither his bilateral nor his multilateral agenda without this linkage.

Competitive politics theory identifies two options for Brezhnev and Kosygin in their efforts to overcome Podgorny's and Suslov's resistance to détente. First, if world events diminished the persuasiveness of one or both critics' grand strategy, Brezhnev and Kosygin could demand concessions on East-West issues. Second, if world events did not come to the rescue, Brezhnev and Kosygin could compromise with one or both critics by offering a concession on one or more issues treated as separable from the East-West package.

The U.S.-Soviet détente of the 1970s developed as the result of two breakthroughs to agreement, the first in May 1971 and the second in May 1972. The first linked the two Soviet proposals (the German treaty and the European conference) to the three U.S. proposals (talks on conventional forces, progress on offensive arms, and a Berlin agreement). The second concluded a wide range of bilateral U.S.-Soviet agreements, particularly SALT I, at the Moscow summit. To get the May 1971 linkage, Brezhnev and Kosygin demanded a concession from Suslov and offered one to Podgorny; to get the May 1972 summit, they offered a concession to Suslov and demanded one from Podgorny.

May 1971: Breakthrough to Linkage in Europe

May 1971 saw a remarkable confluence of changes in Soviet policy. As the Soviets accommodated U.S. preferences on the whole cluster of East-West issues, they became more intransigent on Vietnam and the Arab-Israeli conflict. At the same time there was evidence that Brezhnev was exploiting events that had diminished the persuasiveness of Suslov's strategy of relying on European communists to advance Soviet foreign policy goals.

Europe, the Middle East, and Vietnam

Though they had formally accepted U.S. participation in the proposed European conference in June 1970 and had privately agreed to it in December 1969,[1] during 1970 and early 1971 "in East-West talks the USSR's representatives accepted that a purely regional security

1. Franklyn W. Griffiths, "The Soviet Experience of Arms Control," *International Journal* 44 (1989): 304–64. I thank the author for drawing my attention to this fact.

system was impossible in Europe, but at the same time clarified that this security system could not be drawn into the wake of U.S.-Soviet relations."[2] Their awkward straddling of the issue of linkage ended in May 1971. On May 20 the two governments announced the bargain coupling an ABM treaty with offensive limitations in SALT.[3] The same week both Brezhnev and Kosygin endorsed the NATO proposal for talks on mutual reduction of conventional forces in Europe.[4] A week earlier negotiations between Gromyko and the French foreign minister produced an agreement scheduling a visit by Brezhnev to France for October.[5] The ouster of Walter Ulbricht on May 3 removed a principal obstacle to a Berlin agreement; his successor, Erich Honecker, promptly acceded to tacit linkage of the Berlin agreement and the other East-West proposals.[6] In Brezhnev's June 1971 speeches he omitted the denunciation of linkage which he had repeated as late as May 27, and on June 16 he explicitly linked the German treaty and European conference proposals to a statement of readiness to conclude a Berlin agreement.[7] Having accepted linkage, all the Soviet leaders ceased their demands for prompt summoning of the European conference; they resumed these demands only after the Quadripartite Agreement with the argument that the Berlin agreement and Soviet acceptance of talks on force reductions had removed the remaining obstacles.[8]

As Soviet policy became more accommodating to the United States in East-West issues, it became more intransigent in the Middle East and Vietnam. The shift in policy toward the Middle East was marked on May 25, 1971, when Podgorny arrived in Egypt carrying a draft of a Treaty of Friendship and Cooperation. Arriving with only two days' notice,[9] Podgorny told President Anwar Sadat that the Polit-

---

2. Gerhard Wettig, *Europäische Sicherheit* (Cologne: Bertelsmann Universitätsverlag, 1972), 116.
3. Raymond L. Garthoff, *Détente and Confrontation* (Washington, D.C.: Brookings, 1983), 147.
4. May 15 and 19, 1971.
5. May 8, 1971.
6. A. James McAdams, *East Germany and Détente* (Cambridge: Cambridge University Press, 1985), 114–15; N. Edwina Moreton, *East Germany and the Warsaw Alliance: The Politics of Detente* (Boulder, Colo.: Westview, 1978), 181; Michael J. Sodaro, *Moscow, Germany, and the West from Khrushchev to Gorbachev* (Ithaca: Cornell University Press, 1990), 207–12.
7. Cf. May 27 with June 12 and 17, 1971.
8. September 24, October 26 and 30, December 9, 1971.
9. Lawrence L. Whetten, "The Arab-Israeli Dispute: Great Power Behavior," in

buro considered the treaty (which, although under consideration for some time, had languished) to be "essential right now."[10] The shift in policy toward Vietnam was marked by a meeting on May 9 between Brezhnev and the Vietnamese party first secretary, Le Duan, the principal advocate in Hanoi of a strategy of conventional offensive operations in the South.[11] At this meeting Le Duan evidently obtained Brezhnev's agreement to begin talks on new deliveries of arms necessary to carry out the recently approved Vietnamese plan for a conventional offensive in March 1972. Once again the Soviet policy shift produced an opportunity for Podgorny to go public, as he traveled to Hanoi in October 1971 to place final approval on a new arms agreement.[12]

The new policies in the Middle East and Indochina represented the abandonment of Brezhnev's previous inclusion of both regional conflicts in his overall program of East-West accommodation. With Brezhnev's encouragement, Soviet diplomats had displayed interest in United States plans to broker an Arab-Israeli settlement in mid-1970.[13] Brezhnev also recurrently encouraged the Vietnamese to pur-

---

Gregory F. Treverton, ed., *Crisis Management and the Superpowers in the Middle East,* Adelphi Library no. 5 (Westmead: Gower; Montclair, N.J.: Allanheld Osmun, 1981), 65; the announcement of Podgorny's trip was published only May 24, 1971.

10. Anwar Sadat, *In Search of Identity* (New York: Harper & Row, 1977), 221–30; Mohamed Heikal, *The Sphinx and the Commissar* (New York: Harper & Row, 1978), 227–28. As is usual in respect to Soviet policy toward the Middle East, the sources tell opposite stories, some naming the Soviets as the treaty's sponsors, others the Egyptians. Both agree that the decision to sign the treaty was sudden.

11. May 10, 1971; Thai Quang Trung, *Collective Leadership and Factionalism* (Singapore: Institute of Southeast Asian Studies, 1985), 55–64; Victor C. Funnell, "Vietnam and the Sino-Soviet Conflict, 1965–1976," *Studies in Comparative Communism,* 11 (Spring/Summer 1978), 157–58.

12. On the May date of the Vietnamese decision, see William S. Turley, *The Second Indochina War: A Short Political and Military History, 1954–1975* (Boulder, Colo.: Westview, 1986), 138–39. Although Trung, *Collective Leadership,* 66, says the decision was made in December 1971, after Podgorny's visit, Turley's source is the official Vietnamese history of the conflict; the December 1971 decision apparently confirmed the earlier choice. On the contribution of the arms deliveries agreed to during Podgorny's trip, see Funnell, "Vietnam," 167.

13. George W. Breslauer, "Soviet Policy in the Middle East, 1967–1972: Unalterable Antagonism or Collaborative Competition?" in Alexander L. George, ed., *Managing U.S.-Soviet Rivalry* (Boulder, Colo.: Westview, 1983), 84–86. For Brezhnev's encouragement, see April 15, August 29, 1970. Both Breslauer and Whetten, "Arab-Israeli Dispute," 61–62, claim that the Soviet leadership even exerted "pressure" that compelled Nasser to accept the so-called second Rogers plan as a basis for indirect negotiations to settle the Arab conflict with Israel. In *Sphinx and Commissar,* 201–2, Heikal

sue the then-secret Kissinger-Tho contacts in Paris. In April 1970 and again in October he called upon the Vietnamese to use "diplomatic" as well as "military" and "political" methods to achieve their goals.[14]

The abandonment of Brezhnev's policies on the Middle East and Indochina allowed Podgorny go public with his own strategy: in both regions he rejected negotiations with the United States. The objective of Soviet policy in the Near East remained a "settlement by political means,"[15] but Podgorny now defined a political solution to exclude negotiations with the United States. He accused U.S. leaders of using "honeyed" words about peace to lure the Arabs into a false settlement that would only enable the Israelis to dictate terms.[16] Podgorny argued that Egypt should instead rely on the backing of the Soviet Union and on growing international support for the Arab cause.[17] He urged Sadat both to avoid a war that Podgorny was convinced the Arabs could not win and to refuse U.S.-sponsored negotiations. With the passage of time, he said, growing international pressure would compel Israel to make concessions. This policy would later draw fire from the Egyptian journalist Mohamed Heikal as a policy of "no peace, no war."[18]

Vietnam, in contrast, did not share Egypt's military disadvantages. Podgorny encouraged the North Vietnamese in their plans for an offensive. The U.S. invasion of Cambodia, increasingly frequent offensive operations in the South, attacks in Laos, and air raids against the North, Podgorny said, "cast light on the real essence of Nixon's 'Guam doctrine' and show the actual worth of 'peacemaking' in the U.S. manner."[19] Calling military aid "an internationalist duty" and "a principled course" and promising "modern weapons," Pod-

---

claims that Nasser agreed to the second Rogers plan over Brezhnev's objections. Although, as usual in Mideast issues, the truth is inscrutable, in my view Whetten's and Breslauer's version is correct. Heikal, wanting to embellish Nasser's reputation and to make his "no peace, no war" interpretation of Soviet Mideast policy seem consistently supported by all evidence, conflates Brezhnev's stance with Podgorny's.

14. April 15, October 3, 1970.

15. *Vneshnaia politika Sovetskogo Soiuza i mezhdunarodnye otnosheniia: Sbornik dokumentov,* 1971 (Moscow: Mezhdunarodnye Otnosheniia, 1971), doc. 18, p. 47 (the joint communiqué of Podgorny's May visit). This work is published annually.

16. May 28, 1971. See also May 29, June 11, 1971.

17. October 13, 1971.

18. Mohamed Heikal, *The Road to Ramadan* (Chicago: Quadrangle, 1975), 163–64.

19. October 5, 1971.

gorny signed the agreements that resulted in a threefold increase of Soviet arms, including the tanks and artillery used in North Vietnam's conventional offensive of March 1972.[20]

In sum, Brezhnev obtained Podgorny's acquiescence in linkage in Europe by separating Vietnam and the Middle East from his overall program of East-West negotiations. Brezhnev's and Kosygin's acceptance of U.S. demands for talks on conventional forces in Europe was particularly ill timed from Podgorny's perspective. They conceded the U.S. demands at the very moment when the prospects for Podgorny's strategy of expelling the U.S. from Europe had peaked. Brezhnev's and Kosygin's statements of acceptance on May 14 and 18 occurred, respectively, five and one days before a Senate vote that might have approved Mike Mansfield's amendment to halve U.S. troop strength in Europe.[21]

In return for conceding that "all European issues can and should be decided concurrently,"[22] Podgorny gained the opportunity to go public with his arguments against negotiations with the United States. He used the Arab-Israeli and Indochina conflicts as benchmarks for evaluation of the whole world situation. "Israeli aggression poisons the atmosphere not only in the Near East but far beyond its limits," he said, blaming "the aggressor and his transoceanic patron."[23] He openly criticized the separation of Indochina and the Near East from other world issues: "Sometimes one hears arguments that the world has somehow gotten used to these conflicts, that one may even, so to speak, set them aside and occupy oneself with other unresolved problems. One cannot condone such arguments."[24]

Brezhnev objected to Podgorny's synecdoche. A person who read newspaper accounts of events in Vietnam and the Near East, he said, could get the impression that "few or no positive changes are occurring in the international situation, that the world is running in place. In fact that is not so. Positive changes are occurring, and sometimes very substantial ones."[25] This 1970 statement came only

20. October 4 and 8, 1971; CIA, "Communist Military and Economic Aid to North Vietnam, 1970–1974," SC 01609/75, 4, Lyndon B. Johnson Library, Austin. See also Turley, *Second Indochina War*, 139; Daniel S. Papp, *Vietnam: The View from Moscow, Peking, Washington* (Jefferson, N.C.: McFarland, 1981), 153.
    21. Garthoff, *Détente and Confrontation*, 115.
    22. June 11, 1971.
    23. May 28, 1971. See also October 5, 1971.
    24. September 15, 1971.
    25. April 15, 1970.

Table 3. Number of speeches delivered by three top Soviet leaders, 1970–1972, by type of audience

Audience	Brezhnev	Kosygin[a]	Podgorny
Domestic	41	12	17
Third World	0	22	35[b]
Socialist	22	18	10
Capitalist	8	16	8

[a]Excludes one speech to a U.N. official.
[b]Includes three speeches in Turkey.

two weeks after Podgorny had encouraged exactly that impression in Soviet audiences.[26]

Podgorny's specialization in Third World issues was evident both in the division of labor among him, Brezhnev, and Kosygin during 1970–1972 and in Soviet policy. Table 3 displays the division of labor. Podgorny gave half of all his speeches to Third World audiences, and twice as many as in any other category, while Kosygin's speeches were distributed evenly among audiences and Brezhnev gave none at all to Third World audiences. Soviet policy mirrored Podgorny's long-standing advocacy of economic aid, with new commitments rising from low levels in 1968–1969 to $1.2 billion in 1970 and $2.2 billion annually in 1971 and 1972.[27]

European Security and Eurocommunism

Using a sequential issue trade to secure Podgorny's acquiescence, Brezhnev took advantage of events to demand a concession from Suslov. The emphasis on the favorable prospects for revolution in Europe which distinguished speeches by Suslov and Ponovarev in 1970–1972 was aimed not only to challenge Brezhnev's proposals for East-West détente but also to close fissures in European communism. The invasion of Czechoslovakia had powerfully encouraged the dissenting tendencies, known as "Eurocommunism," which rejected the validity of "really existing socialism" in the USSR as a model for developed capitalist societies and objected to Soviet guid-

26. March 27, 28, and 30, 1970. See also June 12, July 1, 1970.
27. CIA, "Communist Aid Activities in Non-Communist Less Developed Countries, 1979 and 1954–79," research paper, ER 80–10318U, October 1980, Lyndon B. Johnson Library.

ance of foreign parties' domestic political strategy. The Eurocommunists' overt protests against Soviet intervention in Czechoslovakia discredited Suslov's strategy of relying on European communists' loyalty to advance the Politburo's foreign policy objectives.

While Suslov and Ponomarev continued to promote "the unity of the working class," their statements during 1970–1972 differed markedly from those they made in 1965–1967. During 1965–1967, Suslov and Ponomarev had stressed the opportunities for West European communist parties to expand their influence outward by offering coalitions to left social democrats. During 1970–1972 their statements concentrated on West European communist parties' internal disunity. Characteristically substituting description for prescription, Suslov now said that foreign communists "are expelling from their ranks all of those who direct the thrust of their activity not against the class enemy but against really existing socialism." The same fight against "reformism" in domestic politics must be fought against "revisionist instability" in foreign communist parties.[28]

An indicator that Eurocommunism had diminished the persuasiveness of the grand strategy advocated by Suslov and Ponomarev was the intrusion of junior members of the Politburo into their specialty of relations with European communists. In particular, Andrei Kirilenko and Arvids Pelse began to share the responsibility for representing the Soviet Party in meetings with European communists and leftists.[29] This was something new: Kirilenko and Pelse had participated in none of the fifty-four meetings with European leftists reported by *Pravda* between November 1964 and November 1967. Brezhnev encouraged their intrusion into Suslov's specialty, associating with Kirilenko rather than Suslov in the crucial meetings with the French communists in July 1971.[30] Leading Soviet delegations to congresses of the French, West German, and Finnish communists, Kirilenko and Pelse spoke more favorably of Brezhnev's proposals for détente and more pessimistically about the prospects for European communism than either Ponomarev or Suslov.[31] Rivalry between Pelse and Ponomarev was especially manifest in their speeches at ceremonies in June 1972 marking the anniversary of the

28. November 7, 1970; September 30, 1971. See also January 21, February 25, June 3 and 10, July 9, November 18, 1970; March 18, December 22, 1971; June 14, 1972.
29. February 6 and 27, March 7, 1970; January 23, July 6, 18, and 31, August 6, 28, 1971; February 17, 18, and 22, 1972.
30. July 6, 1971.
31. February 6, 1970; November 26, 1971; April 2, 1972.

death of the heroic Cominternist Georgi Dimitrov. In Ponomarev's speech Dimitrov became a symbol for the strategy of seeking peace by building left coalitions in capitalist countries, while Pelse asserted that the legitimate successor to Dimitrov's struggles for peace was U.S.-Soviet détente.[32]

Further evidence of the decline in Suslov's and Ponomarev's credibility on European issues is a change in their behavior. Like Kosygin in response to escalation in Vietnam or Brezhnev in response to the failure of rapprochement with China, they turned to the Third World. During 1965–1967 Suslov's and Ponomarev's meetings with Third World communist and radical parties numbered only three-fourths of the total of their meetings with parties from industrial capitalist states. During 1970–1972 they reversed this priority in favor of an excess of meetings with Third World parties.

May 1972: Breakthrough to the Summit

The Nixon-Brezhnev summit of May 1972 occasioned new concessions by the détente critics Podgorny and Suslov. As Nixon's protocolary counterpart, Podgorny delivered the sole public speech connected with the summit. For the first time he endorsed bilateral negotiations with the United States, though he still withheld explicit endorsement of either SALT or trade.[33] In April, speaking in the capacity of chair of the Soviet of the Union's commission on foreign affairs, Suslov finally ended his opposition to the 1970 German treaty. People who doubted its value to both sides, he said, were "simply engaging in irresponsible demagoguery"; the treaty presented "real opportunities to achieve the goals for which all progressive forces of Europe long have struggled."[34] The interim agreement on offensive arms and the ABM treaty approved at the summit were ratified by the Supreme Soviet at the end of September, when both Podgorny and Suslov finally pronounced themselves satisfied.[35]

Why did Podgorny and Suslov finally agree to détente proposals championed by Brezhnev which they had resisted so long? This question is more pressing than it may first appear, for during the

32. June 14 and 17, 1972.
33. May 23, 1972.
34. April 18, 1972.
35. September 30, 1972. See also August 24, 1972.

winter of 1972 world events seemed to reinforce their case for hesi-
tancy in talks with the United States. Both the Nixon administration's actions and the concession on Indochina offered by Brezhnev
to obtain Podgorny's agreement to the May 1971 linkage of European issues threatened to undermine Brezhnev's argument for closing the U.S.-Soviet deal at a summit. Nixon's trip to Beijing in February 1972 dramatized Soviet concerns that the United States and
China might be moving toward an anti-Soviet coalition, while renewed air raids against North Vietnam in retaliation for the March
1972 conventional offensive in the South seemed capable, in light of
the Politburo's pattern of breaking off talks with the United States in
response to escalation in Indochina, of producing a last-minute can-
cellation of the summit.

A possible reason why Podgorny and Suslov did not try to take
advantage of Nixon's trip to China or the renewal of air attacks on
North Vietnam lies in Brezhnev's bargaining tactics during the preceding eight months. Brezhnev engaged in an issue trade with Suslov on the domestic problem of policy toward ethnic minorities,
while taking advantage of developments in the Middle East to compel concessions from Podgorny.

China, Détente, and Ethnic Policy

Suslov and Brezhnev differed over the significance of Chinese behavior for Soviet policy. Brezhnev reacted to the Nixon visit by
warning against premature alarmism. Calling U.S. diplomatic contacts with China "entirely natural," Brezhnev appealed for a delay in
judgment: "Opinions are opinions, but the deciding word, I repeat,
will belong to facts, to real deeds. Therefore we will not be hasty
with final assessments."[36] In response to the announcement in July
1971 of Nixon's impending trip to China, Suslov had said, "The anti-
Leninist and anti-Soviet line of today's Chinese leaders creates a
great danger for the cause of socialism."[37] The danger was a de facto
alliance between "imperialists" trying to disorganize the communist
parties from outside and Maoists and Eurocommunists pursuing
their "schismatic" line from inside.[38] The de facto alliance was the
target of the shift in polemics by Suslov and Ponomarev from attack-

36. March 19, 1972.
37. Garthoff, *Détente and Confrontation*, 241; September 30, 1971.
38. January 21, 1970; December 1, 1972. See also Suslov, November 7, 1970.

ing "nationalism" during 1965–1967 to denunciations of "anticommunism" or "anti-Sovietism" in 1970–1972.[39] As Ponomarev said, "Nationalism is doubly dangerous when it takes on an anti-Soviet coloration."[40] Thus he recommended "a constant offensive struggle" against "enemies of Marxism-Leninism, outside as well as inside the workers' movement."[41]

Instead of linking the issues of East-West relations and China policy, Brezhnev proposed parallel policies toward West and East. Toward the West he recommended combining ideological struggle with diplomatic and economic negotiations; toward China he advocated a policy combining efforts toward diplomatic normalization with a refusal of any concessions in the dispute over the frontier and a continuation of polemics against "anti-Leninist ideas."[42] The parallel was so exact that the signing of the German treaty in August 1970 was followed in January 1971 by a proposal for an equivalent treaty with China.[43] In March 1972 Brezhnev even advocated "peaceful coexistence" with China.[44]

Suslov's agreement to the separation of China from East-West détente was evidently the product of an issue trade that gave him the lead in formulating policy toward ethnic minorities. As Brezhnev and Suslov considered in September 1971 whether to approve the announcement scheduling the Nixon summit for May 1972, a decision deadline was also looming on ethnic policy. The Politburo was preparing to approve guidance for propaganda in preparation for the fiftieth anniversary of the founding of the USSR, to be celebrated in December 1972.

Both Brezhnev and Suslov chose their stands on ethnic policy by applying the principles defining their respective visions of social order. Brezhnev, who argued that economic expansion ensured loyalty to socialism, claimed that expansion of the economy would intensify exchanges among the republics and result in a gradual erosion of ethnic distinctions. To promote the intensification of economic exchange, he recommended redistribution of resources from the industrially developed republics of the West to the less devel-

39. January 21, February 25, 1970; September 30, 1971; June 21, December 15, 1972.
40. September 30, 1971.
41. November 18, 1970.
42. April 15, 1970. See also April 22, June 13, August 29, 1970; March 31, 1971; December 1, 1972.
43. Brezhnev described this proposal in a speech published December 22, 1972.
44. March 19, 1972.

228   *Public Politics in an Authoritarian State*

oped republics of Kazakhstan, Uzbekistan, and Azerbaijan, headed by his political allies Dinmukhamed Kunaev, Sharaf Rashidov, and Geidar Aliev.[45] Brezhnev has been accurately portrayed as an advocate of Russian nationalism, Russification of Ukraine, and taxation of Ukraine for the benefit of the Muslim republics,[46] but these stands were instrumental to his promotion of ethnic autonomy in Central Asia. Brezhnev's proposals produced real consequences: the six Muslim republics occupied, together with Armenia, the top seven spots in a ranking of share of the turnover tax retained by each of the fifteen republics in 1970.[47]

In the fall of 1971 Suslov promulgated a different emphasis more in keeping with his own vision of socialism sustained by mass persuasion. Suslov now delegitimated the ethnic republics' continuing demands for favoritism in resource allocation by saying that the task of equalizing levels of economic and cultural development of all ethnic regions had been completed. Now Marxist-Leninist theoreticians should assume the responsibility for ensuring "even closer rapprochement of socialist nations."[48] In June 1972 he described a "conciliatory posture toward bourgeois reactionary ideology, conniving at nationalism and chauvinism, money-grubbing, parasitism, bribetaking, and drunkenness," as "incompatible with socialism and communist morality," and summoned ideological workers to ensure that "a representative of any nation or ethnic group in our country be profoundly conscious of . . . membership in a unified multinational Soviet people."[49]

Suslov's guidance informed the propaganda campaign launched by *Pravda* in preparation for celebration of the USSR's founding. This campaign opened with a call for a policy directed against "petty national narrowness, exclusivity, isolation, for consideration of the whole and the general, for the subordination of partial interests to the general interests."[50] Further articles included statements that "borders between union and autonomous republics lose their former

45. November 21, 1964; March 30, 1966; November 4, 1967; April 15, August 29, October 3, November 30, December 1, 1970; March 31, 1971.
46. Grey Hodnett, "Ukrainian Politics and the Purge of Shelest," typescript, 35; July 11, October 24, 1965; November 2, 1966.
47. Donna Bahry, *Outside Moscow: Power, Politics, and Budgetary Policy in the Soviet Republics* (New York: Columbia University Press, 1987), 56.
48. September 30, December 22, 1971.
49. June 21, 1972. See also December 15, 1972; Ponomarev, December 1, 1972.
50. M. Khalmukhamedov, "Obrazovanie SSSR—torzhestvo leninskoi natsional'noi politiki partii," February 29, 1972.

significance" and that "the territorial distribution of productive forces and capital investment policy" should aim "above all at the most rapid economic progress of the country as a whole."[51]

The beneficiaries of Brezhnev's pleas for redistribution of resources to Central Asia objected vigorously—echoing criticisms by Kunaev, Rashidov attacked as a "distortion of our reality" Suslov's preference for the dissolution of separate peoples "into a supernational formation"[52]—but between June 1971 and December 1972 Brezhnev made no public statements at all on ethnic policy. None of the occasions for his speeches during this period particularly required him to address ethnic policy, but other leaders, such as Kosygin, managed to work commentary on ethnic issues into their speeches for other occasions.[53] Moreover, Brezhnev's March 1972 address to the trade union congress offered an opportunity suitable for a statement on ethnic policy had he wanted to make one. Instead he confined his comments on the working class's "proletarian internationalism" to relations among different states instead of relations among nations within the Soviet state.[54] When Brezhnev finally did comment on ethnic issues, in his speech for the fiftieth anniversary of the USSR, he endorsed Suslov's position.[55]

No Politburo member ever drew any explicit link between ethnic policy and East-West détente or policy toward China, but a surmise that the decisions on these issues in the fall of 1971 were unrelated would presuppose that Brezhnev and Suslov did not recognize the consequences of their stand on ethnic issues for the flow of public commentary about détente. Although, as the treatment of Shelepin in 1966 demonstrates (and the direct testimony of Mikhail Gorbachev would later confirm),[56] the top Politburo members barred junior members from direct access to decisions on national security, lesser members of the Politburo nevertheless enjoyed opportunities to endorse or to challenge senior members' policy prescriptions. Petro Shelest, first secretary of the Ukrainian party, had been particularly active both in asserting autonomy for ethnic republics and in

51. E. Bagramov, "Sblizhenie natsii—zakonomernost' kommunisticheskogo stroitel'stva," June 22, 1972.

52. Sh. Rashidov, "Nerushimoe bratstvo," October 6, 1972; D. Kunaev, "Ukreplenie sovetskogo gosudarstva—delo vsekh narodov SSSR," June 30, 1972.

53. October 7, 1971; March 2, October 17, 1972.

54. March 19, 1972.

55. December 22, 1972. This speech is the primary basis for Hodnett's identification of Brezhnev as a Russifier: "Ukrainian Politics," 36.

56. December 10, 1990.

objecting to excessive trust in the United States. Now in May 1972 Shelest lost his post, and with it the opportunity to voice public objections either to Brezhnev's proposals for détente or to Suslov's project of diminishing ethnic autonomy.

Recapturing Control of Mideast Policy

Using a sequential issue trade to gain Suslov's assent to the May summit, Brezhnev extracted concessions from Podgorny by exploiting world events that diminished the persuasiveness of his rival's strategy in the Middle East. At the beginning of 1972 the Politburo abandoned the Mideast policy shaped by Podgorny's strategy of organizing an international coalition intended to isolate Israel and the United States and compel Israel to accept a "political settlement" providing for withdrawal from Arab territory occupied in 1967. The Politburo shifted to a policy of encouraging Egypt and Syria to use "all means at their disposal for liberation of the Arab territories."[57] This phrase, taken from the communiqué of Brezhnev and Kosygin's meeting with the Egyptian premier, Aziz Sidqi, in July 1972, signaled their withdrawal of earlier objections to a new war against Israel.

The decision to give declaratory approval for an attack on Israel by Egypt and Syria has often been attributed to the Politburo's concern that President Sadat's July 1972 expulsion of all Soviet air defense personnel from Egypt would jeopardize the Soviet Union's strategic position in the Middle East.[58] But the attribution of the Soviet policy change to Sadat's expulsion order overlooks evidence that the shift

57. *Vneshnaia politika Sovetskogo Soiuza*, 1971, doc. 57, p. 120. See also Galia Golan, *Yom Kippur and After: The Soviet Union and the Middle East Crisis* (Cambridge: Cambridge University Press, 1977), 23; Dina Rome Spechler, "The USSR and Third-World Conflict: Domestic Debate and Soviet Policy in the Middle East, 1967–1973," *World Politics* 38 (1986): 454–56; Bruce Porter, *The USSR in Third World Conflicts: Soviet Arms and Diplomacy in Local Wars, 1945–1980* (Cambridge: Cambridge University Press, 1984), 122.

58. Philip D. Stewart, Margaret G. Hermann, and Charles F. Hermann, "Modeling the 1973 Soviet Decision to Support Egypt," *American Political Science Review* 43 (1989): 35–59; Spechler, "USSR and Third World Conflicts," 454–56; Whetten, "Arab-Israeli Dispute," 66–68; Harry Gelman, *The Brezhnev Politburo and the Decline of Détente* (Ithaca: Cornell University Press, 1984), 155; Robert O. Freedman, *Soviet Policy toward the Middle East since 1970* (New York: Praeger, 1978), 88, 132–34; Jon D. Glassman, *Arms for the Arabs* (Baltimore: Johns Hopkins University Press, 1975), 103–4; Paul Jabber and Roman Kolkowicz, "The Arab-Israeli Wars of 1967 and 1973," in Stephen S. Kaplan, ed., *Diplomacy of Power* (Washington, D.C.: Brookings, 1981), 441; Kaplan, *Diplomacy of Power*, 185; Porter, *USSR in Third World Conflicts*, 121–22, 221–22.

in declaratory policy began at least five months before Sadat's action, which the Politburo did not anticipate. The communiqué issued after Sadat's own meeting with Brezhnev and Kosygin in April said that because "circles hostile to the movement for progress in the Arab East" have not stopped trying "to disrupt a political settlement . . . , Arab states . . . have every justification to use other means for the return of the Arab lands seized by Israel."[59] Moreover, the two Soviet leaders had stopped pressuring Egypt to pursue Podgorny's "political settlement" as early as February, when the communiqué issued after an earlier meeting between Sadat and the two Soviet leaders omitted reference to a "political" or a "peaceful" settlement for the first time since at least the end of 1969.[60]

The shift in the Soviet declaratory stance can be traced to public statements by Brezhnev and Kosygin beginning in December 1971. Speaking during October, both leaders had echoed Podgorny's calls for a political settlement to be achieved by united action of the radical Arab states.[61] Now in a speech published December 9, Brezhnev described Soviet Mideast policy as designed "to frustrate the plans of the Israeli aggressors and their patrons and to help Arab peoples restore their legitimate rights and to aid the establishment of a just peace in the Near East." By omitting Podgorny's call for a "political settlement" (repeated by Podgorny the same day), Brezhnev left open the possibility of military force as a means of policy.[62] By March 1972, Brezhnev identified himself more unambiguously with the new policy. Noting the "threat of a military explosion" in the Near East, Brezhnev contrasted the Arabs' willingness to reach a political settlement with the Israelis' obduracy, backed by the United States. He then warned: "However, this cannot continue indefinitely. Sober-minded politicians can hardly count on the Arab states to tolerate the occupation of their territory."[63] Kosygin's statements shifted in tandem with Brezhnev's. Four of his speeches in December discuss the Middle East without calling for a "political settlement," and in February he too would warn against the error of supposing that "the Arab peoples . . . will submit to the occupation of their lands."[64]

59. April 30, 1972. See also Glassman, *Arms for the Arabs*, 94; Porter, *USSR in Third World Conflicts*, 122n.
60. *Vneshnaia politika Sovetskogo Soiuza, 1972*, doc. 7, pp. 17–18. Cf. ibid., *1970*, docs. 59, 101; *1971*, docs. 3, 12, 18, 54.
61. October 1, 2, 7, 11, and 28, 1971.
62. December 9, 1971. See also December 8, 1971.
63. March 19, 1972. See also June 6 and 28, October 14, 1972.
64. December 4, 6, 7, and 23, 1972; February 12, 1972. See also July 4, 1972.

This turn to a more confrontational attitude toward Israel responded to mounting evidence from the Middle East that cast doubt on the persuasiveness of Podgorny's strategy. Having declared 1971 the "Year of Decision," Sadat could not be expected to look favorably on Podgorny's calls for restraint, flexibility, "a realistic evaluation of the situation," and "political and diplomatic" struggle while Egypt rebuilt its defenses. Though Sadat, dependent on Soviet arms deliveries for his planned offensive against Israel, temporarily tolerated Podgorny's strategy, from the very outset he told the Politburo publicly that his sole concern was the recovery of the lost Arab territories without regard to means, peaceful or violent.[65] By October 1971 the Soviets were so well aware of Egypt's objections that Podgorny and Kosygin publicly discussed them in nearly identical language. Blaming "anticommunists" for trying to incite "a quarrel between Arab countries and their most faithful friends and allies . . . the Soviet Union and the other states of the socialist commonwealth," Podgorny reassured his audience, as did Kosygin, that experience had taught the Arabs to distinguish their enemies from their true friends.[66]

Podgorny's admission that tensions between the USSR and Sadat were compromising his strategy of assembling a unified Arab coalition around Egypt presented an opportunity for Brezhnev and Kosygin to recapture control of policy toward the Middle East. They dramatized Podgorny's loss of influence in policy making by excluding him from summit meetings with Sadat and Sidqi in February, April, and July 1972, though he had attended every previous Soviet-Egyptian summit during 1970 and 1971.[67] Exclusion from Soviet talks with Egypt deprived Podgorny of a forum he had used during 1971 to go public with attacks on negotiations with the United States. By demonstrating Podgorny's loss of influence to Soviet audiences, the intrusion by Brezhnev and Kosygin into Podgorny's issue specialty enabled them to demand his concessions in May and September 1972 in favor of U.S.-Soviet détente.

Like Brezhnev's exploitation of Eurocommunism to force a concession by Suslov in 1971, the new policy in the Middle East produced an opportunity for a junior Politburo member to go public. Kirill Mazurov, a détente critic who in his government role as Kosygin's first deputy oversaw foreign aid, led a delegation to Damascus in

---

65. January 20, 1971.
66. October 13, 1971; Kosygin, October 7, 1971.
67. See the communiqués cited in n. 60.

February 1972 to sign a new arms deal with Syria. In his speech in Syria for the first time Mazurov gave Brezhnev and Kosygin (but not Podgorny) credit for promoting European security.[68]

While Brezhnev's and Kosygin's recapture of Mideast policy helped them to gain the Politburo's assent to the May 1972 summit, it also stored up trouble for détente in the near future. Brezhnev and Kosygin would presumably have preferred to return to the policy of negotiating a Mideast peace settlement with the United States. At talks with Kissinger in April 1972 to prepare for the May summit, Gromyko made an unexpected concession to the U.S. position on the Middle East. During the summit itself he went even further, for the first time accepting "general working principles" that did not specifically demand Israel's full withdrawal from all occupied territories. However, the two Soviet leaders fully recognized Kissinger's unwillingness to negotiate a Mideast settlement with them. Describing his own participation in the Moscow exchanges as a charade, Kissinger recalls, "Gromyko was experienced enough to know what I was doing."[69] Meanwhile, between the two meetings with Brezhnev and Kosygin in the winter of 1972, Sadat initiated private contacts with Kissinger in the hope of working out a separate deal between Egypt and Israel brokered by the United States.[70]

With Kissinger refusing to negotiate and Sadat threatening to cut the Soviet Union out of a Mideast settlement, Brezhnev and Kosygin tried to appease Sadat by promising to supply the offensive weapons for his proposed attack on Israel. At the same time they tried to prevent an Arab-Israeli war from interfering with U.S.-Soviet détente. The Soviets' usual practice was to offer weapons on credit at low interest rates and flexible terms for repayment.[71] By demanding that Egypt pay cash, Brezhnev and Kosygin took advantage of Egypt's known lack of hard-currency reserves to frustrate Sadat's plans for war.[72]

This policy backfired in January 1973 when Saudi Arabia suddenly

68. February 23 and 24, 1972.

69. Quoted in Alexander L. George, "The Arab-Israeli War of October 1973: Origins and Impact," in George, *Managing U.S.-Soviet Rivalry*, 143.

70. Henry Kissinger, *The White House Years* (Boston: Little, Brown, 1979), 1276, 1292–1300; Garthoff, *Détente and Confrontation*, 315, 361.

71. Roger Pajak, "West European and Soviet Arms Transfer Policies in the Middle East," in Milton Leitenberg and Gabriel Sheffer, *Great Power Intervention in the Middle East* (New York: Pergamon, 1979), 155.

72. *USSR and the Third World* (Central Asian Research Centre, London) 2 (1972): 208; 3 (1973): 93, 246.

granted Egypt a credit of $500 million to purchase Soviet weapons.[73] An Egyptian delegation promptly traveled to Moscow to negotiate the arms deal. The Saudi action left Brezhnev and Kosygin with no option but to fulfill their promise to deliver the arms to Egypt. The June 1973 Washington summit remained at stake; if Brezhnev and Kosygin refused to deliver the arms, the Egyptian protests would lend renewed persuasiveness to Podgorny's accusations that Third World allies were being sacrificed for the sake of détente,[74] and he would be able to demand concessions from Brezhnev. The best alternative was to deliver the arms and try to talk the United States into forcing concessions from Israel. The result was the Yom Kippur War, which would deliver the first powerful blow to popular support in the United States for receptivity to Brezhnev's offers of détente.

73. Alvin Z. Rubinstein, *Red Star on the Nile: The Soviet-Egyptian Influence Relationship since the June War* (Princeton: Princeton University Press, 1977), 242.

74. Brezhnev and Kosygin both addressed these charges, June 28, October 17, November 23, 1972.

Chapter 12

Going Public,
Foreign Policy,
and Political Change

Did the Politburo go public in foreign policy?

Four Politburo members went public after Khrushchev's ouster in the manner of Anthony Downs's competitive advertisers. They advanced alternative visions of social order that promised to preserve socialism at home and distinctive grand strategies that promised to keep peace abroad. Each leader's grand strategy incorporated synecdoches that replicated the symbolism of his own domestic vision. Although each rival specialized in policy toward a particular world region or functional issue, some issues overlapped these specialties, and on those issues the leaders resolved their disagreements by compromises reached either by convergent concessions or by sequential issue trades. When world events contravened a leader's description of world politics or made his policy recommendations seem less feasible or urgent, he made public concessions on issues in dispute, and policy shifted toward the recommendations of his rivals. In 1966 the four rivals acted as a cartel, blocking the attempt of a fifth leader to join the inner core of the Politburo by shaping policy compromises to diminish incentives for a shift of support to the challenger and to display the challenger's inability to control policy.

In 1970 one of the rivals, Brezhnev, changed his grand strategy in the manner associated with constituency expansion by electoral politicians. He selectively incorporated variants of policy recommendations formerly associated with Kosygin; framed his new recommendations to occupy a median on the issue of East-West cooperation

between the positions of Kosygin, its advocate, and Suslov and Podgorny, its opponents; preserved his reputation for attentiveness to
military programs, for promotion of the cohesion of the East European alliance, and for active support of armed rebellion in the Third
World; and justified his shift by claiming that enactment of his earlier policy recommendations had changed world conditions in a direction that justified the new program he had previously opposed.
Despite observable change in international circumstances, the other
three rivals continued to advocate the same strategic principles they
had presented as appropriate for the conditions of 1965. Brezhnev
obtained public endorsements of détente agreements from the opponents in May 1971 and May 1972 by offering them control of policy
on issues treated as separable from East-West détente and by taking
advantage of world developments that undermined the persuasiveness of their grand strategies.

Competition and Policy Inadaptability
without Contested Elections

Observations of going public by members of the Politburo in the
Brezhnev years are inconsistent with arguments, rooted in the institutional distinctiveness of the Soviet Union, that going public was
either useless or perilous for a Politburo member. Public discussion
of policy might not in itself be sufficient to demonstrate conclusively
that Politburo members' behavior was comparable in some respects
to going public among electoral politicians for leverage on policy
bargaining. However, there was a consistent correspondence between (*a*) observed change in Soviet foreign policy on issues publicly
contested among the four Politburo members and (*b*) the expected
outcomes of bargaining, via either convergent concessions or sequential issue trades, among the Politburo members' public stands.
The correspondence of observed policy to the interaction between
going public and bargaining seems hard to explain if we suppose
that going public could not secure bargaining leverage in Soviet politics during the Brezhnev years.

Going public and bargaining success combined to promote tenure
in the Politburo. Table 4 presents a correlation between the reverse
order of the thirteen post-Khrushchev members' removal from the
Politburo and each member's rank by number of speeches published
in *Pravda* between October 1964 and November 1967. A rank-order

Table 4. Rank order of Politburo members by length of tenure and by number of speeches published in *Pravda*, October 1964–November 1967

Politburo member	Rank		Absolute difference $(A - B)$	Square of difference
	A By tenure in Politburo	B By number of speeches		
Pelse[a]	2	12	10	100
Brezhnev[a]	2	2	0	0
Suslov[a]	2	4[b]	2	4
Kirilenko	4	10	6	36
Kosygin	5	1	4	16
Mazurov	6	5	1	1
Podgorny	7	3	4	16
Polianskii	8	8	0	0
Shelepin	9	9	0	0
Shelest[c]	10	11	1	1
Voronov[c]	11	10	1	1
Mikoian[c]	12	6	6	36
Shvernik[c]	13	13[d]	0	0

Note: Spearman's r = .43; Z = 1.49; significance (one-tailed) = .068.
[a]Politburo members who died in office are considered tied for first place, never having been removed; ties are broken by splitting the six points for the first through third places.
[b]Includes speeches by Ponomarev.
[c]Ties between pairs of members formally removed on the same date (Shelest and Voronov, Mikoian and Shvernik) have been broken by the order in which they ceased to hold the outside post that entitled them to Politburo membership.
[d]No public speeches.

correlation is presented because, as I have argued, uncertainty about the distribution of support among Politburo members could indefinitely delay action to remove a member whose support had fallen too low; consequently, not duration of tenure but the order in which Politburo members lost seats is the relevant variable for judging the hypothesis of association among tenure in the Politburo, going public, and bargaining success.

As the theory of competitive politics suggests, the null hypothesis of random variation between opportunities to go public and tenure in the Politburo cannot quite be rejected at the .05 level. The theory holds that not only going public but also success in bargaining, affected by entry into winning coalitions and by favorable development of events, will determine tenure. The right-hand column reveals that 81 percent of the variance between the two rankings is attributable to three leaders: Pelse and Kirilenko, who rank high in tenure but low in number of speeches, and Mikoian, high in speeches but low in tenure. Pelse and Kirilenko, of course, are the two leaders who joined Brezhnev in the coalition for détente when Eurocommunism gave them an opportunity to intrude into Suslov's issue specialty, while Mikoian became isolated in the bargaining on his sole issue of policy toward the Third World in 1965 and lost persuasiveness when radical Third World states rejected his recommended policy of seeking Soviet participation in a new conference of the nonaligned nations.

Moreover, Podgorny was the one member of the Politburo's inner core who finished lower in tenure than his rank in number of speeches would have merited. To maintain a median between détente opponents and Kosygin, Brezhnev did not need both Podgorny and Suslov in the Politburo, and if entry into a coalition with Brezhnev was affecting tenure in the 1970s, one of them was likely to drop earlier than would otherwise have been expected. Mazurov had opportunely joined the coalition for détente in early 1972. An arbitrary small correction in the rank in number of speeches (moving Pelse and Kirilenko up two ranks and Mikoian down two, and adjusting others correspondingly) moves the significance well past the .05 boundary.

Politburo members did go public; some lost but others gained, and those who went public less lost more. Politburo members in the Brezhnev era were advocates, not just infighters or brokers. Infighters would have penalized anyone who looked beyond the Politburo for support, while brokers would have avoided public statements likely to polarize bureaucratic disputants. The Politburo did broker bureaucratic disputes, and its members did try to outmaneuver each other in the back room, but like politicians in an electoral polity, they embedded these activities in a larger public contest for support.

This conclusion does not necessarily contradict the argument that the Politburo members owed their seats to control of appointments, which enabled them to depend on the circular flow of power. In principle, of course, they could have depended both on control of appointments and on going public. Moreover, it might be true that they went public to appeal to the Central Committee members whose votes formally determined whether they were in or out of the Politburo. This possibility seems most implausible, however. While Central Committee members were surely among the audiences to whom Politburo members directed their speeches, all the evidence I have cited of going public comes from texts printed in *Pravda*. With a circulation in the millions, this newspaper would have been a cumbersome means of communicating to a Central Committee voting membership numbering in the few hundreds. When the Politburo wanted to communicate solely to Central Committee members, it convened them in closed session, sent them circulars not available to the public (not even to lower-ranking Party officials), or summoned them individually to Party headquarters. Brezhnev reportedly used to spend two hours every morning on the telephone to the provincial Party committee heads who composed a plurality of the Central Committee and otherwise made himself regularly accessible to them.[1] All the Politburo members toured the provinces for private consultations with Central Committee members. The audience for going public seems to have been much broader than the Central Committee membership.

The implications of going public do less to contradict the circular flow of power than to duplicate its explanatory power. Unquestionably control of appointments helped to secure the power of the Politburo as a whole against outside challengers, but the circular flow of power is also advanced as an explanation for the dominance of successive general secretaries against challenges from within the Politburo. Competitive politics, substantiated by observations of going public and bargaining, offers an alternative explanation of how Brezhnev won the contest, and of course in electoral polities success in public contests for support is the source of a candidate's ability to control appointments. Two explanations for the same phenomenon are one too many. While extensive documentation has been adduced for the circular flow of power, that model does not provide any obvious explanation for the observations to which the competitive politics theory directs our attention, and the older model led its originator to dismiss the possibility of finding the evidence presented in this book.[2] Moreover, despite extensive documentation of the circular flow of power, the extreme secrecy surrounding Party appointments has prevented the originators of the model from ever directly observing the process of appointment. Like the competitive politics theory, it is an "as if" model, relying on hypotheses about

1. Fedor Burlatskii, "Brezhnev i krushenie ottepeli: Razmyshlenie o prirode politicheskogo liderstva," *Literaturnaia Gazeta*, 1988, no. 37 (September 14), 13–14. See also Shelepin in *Trud*, March 15, 1991; Egorychev in *Ogonek*, February 4–11, 1989.
2. Robert V. Daniels, "Political Processes and Generational Change," in Archie Brown, ed., *Political Leadership in the Soviet Union* (Bloomington: Indiana University Press, 1989), 117.

other observations to establish the plausibility of the mechanism to which it ascribed Brezhnev's dominance. Especially if an opening of the Party archives lifts this secrecy, the circular flow of power deserves reexamination.

Observation of competitive politics is certainly very far from contradicting the interest-group models of Brezhnev-era politics—institutional pluralism, participatory bureaucracy, bureaucratic pluralism—to which the circular flow of power led. One of the originators of the interest-group model has criticized an early version of this theory for reducing Soviet politics to "introverted political competition among Politburo members,"[3] but of course the theory no more reduces Soviet politics to leadership struggles than does the same theory in application to an electoral polity. Competitive politics and interest groups are found together in electoral polities, and the more open the contest, the more active the interest groups.

Nor do the observations associated with competitive politics force us to reject the finding, amply documented in studies of foreign policy by Bruce Parrott, Michael Sodaro, Franklyn Griffiths, Dina Rome Spechler, and others, that in going public Politburo members participated in "rational deliberation" of policy options in interaction with policy experts. But the observations do reveal that rational deliberation for influence on experts is incomplete as a characterization of the Politburo's public statements. Politburo members sought to get the experts on their side. But despite their public statements calling for a "scientific" policy to replace Khrushchev's alleged voluntarism, a striking regularity is observable in all five grand strategies identified here. Each Politburo member presented descriptions of world conditions or policy recommendations that disagreed with information or preferences widespread among policy experts on that issue. Brezhnev denied the divisiveness of the MLF in NATO, Suslov implied that the French and Italian communists exercised an effective veto over European capitalist governments' decisions on war and peace, Podgorny recommended continuing to decide economic aid commitments by political criteria, Kosygin claimed that lack of politi-

3. Franklyn Griffiths, "Soviet Policy toward the United States," in George W. Breslauer and Philip E. Tetlock, eds., *Learning in U.S. and Soviet Foreign Policy* (Boulder, Colo.: Westview Press, 1991), 670. Griffiths objects sharply to my paper in the same volume while reaching virtually identical conclusions about the Brezhnev leadership's inability to learn and its consequences in blocking adaptation in Soviet foreign policy.

cal will among capitalist governments was the main barrier to Soviet exports of industrial products, and Shelepin argued that communist takeovers were the only path open for development of Third World countries and that Nazis were influencing U.S. policies.

Not only did the Politburo members display a surprising tendency to disagree with the experts;[4] their arguments seemed remarkably ill suited for influence on experts. In addition to synoptic propositions of the kind convincing to experts, the Politburo relied heavily on synecdoche—individual instances that stand for more general phenomena regardless of whether the instances are typical. In contrast to the expert, the inexpert find argument by vivid example persuasive. Synecdoche avoids presentation of more information than the inexpert can recall, and persuades by converting the political leader into a personification of the audience. The politician appears to the constituents to be facing the same circumstances they face and to be acting as they would act. If Politburo members went public to engage in political competition, their arguments should have been aimed mainly at the inexpert. In a national bureaucracy, as in an electorate, the inexpert on any given issue far outnumber the experts. When the contest is resolved by the distribution of support, the inexpert outweigh the expert.

Observation of going public reinforces the conclusions originally advanced by George Breslauer concerning the fundamental requirement for authority building even in the Soviet institutional context. Institutionalists sometimes discount political competition as a cause for the policy sclerosis increasingly displayed by the Politburo toward the end of Brezhnev's term as general secretary. In *Crisis amid Plenty*, an admirable study of energy policy that deserves wide attention for its rich documentation and careful execution, Thane Gustafson convincingly attributes "self-defeating" decisions in regard to energy to "the power and inertia of the vast vertical hierarchies, only weakly offset by the available mechanisms for central oversight and horizontal coordination." The Politburo, "rather than offsetting the biases and tendencies imparted by the system, aggravated them instead, not because of conflict within the leadership but because of the character of Brezhnev as a leader." In particular, Brezhnev approved a crash program of expansion of oil output in the near term, at the expense of alternative proposals for conserva-

4. As Griffiths, "Soviet Policy," also notes (670).

tion, because to do otherwise might have interfered with his long-term programs for modernization of agriculture and accumulation of military power.[5]

Despite the thorough research and careful weighing of alternatives, Gustafson's empirical findings may not really disprove the hypothesis that competitive politics shaped Soviet energy policy. Competitive politics theory leads us to expect rival leaders to present alternative visions of social order and to decide their positions toward particular issues, such as energy, by the criterion of finding symbolism consistent with their overall visions. From his very first speech in October 1964, Brezhnev stood for a vision of inspirational accomplishment, made concrete with examples of expansion of output achieved by central oversight of vertical organization. From his own first speech, Kosygin stood for a vision of efficiency to be achieved by strong horizontal coordination. When energy was at issue, Brezhnev was likely to advocate expanding supply while Kosygin was likely to focus on more efficient use. After 1969, when Brezhnev became ascendant, he was likely to respond to developments that diminished the persuasiveness of Kosygin's policy recommendations by selectively incorporating variants of Kosygin's efficiency proposals in his own larger program of inspirational accomplishment.

When one turns to Gustafson's evidence on Soviet energy policy, one finds that in fact Brezhnev stood for expansion of oil production, Kosygin for conservation; when mounting energy costs discredited Kosygin's stewardship of energy issues, in 1977 Brezhnev expanded his own role with a new program of an "all-out oil offensive," into which he blended calls for conservation. The substitution of symbol for objective problems had the usual self-defeating consequences. Brezhnev's promises of a steady rise in oil production diminished incentives for Soviet bureaucrats to heed his calls for conservation. Gustafson argues that this pattern does not reveal political competition in action because "Brezhnev's precedence had been settled a decade before, and . . . Kosygin was a sick man with no political ambitions."[6] But if going public is necessary for a leader to retain office as well as to advance, precedence is never finally settled, and ill health does not exempt a leader from the requirement

5. Thane Gustafson, *Crisis amid Plenty* (Princeton: Princeton University Press, 1989), 290–91, 324–27, 331.
6. Ibid., 320–21, 327.

to continue advocacy of the vision that attracts his or her supporters. These remarks do not detract from the persuasiveness of Gustafson's findings about the inefficiencies of vertical economic organization, but they do suggest that competitive politics exacerbated systemic dysfunction.

My observations of going public not only reinforce Breslauer's conclusion that the leader's power depended on authority building but extend his findings by pointing out the difference between a situation in which one or two persons build authority and a situation in which the presence of a third authority builder provides an ascendant leader with a chance to occupy a median. The median explains both the stability of the leader's hold on office and the inflexibility of policy. Brezhnev's moderation, often noted, has been attributed to his character. In fact from 1965 to 1967, in foreign policy at least, Brezhnev was evidently an extremist—not so extreme as Shelepin, but still more averse to cooperation with noncommunists than any other senior leader. Despite its advantages, a move into the median was not available to him before 1969 because centrist positioning would not have let him differentiate his reputation. Only with ascendancy after 1969 did he become a moderate.

Occupation of the median perpetuated Brezhnev's ascendancy. When leaders can position themselves along more than one issue dimension, rivals can easily dislodge a contender from the median by small shifts in their own positions, but if the costs of inconstancy to their reputation among constituents outweigh the gains in bargaining influence by eliminating the median, the rivals will not shift. If retention of constituents compels the rivals of an ascendant leader to repeat their previous themes (as Kosygin, Podgorny, and Suslov all did during 1970–1972), a leader in the median can continue to control policy over time. If other issue dimensions arise, the ascendant leader can offer concessions by treating those issues as separable, as Brezhnev did with the Middle East, Vietnam, China, and ethnic policy in 1971.

In the absence of term limitations, an ascendant leader's continuing control of policy makes him hard to displace. If political competitors can afford to change the themes of their visions and grand strategies (as opposed to stands on particular issues) only when they achieve ascendancy, once a leader achieves it, the vision is unlikely to change again. Kosygin and Suslov occupied the same posts with the same visions until the former's illness in 1980 and the latter's death in 1982; if Brezhnev continued to occupy the median between them, new departures in Soviet policy were not to be expected. The Politburo may have been trapped by Soviet institutions, but the dynamics of competition for bureaucratic allegiances exacerbated the effects of institutional misdesign. If Soviet bureaucrats could register approval or disapproval for a Politburo member mainly by enthusiasm or sabotage in the execution of that member's policies, as I suggested in Chapter 2, the process of leadership maintenance would have imposed a heavy burden on organizational effectiveness.

These observations have implications for the field of comparative politics beyond the study of the Soviet state, implications concerning the explanatory power of institutional differences between states. It is well established that differences in electoral institutions vary the competitive strategies of politicians and parties and that variation in political strategies in turn changes political outcomes.[7] Downsian competition, however, appears to be a more general phenomenon than the institution of contested elections to which it is normally attributed. It appears to represent a phenomenon found regardless of the presence or absence of the electoral institution. The process of recruiting political allegiances may vary with electoral laws but is not attributable to them.

Domestic Competition and Maladaptive Foreign Policy

Political competition caused Soviet foreign policy to be maladaptive to international circumstances. Maladaptation occurred because symbols displaced objective problems; because issue separation eased the search for compromise at the expense of attention to substantive interactions among the effects of policy; and because logrolling combined policies with mutually incompatible substantive goals.

The Soviet decision to pursue offensive détente after 1969 may potentially have been either (*a*) a maladaptive logroll among leaders who disagreed over whether to pursue an offensive against capitalism or détente or (*b*) an adaptive response to new domestic and international circumstances that emerged in that year. Since the adherents of the latter analysis describe the conditions of 1969—U.S. and West German willingness to negotiate, Chinese antagonism, U.S. retreat in Vietnam, economic slowdown—as favorable to a decision

---

7. For a recent review, see Arend Lijphart, "The Political Consequences of Electoral Laws, 1945–1985," *American Political Science Review* 84 (1990): 481–96.

for offensive détente, evidence that the policy was also a logroll does not contradict their claim that it was an adaptive response to world developments. Certainly, imaginable but sufficiently unfavorable counterfactual international circumstances—such as the United States' resort to nuclear weapons in Vietnam—would presumably have deterred the Politburo from approving détente. Certainly, too, the evidence of logrolling in connection with détente can be given other interpretations. Perhaps Brezhnev's insistence on one-sided advantages in arms-control talks and his security-first, economics-later approach to East-West cooperation were simply his preferences, not occupancy of the median, and maybe Brezhnev approved Podgorny's approach to the Middle East and Vietnam merely in reaction to Israeli and U.S. recalcitrance in these regions, not as a compromise.

Even though, when viewed in isolation, the Soviet shift to offensive détente in 1970 might be seen as adaptive to circumstances, consideration of the features found more generally in the other Soviet policies examined here suggests that offensive détente was probably a logroll too, propitiated by some (not all) of the international circumstances of 1969 but determined by competitive politics. The most egregious example of maladaptive logrolls was the 1965 offer of reconciliation to China coupled with a refusal of any substantive concessions on the issues in dispute. Offers of reconciliation without readiness to compromise are adaptive to circumstances only when the other side has no option but to accept. If the idea was to score propaganda points by appearing willing to end the dispute on reasonable terms without really wanting to, why insist on transparently unreasonable terms? If the Politburo did not want to make concessions, why offer reconciliation at all? Logrolling explains this policy, circumstances do not.

Compromise policies toward every world region betrayed the propensity of logrolls to produce self-defeating policies. The Politburo approved economic reforms in Eastern Europe while reducing the subsidies necessary to enable the reforms to succeed, with the result that the rule of the limited reformers in Czechoslovakia collapsed inside two years. The Politburo tried to combine pleas for the North Vietnamese to enter negotiations for a settlement of the Vietnam conflict with delivery of air defense weapons that made the North Vietnamese feel safer in rejecting negotiations. By separating its policies on security and economic aid, the Politburo found itself urging Third World radicals to provide more support for Soviet foreign policy goals at the same time that it was reducing the rewards to them for support. The Bucharest program combined pressure on West European governments to negotiate economic and security issues with demands for exclusion of the United States from the negotiations even though U.S. participation was the one condition that might have made the Soviet offer acceptable to the West European allies.

Not every logroll need be self-defeating, and some of the Politburo's were not. The Soviet Union could decide in 1966 to àid radical Third World regimes without impairing its aid to countries on the capitalist path. Also, when the Politburo avoided logrolling by separating issues, its policies avoided the internal contradictions that frustrated accomplishment of these policies' manifest objectives. The compromises reached by convergent concessions on aid to Vietnam during most of 1965 and on the redirection of economic aid to developing states with capitalist institutions in the same year, and the decisions in 1966 to increase aid to Vietnam and to accelerate economic reform, reached by closing the public gap between Kosygin and Brezhnev, all worked smoothly. The issue separation necessary for compromise by convergent concessions did produce some awkward consequences in other areas. Increased arms deliveries to Vietnam handed weapons to Chinese Red Guards, who stole them from southbound trains, and aid to capitalist developing nations rewarded international opponents of the Soviet refusal to negotiate on Indochina.

Propitious international circumstances were present whenever the Politburo approved any of its self-defeating policies. U.S. enmity toward China was a factor pressuring the Maoist leadership to entertain a Soviet bid to end the split. Unlike the Chinese, the East Europeans could not reject Soviet terms outright. After the November 1964 elections, the United States seemed to be on the verge of pulling out of Vietnam anyway and might well have accepted some face-saving formula for negotiations that a more secure leadership in Hanoi might have been more prepared to enter. U.S. escalation in Vietnam, coupled with intervention in the Dominican Republic, might have frightened radical regimes elsewhere in the Third World enough to make them more interested in Soviet security assistance than in economic aid. De Gaulle's expulsion of NATO headquarters from France might have indicated that his proposals to broker a U.S.-Soviet rapprochement were a temporizing measure on the way to a realignment with the Soviet Union. A coup in Damascus suggested that the prospects for radicals to take power in Third World countries might be improving.

These seemingly favorable aspects of the world scene exerted undue influence on Soviet policy, however, because going public made policy selectively responsive to circumstances. Selectivity was consistently associated with the Politburo rivals' recourse to synecdoche. NATO's MLF proposal was a circumstance that influenced Soviet policy, but divisive effects of the MLF on NATO were not. The military threat posed by the United States influenced the Politburo to offer reconciliation with China, but Chinese objections to Soviet domestic and foreign policies were temporarily set aside until the proffered reconciliation had been rejected. Escalation in Vietnam was an indicator of global U.S. intentions, but President Johnson's offers to negotiate were not. Electoral successes by the French and Italian parties influenced the Soviet program toward European communism, but defeats suffered by other European parties did not. The Syrian coup revived the Politburo's willingness to offer economic aid to Third World radicals while three coups indicating the instability of the recipient governments were ignored. The Syrians' desire for the Euphrates dam, symbolic of continuity with the Third World policy made concrete (literally) by Aswan, shaped Soviet policy when the Iraqis' protests did not, even though the aid was associated with an attempt to arrange an alliance between Iraq and Syria. France's public withdrawal from NATO's military organization counted, but its continuing participation in NATO's political council and private cooperation in military planning did not count. As far as Brezhnev was concerned, escalation in Vietnam in 1965 outweighed President Johnson's offers of East-West talks, while President Nixon's offers of East-West talks outweighed U.S. actions in both Indochina and the Middle East in 1970; as far as Podgorny was concerned, nothing had changed.

Maladaptation caused by logrolling, issue separation, and symbolism that produced selectivity in responsiveness is, of course, not the same as unresponsiveness to international circumstances. I have not examined any issues on which the Soviet leaders did not go public and therefore cannot comment on how their policies on those issues interacted with developing international conditions.[8] Whenever Politburo members did go public, international circumstances influ-

8. Because competitors want the international scene in general to develop in a manner favorable to their grand strategies, their preferences even on issues that do not become public controversies are likely to be shaped by the policy preferences they do declare in public. In the absence of the private record, however, this hypothesis is not testable for the Politburo.

enced policy compromises by their effect on the relative persuasiveness of the rivals' respective descriptions of world conditions and policy recommendations. Four tests have been offered of the effects of international circumstances on persuasiveness.

First, changes in relative persuasiveness explain why events or trends affecting the feasibility of policy recommendations toward one region or issue compelled leaders to make concessions on policy toward other regions or issues. Kosygin lost persuasiveness in Vietnam and made concessions on policy toward Western Europe. Brezhnev lost persuasiveness on China and the MLF and made concessions on economic relations with Eastern Europe as well as diplomacy toward Western Europe. Suslov lost persuasiveness because of Eurocommunism and made concessions on linkage of European security issues. Podgorny lost persuasiveness on the Middle East and made concessions on strategic arms control.

Second, whether comparable events or trends affected Soviet policy depended on how they affected the distribution of persuasiveness. Of course, because international circumstances can only be comparable, not identical, and because relevant pairs are likely to be rare, the results of this test cannot be conclusive. One pair of comparable events with different effects on the distribution of persuasiveness consists of (*a*) the U.S. military intervention in Vietnam in 1965 and (*b*) the covert intervention in Chile from 1970 to 1973. Because Kosygin promised that the United States would observe restraint in Vietnam, escalation there damaged his persuasiveness and resulted in policy change. Although Podgorny blamed the United States implicitly for intervention against the government of Salvador Allende, Brezhnev separated the argument for his détente program from this issue (as from other Third World problems).[9] Thus covert intervention in Chile neither impaired Brezhnev's persuasiveness nor exerted observable effects on Soviet policy toward the United States (and the same is true of the eventual coup against Allende).

Another pair of comparable developments with contrasting impacts on the distribution of persuasiveness consists of (*a*) the failure of the 1965 initiative for reconciliation with China and (*b*) hostile Sino-Soviet relations during 1970–1972. In 1965 the failure of

9. Cf. Podgorny's reference to "internal and external reaction" and the use of "all means of political and economic pressure . . . to disrupt the process of revolutionary renewal of" Chile (December 7, 1972) with Brezhnev's warning that both "past experience" and "current events" pointed to the possibility of "overthrows and zigzags" during political struggles in Latin America.

Brezhnev's initiative toward China compelled him to offer a concession authorizing pursuit of rapprochement with Western Europe; because he had separated the issue of China from the persuasiveness of his East-West program, not even China's rapprochement with the United States in 1971 kept him from pursuing East-West détente.

Third, the effects of the changing distribution of persuasiveness within the Politburo on Soviet foreign policy are also evident in those cases in which comparable international events evoked opposite Soviet responses. Of course, the overall international context can never be held constant, but still these cases are striking. Escalation in Vietnam in February 1965 suspended Soviet diplomatic initiatives toward Western Europe; further escalation of the Vietnam conflict six months later led to resumption of the initiatives toward Western Europe. In 1965 the Soviets rejected East European requests for increased economic subsidies; in 1966 and 1971 they approved the same requests.

Brezhnev's constituency expansion exerted especially pronounced effects on Soviet responses to developments in both Vietnam and Western Europe. Limited air raids on military targets in the southern periphery of North Vietnam in 1965 inhibited even low-level U.S.-Soviet contacts, but massive air raids on civilian zones of Hanoi in 1972 did not obstruct a U.S.-Soviet summit. Soviet policy sought the expulsion of U.S. influence from Western Europe in 1966–1967; Soviet acceptance of talks on reducing conventional forces helped preserve the U.S. position in Europe in May 1971.

Fourth, in a series of instances efforts to change the distribution of persuasiveness in the Politburo resulted in changes in Soviet policy that preceded the development of international circumstances without anticipating them. Aid to North Vietnamese air defense was approved before the United States escalated the air war in February 1965; it was approved on the assumption that the United States would not escalate (and despite the Soviets' refusal of aid after the August 1964 attacks). In 1965, reduction of Soviet economic aid to the Third World preceded the coups against allies in Indonesia, Ghana, and Algeria; efforts to undermine Shelepin's reputation for ability to control policy then produced dramatic expansion of aid commitments during 1966. Sadat obtained declaratory approval of his intention for war against Israel, and an offer of arms for cash, before he expelled Soviet advisers and air defense forces in July 1972. The expulsion had no evident effect on the Soviets' willingness to continue to approve Sadat's aims or on their insistence on cash in exchange for weapons.

In short, the interaction between Soviet foreign policy and international circumstances was contingent on symbolism, on logrolling, and on the emergence of Brezhnev as an ascendant leader. Each leader's grand strategy in world politics replicated the symbolism of his self-presentation in domestic politics, while Brezhnev's grand strategy in 1970 changed in parallel with his selective incorporation of variants of recommendations by Kosygin for domestic policy.[10] These observations should raise suspicions about the adaptiveness of Politburo members' individual grand strategies to world conditions, which, produced by the interaction of the behavior of many countries, surely bear only a weak relation to the domestic politics of any particular country.[11] To single out the decision for offensive détente after 1969 as an adaptive response to international conditions, when it equally well may have been a logroll, is to neglect the effects of symbolic politics and logrolling on other Soviet policy choices when going public by Politburo members is observed. It is of course also relevant that if offensive détente was adaptive to international circumstances in 1969, it did not remain adaptive very long. Brezhnev's intrusion into Podgorny's control of Mideast affairs, evidently a means of compelling the concessions by Podgorny that allowed the May 1972 summit to go forward despite renewed U.S. air raids in Vietnam, produced a Soviet policy of declaratory approval for a renewal of warfare between the Arabs and Israel. When unexpectedly Egypt obtained the cash to convert declaratory approval into sales of arms, it launched the attack on a U.S. ally that severely exacerbated public distrust of détente in the United States.

The U.S. public's growing suspicion of Soviet motives failed to persuade the Politburo to adjust its policy of offensive détente. Although I have examined only six years of Soviet foreign policy, the evidence provided here prefigures the main outlines of offensive détente during the 1970s. Brezhnev's 1965 commitment to use arms aid

10. For the domestic side, see George W. Breslauer, *Khrushchev and Brezhnev as Leaders* (London: Allen & Unwin, 1982), 179–99.
11. Ronald Rogowski argues that over the very long term, political conditions within countries are strongly related to shifts in international commerce, but even Rogowski argues that commercial trends influence only class or sectoral cleavages within countries and do not determine how these cleavages are reconciled: *Commerce and Coalitions: How Trade Affects Domestic Political Alignments* (Princeton: Princeton University Press, 1989).

for influence in the Third World and his criterion of adoption of socialist policies for evaluating a Third World country's suitability for aid presaged armed interventions in Angola, Ethiopia, and Afghanistan. Soviet rejection of U.S. demands for linkage between U.S.-Soviet relations and Third World issues is usually attributed to differences in the two sides' beliefs about international relations, but comparison of the U.S. and Soviet positions on this question in the 1960s reveals that the two sides flip-flopped. Until the late 1960s the Soviets insisted on linkage between Vietnam and U.S.-Soviet cooperation, while the Johnson administration promoted separation of these two issues. Rather than expressing lasting beliefs, the Soviet position on linkage at the international level was instrumental at the domestic level. It allowed Brezhnev to separate Third World issues for sequential issue trades at the Politburo level and to preserve his reputation at the level of Soviet officialdom as a heroic anticapitalist, while activism in the Third World both before and during détente let Politburo members share opportunities to claim credit for policy accomplishments. Brezhnev's insistence on the exclusivity of the Soviet preserve in Eastern Europe and his obduracy with regard to the one-sided strategic advantages won by the principle of "equal security" in SALT I also helped to perpetuate his reputation to officials and his presence in the median between Kosygin and Suslov.

These policies maintained Brezhnev's ascendancy in the Politburo, but how adaptive were they for the Soviet Union? The one-sided strategic advantages won in SALT I—the three hundred heavy missiles, permission for deployment of extra submarines, the SS-19 with its MIRV potential unexpected by the U.S. side—proved to be entirely symbolic. The Soviet Union never achieved even a notional capability for a first strike even against land-based U.S. missiles, let alone the sea-based forces or the bombers. Deterrence the Soviets had already achieved without insisting on the additional forces justified by "equal security." Meanwhile, insistence on retention of these forces complicated negotiation of SALT II, tried the patience of détente advocates in the United States, and provided telling ammunition to U.S. critics of arms control. Together with Soviet behavior in the Third World and repression at home and in Eastern Europe, Brezhnev's insistence on "equal security" helped to elect in 1980 the most vociferous opponent of détente in U.S. politics. He launched a huge arms buildup, while shipping the weapons that bloodied the Soviet army in Afghanistan. Were Reagan's policies a desirable consequence of offensive détente for the Politburo?

Competitive politics theory is sometimes considered inadequate to explain offensive détente, because it ascribes foreign policy to leaders' search for constituencies but does not provide any evidence of constituents' interests. In his extraordinary *Myths of Empire*, Jack Snyder, who originated the term, argues that offensive détente is the less damaging of two forms of self-defeating overexpansion, the other being "multiple expansion," the simultaneous pursuit of "several distinct imperial projects" that may be feasible individually but together generate self-encirclement by hostile foreign states. Snyder ascribes both forms of overexpansion to an alliance between cartelized economic interests that develop in the course of industrialization and the government bureaucracies that spend their procurement budgets on the cartels' industrial products. He provides evidence that this hypothesis is superior to realist and cognitive explanations of overexpansion.[12]

Snyder argues, however, that leadership contests can make the difference between offensive détente and multiple expansion and even, when sufficiently strong leaders emerge or when institutional rules in force in a polity enable them to draw on popular support against the cartels and their bureaucratic patrons, preclude either form of overexpansion. He also notes that Nazi Germany decided for multiple expansion only after Hitler had finished subordinating the "Junkers, industrialists, and the military" to his control. And Snyder particularly argues that cartelized economic interests explain less in centralized states exemplified by the Soviet Union.[13] Competitive politics is at least an intervening variable in the explanation of foreign policy.

A competitive politics theory certainly does not rule out politicians' responsiveness to compact interests, and Snyder's hypothesis that logrolling the interests of industrialists and bureaucrats shapes foreign policy has a certain instant plausibility as a proposition about the Soviet Union's command economy. Though Snyder's causal variable of cartelized economic interest is valid for the cases he examines, it faces one difficulty. Imperial myths and imperial overextension are more universal than the cartels that arise during industrialization. To pick just one example, Snyder's term "El Dorado myth" harks back to the Conquistadores, whose search for gold ulti-

12. Jack Snyder, *Myths of Empire* (Ithaca: Cornell University Press, 1991), 31–65.
13. Ibid., 105, 308–11.

mately helped to ruin Spain and whose interests were certainly pecuniary but not industrial. Grand strategies in foreign policy help leaders convince their following of their indispensability whether or not their state is industrial. Industrialization does exacerbate tendencies to overexpansion. Expansion of industry at home encourages leaders to identify themselves with expansive visions of the domestic social order that find symbolic replicas in grand strategies of foreign expansionism. The physical tools supplied by industry—"We have the Maxim gun and they don't"—enable proposals for foreign expansion to succeed, augmenting the persuasiveness of expansionist grand strategies to domestic audiences. Snyder presents convincing evidence that persons employed in industrial sectors were more responsive to imperial myths than employees of other sectors in several of the polities he examines (although of course for the Soviet Union he can present only "anecdotes").[14] The observation that imperial myths are more general than cartelized industrial interests by no means contradicts Snyder's argument that in his cases industrial cartels generated overexpansion, but it does suggest that his political variable may be more powerful than the economic variable.

Even sympathetic readers sometimes suspect that the theory of competitive politics is tautological. Constituencies support leaders for differentiating visions of social order and grand strategies and for entering winning coalitions; differentiation of visions and grand strategies and entry into coalitions offer evidence that leaders seek constituency support. If the argument held that constituencies caused Soviet foreign policy, these suspicions of circularity would be fully justified. But the argument does not start with constituencies. It begins with the observation that a Politburo of ten or fifteen men could mandate the behavior of a population in the hundreds of millions. The observable disproportion between the few rulers and the many ruled presents a problem universal to political leaders: to enforce their rule, they need help. Leaders can solve this problem by rhetorical appeals for aid; the theory of competitive politics investigates whether the politicians of any given country do rely on the rhetorical solution to the universal problem they face. Not the constituencies but the leaders' solution to the problem of recruiting constituencies is the independent variable of a political competition theory of

14. Ibid., 243.

foreign policy. Because the observation of a numerical disproportion between rulers and ruled is distinct from observations of foreign policy, the theory is not circular.

Symbolic grand strategies with a tendency to misrepresent international conditions and to logroll into maladaptive foreign policies help political competitors to maintain the distinctiveness of domestic visions that is constantly compromised by their need to bargain over domestic policy. This is a general proposition, and therefore it is refutable if a search fails to find the observations I have offered—symbolic coherence between differentiated domestic visions and associated grand strategies in world politics, logrolling, maladaptiveness of policy—in any state for which an adequate documentary record is available. (Lest I be misunderstood, a Stalin can win the contest and temporarily interrupt evidence of political competition by predictable changes in institutions and policies.) For each country a specialist on that country must undertake the task; here I can only offer my contribution to it.

A sympathetic critic has written that the competitive politics view of foreign policy "paints a portrait of Soviet decision making as autistic."[15] Uncommunicative, self-injuring, given to outbreaks of violence against others—is autism such an inappropriate metaphor for the historical record of global conduct by states?

Gorbachev, Yeltsin, and Beyond

Competitive politics became a dynamic of change during the Gorbachev years. Differentiation among leaders, continuity of symbolism from domestic vision to grand strategy in foreign policy, logrolls, and the effects of diminishing persuasiveness all drove the transition to democracy that began in 1985. A study of foreign policy in the early Brezhnev years cannot pretend to provide documentation for claims about the transition to democracy two decades later, but the outlines may be sketched.

Promising in his first speech in March 1985 to reform the faltering Soviet economy, Gorbachev faced from the beginning the task of convincing people—the nomenklatura, the Soviet populace, for-

15. Philip E. Tetlock, "Learning in U.S. and Soviet Foreign Policy: In Search of an Elusive Concept," in Breslauer and Tetlock, *Learning*, 48.

eigners—that he was not simply another Brezhnev, willing to approve reforms early only to roll them back later. Gorbachev differentiated his proposals not only from Brezhnev's, but also from those offered by Kosygin and later by Andropov, when for the first time he combined economic reforms with glasnost: a policy of giving more information to the public and of listening to its opinions.

The actual practice of both glasnost and economic reforms remained far more limited than Gorbachev's proposals. If it is true, as the theory of competitive politics claims, that policies must be chosen by bargaining, then the presence of conservatives in the Politburo explains why Gorbachev promised more than he delivered. He wanted perestroika, "restructuring"; they wanted *uskorenie*, "acceleration"; and he promised both. As the main requirement of perestroika was an end to the overweening concern with economic expansion communicated by uskorenie, the logroll had its characteristic self-frustrating consequences. When leaders have adopted compromise policies that will not work, they anticipate that their persuasiveness will decline, and they try to reinforce constituents' loyalty by replicating the symbolism of their domestic visions in grand strategies for world politics.

Thus Gorbachev began immediately to revise Soviet foreign as well as domestic policies. Eduard Shevardnadze's main accomplishment in drafting Gorbachev's report to the XXVII Party Congress in 1986, he recalled, was elimination of the words "specific form of class struggle" from the definition of peaceful coexistence. "This was definitely not a scholastic definition. 'Form of class struggle' inescapably entailed a view of the world as a field of permanent conflict of systems, camps, blocs, and an 'enemy image' gripped the consciousness of millions in all parts of the earth." Gorbachev's foreign minister "knew what opposition various provisions had met" as the Politburo traded demands for revisions of the draft. At stake, Shevardnadze "would risk saying," were the "interests and positions of various forces, rather broadly represented in the membership of the Politburo." Gorbachev was "walking into a bonfire that was anything but figurative." The victory in drafting Gorbachev's report provided Shevardnadze with "working guidance" that authorized him to press forward with the diplomacy that led to the series of breakthrough East-West agreements that defined the end of the Cold War. "Everything that we achieved in consequence—the new quality of Soviet-American relations, the dialogue that crowded out confrontation, the shift of accents from forcible confrontational methods to political means of resolving international problems—became a result of practical orientation on these conclusions."[16]

Shevardnadze testifies that an end to class struggle abroad was a symbol to express democratization at home. "If you begin democratization of your own country, you don't have the right to block this process in other countries. And if you reject adherence to the 'philosophy of tanks' in relation to bordering countries, then as a minimum you must not think in its categories in relation to your own country."[17] Tanks abroad stood for authoritarian coercion at home, talks abroad for democratic dialogue at home.

While Gorbachev coordinated his domestic vision of reform with a grand strategy of East-West cooperation, foreign policy remained a compromise. Conservatives led by Egor Ligachev retained seats in the Politburo and continued to go public with criticism of East-West agreements and demands for continuation of the forward policy in the Third World.[18] As during the Brezhnev era, Gorbachev reconciled the disputes with the conservatives by separating issues and logrolling. Soviet policy continued to feature offensive détente, funding anti-Western Third World governments and fighting in Afghanistan while negotiating on European and U.S.-Soviet issues.

In contrast to Kosygin, Gorbachev could now win the contest. Ligachev's proposals were much less persuasive than the same proposals by Brezhnev had been in 1965, because now the failure of policies symbolized by Brezhnev's grand strategy was so pronounced on every issue facing the Politburo. Consequently Gorbachev and Shevardnadze exercised a much freer hand in pursuing détente. Even if they could not pull out of Afghanistan and other Third World conflicts unilaterally, they could enter serious negotiations with the United States on ending regional disputes.

Compromise within the Politburo remained costly to Gorbachev. As general secretary he continued to bear responsibility for what his emerging rival, Boris Yeltsin, would later call "half measures" and "indecisiveness, compromises, and balancing between the interests of the apparatus and society."[19] As Politburo resistance required him to compromise on halfhearted economic reforms and encouraged

16. Eduard A. Shevardnadze, *Moi vybor* (Moscow: Novosti, 1991), 93–96, 99, 103.
17. Ibid., 14.
18. Bruce Parrott, "Soviet National Security under Gorbachev," *Problems of Communism*, November-December 1988, 1–36.
19. December 17, 1989.

bureaucratic sabotage of the compromise, the economic decline worsened while Gorbachev's popularity among ordinary citizens entered a rapid downward spiral.

Despite the decline of his own popularity, Gorbachev remained preferable in the population's eyes to Ligachev and the other anti-reformers, and during 1990 he used growing popular pressure on the Politburo to extract two further concessions from them. One concerned the Politburo itself. Its practice of collective responsibility obscured the differences between what Gorbachev wanted and what conservative pressures compelled him to accept, and continuing suspicions among the Soviet populace that he remained just another Communist seemed to be confirmed by the halfheartedness of reform. If the Politburo was compelling Gorbachev to accept popular blame for policies it constrained him to accept, he would set himself sharply apart from it. He organized his own election as president and began to rule by personal decree, while at the XXVIII Party Congress he gained assent to the abolition of the old Politburo. The conservatives managed to force retention of the name of the institution, but Gorbachev gained its transformation into an assembly dominated by representatives from the parties of the ethnic republics whose monthly (instead of weekly) meetings turned them from a policy executive into a consultative assembly.

Though this move freed Gorbachev from identification with the Politburo conservatives who were swept from office, it forced him to accept even more responsibility in the eyes of the populace for the failure of his reforms, which government and party bureaucracies continued to sabotage. Moreover, deprived of their Politburo representatives' ability to keep Gorbachev in check, conservatives in the defense industry and in the military intervened directly, demanding in the fall of 1990 that Gorbachev take action against ethnic separatists, strikers, radical democrats, and proponents of private property.[20] He responded with the notorious "turn to the right" of November 1990. Although, after mass demonstrations and a renewal of strikes, a new coalition with Yeltsin in April 1991 reversed the turn to the right, what was left of Gorbachev's reputation among the Soviet population suffered permanent damage, and the conservatives struck with the August coup. A popular rally behind Yeltsin saved

20. Aleksei Kiva, "V plenu maksimalizma: O politicheskoi situatsii v strane posle IV S''ezda narodnykh deputatov SSSR i sobytii v Pribaltike," *Izvestiia*, January 24, 1991.

Gorbachev's life but not his presidency. When Communists still in the majority in the parliaments of various ethnic republics moved to avoid falling under an extension of Yeltsin's ban on the Communist Party in Russia, they formed a coalition with local separatists to lead a parade of independence declarations that broke the Soviet Union apart.

As Yeltsin leads Russian democracy, a theory drawn from the experience of electoral polities may not gain but certainly does not lose relevance. The first consequence of the reestablishment of Russian statehood was competitive differentiation among Yeltsin's colleagues in the leadership, as Ruslan Khasbulatov and Aleksandr Rutskoi began to challenge their erstwhile champion. Each of the new rivals turned to building a public following through the establishment of political parties, and the orientation of foreign policy became entangled in the competition, as Yeltsin turned to the West, Khasbulatov to the new Muslim states of the Commonwealth, and Rutskoi to the defense of ethnic Russians residing beyond the boundaries of the Federation. Complex bargaining between the presidency and the legislature delayed both the adoption of a new constitution and the privatization of state-owned industry. Both symbolic politics and logrolling were evident as Russian nationalists and representatives of ethnic minorities defined themselves by contending over the official name of the country, compromising on a name that combined both proposals: "Russia (Russian Federation)." All of the rivals lost public confidence as economic conditions steadily worsened.

My version of competitive politics theory emphasizes symbolic politics over economic interest, a point of particular importance for the contemporary situation, when constant delays in privatization are causing a calamitous economic situation steadily to deteriorate. Competitive theories of politics do not foretell the fate of democracy in Russia. These theories emphasize path dependence and contingency, and their predictions are tests of hypotheses, not forecasts of the future. A study of four Politburo members allows the observer to rely on far simpler bargaining games than the complex mathematical exercises needed to analyze a parliament, or the interactions among a parliament, an executive, and its agencies. The complexity of these games (not to mention my lack of the mathematical training to compute their outcomes) makes the future inscrutable. If the political following assembled by Brezhnev collapsed with his death, a Yeltsin with far fewer organizational levers to keep followers in line may find his support even more evanescent. Analysis of contemporary

Russian politics must focus on both the horizontal bargaining—the interactions between Yeltsin and the parliament as well as within his government—and the vertical ties linking Yeltsin and his rivals to their respective popular and bureaucratic followings. With all the uncertainties, the Russian democratization raises anew an old and vital question: Is democracy stable because of its scope for the pursuit of economic self-interest or because of its affirmation of the symbolic equality of persons? If democracy survives amid the economic turmoil in Russia, a theory of symbolic politics will have put the emphasis in the right place.

Index

Massamba-Debat, Alphonse, 164
Mayhew, David, 28, 77
Mazurov, Kirill, 232–33
Median, 86, 235–36, 238, 251; and
  Brezhnev, 196–201, 206–8; defined,
  83–84; and tenure in office and policy
  stability, 243
Median voter theorem, 63–64
Middle East conflict, 190–93; and arms
  control, 248; and political settlement,
  221, 230–34
Mikoian, Anastas, 158, 163, 238; on eco-
  nomic aid and trade, 148, 153–55
Military aid, 138, 163–64, 171; to Congo-
  Brazzaville for Angola, 164; to Egypt,
  233–34, 250; to Syria, 233; to Third
  World revolts, 157–58; to Vietnam,
  131–40, 143, 178, 220–22; to Zambia
  for Zimbabwe, 181
MLF (multilateral force), 100–103, 106,
  108–10, 240, 248; as synecdoche, 102,
  247
Mongolia, 167–69
Moreton, N. Edwina, 209
Morocco, 181
Moscow, Communists of, 40
Moscow summit, 207, 225–26
Muhri, Franz, 121

Nasser, Gamal Abdel, 153–54, 190–91
North Atlantic Treaty Organization
  (NATO), 14, 102–5, 110, 181; divisive-
  ness in, 103, 144–45, 149–51, 185–86,
  189, 213–15, 247
Nazis: in U.S., 167, 171, 241; in West
  Germany, 171, 184
Ne Win, 153
Nixon, Richard, 14, 195, 207, 221, 225–
  26, 247
Nonexperts, 61, 69–72, 241; influence of,
  16–18; leader reputation and, 18. *See
  also* Policy experts
Nonproliferation Treaty, 213
Norway, 129, 142
Novotny, Antonin, 105
Nuclear Planning Group (NATO), 103

Obote, Milton, 153
"Offensive détente," 20, 244–45, 252–53;

defined, 13; as logroll, 19; as maladaptive policy, 250–51
Oversimplifications, by politicians, 24

Page, Benjamin, 79
Pakistan, 153, 159, 162, 164, 181
Parliamentary strategy, 112–114, 116,
  158
Parrott, Bruce, 10, 51, 240
Pelse, Arvids, 224, 237–38
Perestroika, 40, 255
Persuasion vs. bargaining, 23, 74
Persuasiveness, 62, 65, 71, 78–83, 187;
  and Soviet policy, 247–51
Poland, 105, 109, 205, 209
Policy experts, 13, 29, 73, 240; and Ko-
  sygin, 131; and Politburo, 9. *See also*
  Nonexperts
—views of: on Eastern Europe, 106; on
  economic aid, 152; on European com-
  munism, 115; on foreign trade, 130;
  on Third World communists, 169–70
Policy maladaptiveness, xii–xiii, 31, 61,
  78, 80, 111, 125, 127, 145, 148, 164,
  244–51, 254; possible causes of, 4–6
Policy obstruction, as bureaucratic opinion, 52–55, 195, 244, 257
Policy oscillation, 62, 78, 80
Politburo: procedures of, ix–xi, 4, 6–9,
  12, 22, 26–29, 35–36, 48–49, 54–57,
  149, 188, 239; *protokol* of, 21
Politburo members: as advocates, 4, 33,
  238; as brokers, 4, 9, 10, 18, 33, 57,
  238; as infighters, 4, 7, 10, 33, 238
Polsby, Nelson, 43
Portugal, 164
Portuguese Guinea, 163
Prokof'ev, Iurii, 40

Rashidov, Sharaf, 228–29
"Rational deliberation," by Politburo, 10,
  13, 240
Reagon, Ronald, 68, 71, 83, 251
Regional economic equalization, 227–28
Reputation, 62, 64–65, 89, 236
Rhodesia, 163. *See also* Zimbabwe
Romania, 105, 106, 108
Rostov, 43
Rutskoi, Aleksandr, 258

Library of Congress Cataloging-in-Publication Data

Anderson, Richard (Richard Davis), 1950–
  Public politics in an authoritarian state : making foreign policy during the Brezhnev
years / Richard D. Anderson, Jr.
    p.   cm.
  Includes bibliographical references and index.
  ISBN 0-8014-2900-5 (alk. paper)
    1. Soviet Union—Foreign relations—1953–1975.   2. Brezhnev,
Leonid Il'ich, 1906–1982.   I. Title.
DK282.A53   1993
327.47—dc20   93-15240